ECO TOURISM

The Top 50 Sustainable Destinations to Travel Green

Contents

Introduction

The earth is fragile. Unless we are all prepared to take part in its preservation, unique, beautiful destinations might no longer be there for future generations, perhaps not even for this generation.

As a whole, the tourism sector is responsible for the emission of almost 5 billion tons of CO_2 a year, which corresponds to 8% of total emissions. Apart from pollution produced by travel (air travel alone produces 12% of the sector's total emissions and 2% of global emissions), we should mention the pollution produced by building and maintaining facilities, by retail sales of foods and beverages linked to tourism, and by the production of souvenirs travelers traditionally buy.

Thus—paradoxically—the tourism sector in its current, mass-market form contributes to climate change, which, in turn, could bring about its demise.

It is a vicious circle. And the highest price is paid by exotic paradises, precisely those where everyone dreams of going, sooner or later.

Of course, tourism takes us to wonderful places, incredible countries, astonishing in their beauty and very different from those we already know. But if we care about our life and our planet, if we want our great-grandchildren to live in a marvelous world, and if we value people, then we must be aware of the environment and its preservation.

When we travel, we have to be conscious about it.

So, an ecotourist is an environmentally aware tourist. Someone who visits a place and leaves it in a better state and with happier people.

To describe the relationship between tourism and sustainability, today we use words like "ecotourism" or "sustainable, responsible, eco-sustainable tourism." However, concern for the places we visit and the welfare of the local people started as early as the late 1980s. It was thus summarized by the World Tourism Organization (UNWTO):

"Sustainable tourism development meets the needs of present tourists and host regions while protecting and enhancing opportunities for the future. It is envisaged

3 A trekker on a suspension bridge in the Annapurna Conservation Area, the largest protected area in Nepal, which stretches across the districts of Manang, Mustang, Kaski, Myagdi, and Lamjung.
5 Tourism on horseback is one of the most authentic and low-impact ways to explore every corner of the planet.
8–9 Vinicunca, the Mountain of Seven Colors, is one of the most beautiful sights that nature has to offer.

as leading to management of all resources in such a way that economic, social and aesthetic needs can be fulfilled while maintaining cultural integrity, essential ecological processes, biological diversity and life support systems."

Set aside proclamations and definitions: it is the ecotourist's attitude that makes all the difference while traveling green. It all begins before leaving. Find out about the geography, customs, good manners, and culture of the region you are traveling to. When choosing the means of transport to reach your destination, choose trains, buses, and public transportation in general, or car sharing if you really need to travel by car. If you cannot go without flying, calculate your environmental impact and try to compensate for it by planting trees (although it is not easy to establish how much you will pollute with a flight). Hopefully, the transport industry will invest more and more on eco-friendly solutions, fostering innovations that can lessen the human carbon footprint during travel.

As far as accommodation is concerned, choose hotels, bed and breakfasts, farm holidays, and mountain shelters that separate their waste, use renewable energy sources, have green buildings, involve the local community, and have qualified staff who are well trained in the fundamental principles of conservation. If you do not insist on having your sheets and towels changed daily, you can save water and energy. Conscious tourists committed to a green way of life do not give it up when they go on vacation: that is why tourist facilities are investing more and more to gain an environmental certification.

When you arrive at your destination, it's time to discover the area slowly, profoundly, and with a low environmental impact. Follow marked trails and have respect for animals, plants, and habitat. Carry your own waste with you and leave every element of the sea and the earth in its place (it is not a souvenir to take back home). Take photos only: no graffiti for posterity, nor unnecessary noise that could frighten the animals. Then respect the people you meet, their work and their property, their privacy and their dignity, and check first whether they want to be photographed. Devote time to listening to them and encourage efforts to preserve the place. Appreciate what is offered to you, give priority to the local economy, and spend your money to benefit the people who work and live there. Avoid purchasing products made from endangered plants or animals, like ivory, turtle shells, animal skins, and feathers.

You should encourage eco-friendly attitudes in people that accompany and welcome you (guides, restaurants, hoteliers, etc.), first by giving a good example yourself, then asking them to adopt environmentally sustainable practices. Each place has its own surprises, and it is very difficult to choose among them because the ways into nature and the wonders you find in following them are infinite. Those who have tried know that traveling through nature is good for the body and the spirit, reduces stress, and stimulates feelings of well-being and optimism. Nature helps us discover more about ourselves. Climb mountains or dive into the sea, travel to the end of the world, or get to know new civilizations. Travel through woods, villages, and refuges, along rivers or prairies, on volcanoes or through swamps, and you will surely return home having gained something, especially from meeting people of different cultures, listening to their stories, learning their customs, trying their food.

This book could be useful, and maybe inspire you to journey through nature in an eco-sustainable way, for iconic itineraries in different countries. The common theme is beauty and environmental, economic, and social sustainability.

Each itinerary features a presentation, the daily stages, practical advice, and ecological suggestions. All can be modified and adapted to different needs.

Every tour only suggests the actual number of days on foot, on a bike, on horseback, or in a canoe, and everyone is free to do it in his/her own time. It is certainly true that you often use other means of transport to arrive at the starting point and that sometimes you have to take a ferry or a cableway to discover unique places. But the routes suggested here pollute the least possible and do not change what they touch. There are different levels of difficulty, and some trails require you to be well prepared and equipped, both physically and psychologically. It is of fundamental importance that you carefully inform yourself about travel documents and contacts with your country's embassy or consulate in the region you are visiting, that you register online to communicate your itinerary, and that you take out insurance to cover medical expenses and a possible flight home. This is apart from studying the meteorological and health aspects of a region, or the war situation if you are going to a place where there is political unrest. And last but not least, it is better to travel with another person to share experiences and support each other.

Ecotourism is an investment. It needs vision, care, wisdom, and time, but in the end, the capital grows and produces satisfying results. We must preserve instead of throwing away what we have and find solutions so that all can enjoy a healthier future for our entire global ecosystem.

Itineraries on Foot

Thirty minutes a day: this is the minimum time every adult should dedicate to moderate aerobic exercise—for example, walking, a healthy, natural activity that can be done in every season and at every age.

Walking is the most natural, green, and cheap way to move from one place to another. And also the slowest. It is the oldest way of traveling and brings together people and places. It helps release tension and recharge energy, restores good moods and serenity, and allows you to enjoy new experiences and make new discoveries, about the world and also about yourself. There are no side effects.

So let's walk, then—especially in nature, where light, space, colors, rhythms, and sounds are different, amplified, pleasant, and unforgettable. This way of traveling is an expanding social phenomenon, attracting more and more people every year.

The way of St. James and the Via Francigena are the main pilgrim routes of Christianity, one of which dates back to the first half of the 9th century and the other to the year 990 AD. Yet, trekking as we know it today began only at the turn of the 19th century in Europe and North America.

Every country has its own rules and ways to indicate the routes: some tracks are well marked, while others are less visible, perhaps regularly hidden or worn out by the forces of nature; some have been created recently. Sometimes, there are no maps for the routes, and to find them you must rely on local experts, who love their land and will tell you everything about it.

Here we present many different paths, easy and difficult, to be followed with or without a guide. In the mountains, along the coast, on a plateau, through the woods, in the desert, in the "happiest" country or in the best organized, most ecological, most spiritual one; along lake shores, in the footsteps of ancient Romans, brigands, or fishermen; in holy lands, on islands, among geysers or volcanoes—a vast choice, always in the midst of nature, and taking account of environmental characteristics. We indicate the best season to begin the walk and the number of days required, which can vary according to the speed and detours you want to take.

However, before you decide to leave, you must assess your physical and mental condition: if you are trained to walk or do regular aerobic activity, you may have an advantage. If you

11 Trekking at the foot of the Himalayas, a very demanding destination. It is necessary to be mentally and physically prepared before the start.

intend to travel solo, you will need a good sense of direction, provide yourself with maps, and take a first-aid kit.

Once you have chosen your destination and found out more about it, you should calculate how many days you have available and the average distance per day you intend to cover.

Then you need to decide how to reach the starting point: if you want to be really eco-sustainable, flying is the last resort.

Now it's time to plan where and how to stay the night, and thus the equipment to take with you, and how to be supplied with food and water on your walk, keeping in mind that some stages have no contact with civilization. You must be able to read the signage and know the rules for access to parks and reserves, which sometimes need to be booked. Of course, always follow the *Leave No Trace* rule.

As far as baggage is concerned, in each itinerary we indicate what is necessary: packing a tent means adding a mat, sleeping bag, camping stove, and saucepans, which increase the weight on your shoulders. Therefore, it is better to know in advance whether free camping is allowed in the country in question. Staffed or unstaffed refuges may have useful tools available, but it is always wise to find out beforehand what you will find in the place. If you are thinking of staying in tourist facilities, always favor eco-sustainable ones and in any case book them some time ahead: you don't want to risk not finding a place to stay at the end of a particularly tiring stage.

It is a good idea to have a camera with you to record your journey: you can take photos of unique encounters and places, but remember to enjoy the trip without being obsessed with perfect photos. No less important: always remember you are a guest in wild nature and behave accordingly.

12–13 A group of people hiking in the Langtang National Park in Nepal. The park's climate is dominated by the southerly monsoon, which occurs between June and September, so suitable clothing is necessary during the trek.

ICELAND

Start: Landmannalaugar
Finish: Thórsmörk
Distance: 33.5 mi (54 km)
Time: 4 days
Difficulty: difficult
Accommodation: You can choose between shelters (book months in advance, bring a sleeping bag) or tents (be aware of the weather conditions: constant rain and strong winds can cause discomfort). Tents can only be pitched near the shelters (there is a small fee), and it is forbidden to enter the shelters if you are not a client.

Eco because: Colorful vistas, incredibly long days, magnificent and contrasting landscapes, a unique ecosystem: an exclusive heritage to be protected from the flow of tourists who increasingly invade this precious and original land.

Laugavegur Trail

Land of fire and ice, Iceland has dramatic landscapes where everything thrills and attracts: pools of mud, geothermal hot springs, glaciers, and waterfalls. It is one of the most active volcanic areas on Earth, and its spectacular landscapes are the result of the interaction between the volcanic activity and the natural elements. Among the benefits of this impetuosity is the environmentally friendly geothermal heating for almost all the homes of Iceland and the hydroelectric power, supplied by the meltwater from the subglacial volcanoes, that meets the energy needs of the country. Iceland is also the ideal place to admire the northern lights (from mid-September to mid-April) and splendid animals such as puffins and whales, to be seen from land or at sea.

To fully enjoy the unusual beauty of this land, one of the most popular trails of Iceland is the Laugavegur Trail (or the Hot Spring Trail) between Landmannalaugar and Thórsmörk. Crossing rhyolite mountains, hot springs, lakes, and deserts of black sand, it ends in a verdant woodland. The trail is well signed, but it may be foggy and snowy even in July, so take great care during the trek. While some rivers are equipped with a footbridge, others must be forded.

Landmannalaugar

Hrafntinnusker

- Day 1
- Day 2
- Day 3
- Day 4

Alftavatn

Emstrur

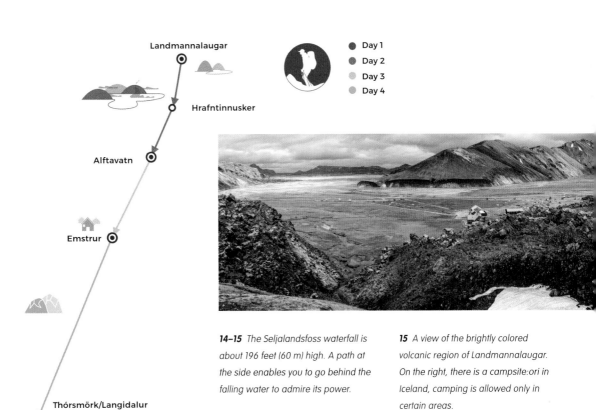

Thórsmörk/Langidalur

14–15 *The Seljalandsfoss waterfall is about 196 feet (60 m) high. A path at the side enables you to go behind the falling water to admire its power.*

15 *A view of the brightly colored volcanic region of Landmannalaugar. On the right, there is a campsite:ori in Iceland, camping is allowed only in certain areas.*

When to go: The trail is—or at least should be—open from June 25 to September 15, but its feasibility depends on the weather and the snowfall.

How to get there: The international airport of Keflavik, near the capital Reykjavik (Reykjavik Keflavik Nas), is the main gateway to the country from abroad. From here, you take a bus to Landmannalaugar (about 137 miles [220 km]).

What to pack: A tent, a sleeping bag, food (the shelters do not sell food! In some rare cases you may find freeze-dried products, but prices will be high: better not to depend on their availability), a canteen. Good quality, strong hiking boots and equipment. Wind- and waterproof clothing. Bathing suit. First-aid kit. Anti-blister bandages. Painkillers and disinfectant for minor wounds. Headlamp. Waterproof coverings for cameras and video equipment. Maps in your own language.

DAY 1: Landmannalaugar

The trek starts in the beautiful rhyolite area of Landmannalaugar, where you can take relaxing walks through the enchanting colored landscape. A flow of black obsidian forms a magnificent contrast with the hills striped in green, white, red, and yellow. The coloring is due to the volcanic activity. Landmannalaugar is one of the few places where you can swim in a natural hot pool, surrounded by a magnificent landscape. At night, the local shelter can house about 80 guests.

DAY 2: Landmannalaugar–Hrafntinnusker–Alftavatn

This day's stage is quite long and challenging. The first part of the trail climbs slowly to the hot springs of Storihver, where the contrast between the snow and the springs creates a fascinating panorama. After passing Hrafntinnusker, you enjoy a breathtaking view over the highland. Then, after some ups and downs, you descend to the shelter on the Alftavatn lake, where you will stay the night (about 70 places available).

DAY 3: Alftavatn–Emstrur

During this stage, you walk across wide gravel and sand stretches, crossing some very cold rivers. Here you can appreciate the isolation and the enchanting vastness of the area. The terrain is fairly flat and offers a wonderful view of the surrounding mountains and glaciers. You stay at Emstrur for the night (about 60 places available)

DAY 4: Emstrur–Thórsmörk/Langidalur

Today your walk starts to the east of the shelter, passing through a colored canyon, from which there is a wonderful view of the Mýrdalsjökull glacier. You cross a bridge over the Sydri-Emstrua River and continue on an easy trail beside the Markarfljót River. You ford the Thronga River to approach the verdant valley of Thórsmörk: here you will understand why Iceland is called the land of contrasts. The climb up the Valahnúkur hill is a must-do to enjoy a beautiful view over the valley, the glaciers, and the rivers. Your last stay is at the Thórsmörk/Langidalur shelter (75 places available).

*16 **top*** *Iceland's great variety of hot springs and geysers is the result of the intense geothermal activity caused by its volcanoes.*

*16 **bottom*** *The bridge crossing the Sydri-Emstrua canyon: this is on the fourth and last day of the itinerary, in the Emstrur area.*

17 Along the trail, between the refuges of Alftavatn and Emstrur. There is an amazing variety of landscape: from black deserts to blue glaciers, from rainbow mountains to green hills.

ECO-TIPS

IT IS ABSOLUTELY FORBIDDEN TO LEAVE WASTE OR TRASH BEHIND, INCLUDING TOILET PAPER AND FOOD WASTE. CARRY IT WITH YOU AND DISPOSE OF IT IN THE APPROPRIATE BINS. IT IS ESSENTIAL TO REMAIN ON THE TRAILS AND PATHS, CAMPING ONLY IN APPROVED SITES, TO AVOID TRAMPLING THE LICHEN OR LEAVING MARKS OR TRACES WHERE THERE WERE NONE:
IF YOU LEAVE EVEN A FEW FOOTPRINTS, OTHERS WILL FOLLOW, ALTERING THE LANDSCAPE OVER TIME. THE GENERAL RULE IS TO LEAVE NOTHING OTHER THAN FOOTPRINTS ON THE TRAIL AND TAKE ONLY PHOTOGRAPHS AS A SOUVENIR.

Useful Websites
inspiredbyiceland.com
www.fi.is/en/mountain-huts

Karhunkierros Trail

Start: Hautajärvi or Sallantie (Ristikallio)
Finish: Rukatunturi Fell
Distance: 51 mi (82 km)
Time: from 4 to 8 days
Difficulty: easy-medium
Accommodation: tents and shelters

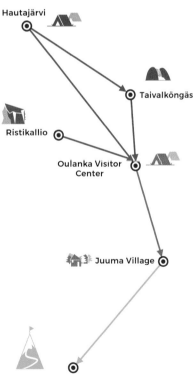

Hautajärvi

Taivalköngäs

Ristikallio

Oulanka Visitor Center

Juuma Village

● Days 1–2
● Days 3–4
● Days 5–6

Rukatunturi Fell

18 An abandoned fisherman's house on the Oulankajoki River.
19 Aerial view of the boreal forest, or taiga, one of the main terrestrial biomes in the Oulanka park. It mainly comprises conifers.

Finland is an immense green and blue country: more than 70% is covered in forest, and there are more than 188,000 lakes and numerous islands. The country's 40 national parks are distributed throughout the territory, in Lapland to the north, in the lake district, along the coasts, and on the archipelagos. These uncontaminated places are home to thousands of wild animals and birds: it is estimated that there are about 1,500 brown bears in the forests of Finland. The country is also home to rare species: for example, on the Saimaa lake it is possible to see the ringed seal, one of the species at the greatest risk of extinction in the world.

The midnight sun in summer, the northern lights from September to March, and the pure air instill the desire to fully experience the magic of nature. Finland is one of the best destinations in Europe for hiking: it is also popular with people who practice *Nordic walking*, the total body version of walking, performed with specially designed walking poles, similar to ski poles. It is also considered one of the most environmentally friendly countries in the world: its battle in favor of widespread eco-sustainability centers on the elimination of coal, gas, and fossil fuels as energy sources.

There is much to see along the Karhunkierros Trail, which winds through the Oulanka National Park, in the northeast of the country: rivers, rapids, cliffs, forests, pinewoods, meadows, moose, and reindeer. Also known as the Bear's Trail or the Bear's Ring, the walk can be divided into four sections, each with some challenging parts. The hike can start from various points; here we suggest two—Hautajärvi and Sallantie. If you keep up your pace, you can complete the trail In four days. You can also follow part of the itinerary in a canoe.

Eco because: The Oulanka National Park is renowned for its biodiversity. Considerable attention is paid to the preservation of the environment: in fact, along the Karhunkierros Trail, there are numerous recycling stations, where visitors can deposit metal, glass, plastic, and paper, or even dangerous waste like batteries.

20 *A wild orchid, with very colorful flowers, a widely distributed species.*

21 top *A magnificent view on the Aventojoki River, which flows through vertical rock walls. This place is 3 miles (5 km) from Ristikallio, one of the two starting points for the trek.*

21 bottom left *At the end of the winter, visitors may hear the tapping of woodpeckers on tree trunks.*

21 bottom right *A reindeer in the park. The number of species in Oulanka is not certain, but today almost 400 protected species live and grow in at least 4,400 habitats in the area.*

DAYS 1–2: Hautajärvi–Oulanka Visitor Center

The northernmost section of the Karhunkierros Trail begins in the village of Hautajärvi and ends at the Oulanka Visitor Center, on the Liikasenvaarantie road. This section passes through the forest, but there are also sections through ravines and gorges. You cross the Oulankajoki River on the suspension bridge at Savilampi to reach the Taivalköngäs rapids. Along the way you will encounter numerous resting places: the Runsulampi camp and, at the end of the stage, Oulanka Camping Ground and Oulanka Visitor Center.

TRAVEL TIPS

When to go: The best time for this trek is from June to the end of September.

How to get there: From the Helsinki international airport, you take a flight to Kuusamo and from there travel about 43 miles (70 km) north by car, to the village of Hautajärvi, where the trail starts.

What to pack: Sleeping bag, mattress, tent, water purification tablets or water filter, hiking boots and trekking poles, technical garments, sunscreen.

DAYS 1–2: Sallantie Parking Area (Ristikallio Starting Point)– Taivalköngäs

The alternative starting point for this trek is Ristikallio, near the Sallantie road (road 950). This was the first part of the Karhunkierros Trail to be signposted. The trail leads to the Ristikallio cliffs. Along the trail you pass through woodland and meadows on the banks of the river, amid the barns and sheds of the local shepherds. The first part of the trail follows the Aventojoki River. From here, with a one-day excursion, you can reach the Ristikallio shelter (about 3 miles [4.8 km] away), where the trail leads to the Taivalköngäs rapids. You continue walking beside the Aventojoki River, crossing it on two suspension bridges, then you camp at the end of this stage near the Taivalköngäs shelter.

▶ ECO-TIPS

WHEN SLEEPING OVERNIGHT IN THE SHELTERS, IT IS ESSENTIAL TO READ THE RULES AND INSTRUCTIONS ON HOW TO USE THE EQUIPMENT PROVIDED. THERE ARE ALSO NOTICES USEFUL FOR HIKERS. IT IS FORBIDDEN TO SMOKE IN THE SHELTERS. IT IS ESSENTIAL TO FOLLOW THE INSTRUCTIONS FOR THE MANAGEMENT AND DISPOSAL OF TRASH: BIODEGRADABLE WASTE SHOULD BE LEFT IN THE COMPOST BINS OR IN THE COMPOSTING TOILETS; EVERYTHING ELSE MUST BE CARRIED TO THE NEAREST RECYCLING STATION. IT IS FORBIDDEN TO ABANDON ALONG THE TRAIL ANY OBJECTS OR FOOD THAT COULD ATTRACT VERMIN, AND IT IS ONLY POSSIBLE TO BURN CLEAN PAPER.

Useful Websites
www.visitfinland.com
outdoors.fi
www.nationalparks.fi/karhunkierros
www.nationalparks.fi/oulankavisitorcentre
www.ruka.fi/en/national-parks

22 top A summer view of the Ruka Ski Resort. The trek concludes precisely in the central square of the ski center, one of the largest skiing complexes in Finland.

22 bottom Summer landscape view from Rukatunturi, a hill 1,608 feet (490 m) high. Besides downhill skiing, cross-country skiing is practiced here in winter.

22-23 Today Oulanka, founded in 1956, is an internationally recognized protected area.

DAYS 3–4: Oulanka Visitor Center–Juuma Village

The start of this stage to the Kiutaköngäs waterfall is quite challenging, but after this section, the trail becomes easier and runs through the forest. This 4-mile (6 km) section can also be traveled in a canoe, starting under the Kiutaköngäs waterfall and paddling toward the Ansakämppä shelter. Sometimes, it is possible to see moose and reindeer along the route. If traveling on foot, after the waterfall, the trail enters the pinewoods and descends toward a stream hidden in the woods, running along the banks of the Oulankajoki River to the Ansakämppä shelter. From here you turn toward the area of Kitkanniemi, and after passing the Jussinkämppä

shelter, you descend the steep, rocky slope of Päähkänäkallio and follow the banks of the river Kitkajoki in the direction of the village of Juuma. Under the Päähkänäkallio cliffs, the trail joins the Pieni Karhunkierros Trail. Hikers can choose whether to take the trail clockwise or counterclockwise. In the counterclockwise direction, the structures and sights on the trail are the Myllykoski and Niskakoski suspension bridges, the Kallioportti viewpoint, and the shelter for one-day trips at Myllykoski. If traveling clockwise, hikers will pass the magnificent Jyrävä waterfall, the Siilastupa shelter, and the Harrisuvanto and Niskakoski suspension bridges. Both options lead to the village of Juuma.

DAYS 5–6: Juuma Village–Rukatunturi Fell

The last stage of the trail runs through hilly landscape. The start is through fairly easy forest, but the trail becomes more challenging as you advance. You reach the Porontimajoki River, and as you continue toward the Kumpuvaara hill, the difficulties of the trail increase.

Toward the end of the stage, walkers must climb the slopes of the Konttainen and Valtavaara hills, which reach 1,611 feet (491 m) above sea level, the highest point of the hill chain. The trail ends at the foot of the Rukatunturi Fell, in the central square of the Ruka Ski Center.

SCOTLAND (UNITED KINGDOM)

Start: Milngavie
Finish: Fort William
Distance: 94 mi (152 km)
Time: 8 days
Difficulty: medium
Accommodation: tents, inns, B&Bs

24–25 Milngavie: aerial view of Mugdock Castle and estate from the 14th century, now a country residence in east Dunbartonshire.

Eco because: The trail allows anyone to discover the most seductive side of Scotland on foot. It is one of the last pure natural places, with uninhabited lands of harsh beauty and unique wildlife. The majority of the landscapes are still unspoiled or protected.

West Highland Way

Scotland and its islands occupy one-third of the land of Great Britain. Rich in castles, monuments, museums, and traditions, the country teems with charm and cordiality: in order to get to know it, in the evening you should visit traditional pubs and drink single malt whiskey, like the inhabitants of the Highlands. However, it is nature, with its spaces, its open skies and unspoiled areas, that is the true heritage of this land, a paradise of wild moors and mysterious places.

For many years, Scotland has been encouraging ecotourism and respect of the landscape and the local communities, attracting an increasing number of "green" tourists. Among the aims of the government, the most ambitious is a 90% cut in harmful emissions by 2050, accompanied by the promotion of renewable energy sources and green economy projects.

Among Scotland's Great Trails, the national walks that run through the country's magnificent landscapes, the West Highland Way is the oldest official hiking trail and one of the most spectacular. In the inimitable panorama of the Highlands, this walk crosses Loch Lomond and the Trossachs National Park through wide and narrow glacial valleys (glens), across mountains and moors, and alongside rivers, streams, canals, and lakes (lochs). A dreamlike atmosphere.

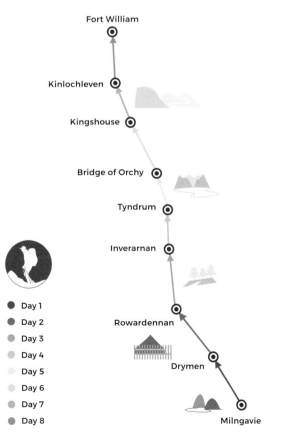

Fort William

Kinlochleven

Kingshouse

Bridge of Orchy

Tyndrum

Inverarnan

Rowardennan

Drymen

Milngavie

- Day 1
- Day 2
- Day 3
- Day 4
- Day 5
- Day 6
- Day 7
- Day 8

25 A view of Loch Lomond, situated in an area that has had great strategic importance through history, as shown by the many castles.

DAY 1: Milngavie–Drymen

The walk that links Milngavie—a quiet village northwest of Glasgow—to Drymen will give you a sample of the diverse landscapes you will meet along the West Highland Way. Following small lochs and rivers, you reach Drymen, near Loch Lomond—the largest lake in the UK—in the Loch Lomond and the Trossachs National Park. Drymen is the stopping place for the night and your gateway to the Highlands.

DAY 2: Drymen–Rowardennan

The second day you enter the Highlands, in the area of Loch Lomond. First, you arrive at Conic Hill to enjoy the view of Loch Lomond, one of the most enchanting in Scotland. The trail descends from the hill toward Balmaha, one of the preferred stops for hikers because it is about halfway along the path. The final part of this stage runs along the banks of Loch Lomond for about 19 miles (30 km). It is worth making a short detour to see the crannog at Strathcashel Point.

When to go: From April to October.

How to get there: The nearest international airport is Glasgow. To reach Milngavie, which is about 12 miles (20 km) away, take a train or a bus.

What to pack: Tent, sleeping bag, suitable equipment for rainy weather (jacket and pants). Hiking boots, warm clothing. Waterproof coverings for cameras and video equipment. Hat and sunscreen. First-aid kit and insect repellent. Canteen and food for a couple of days.

Crannogs are mysterious artificial islands from the Neolithic period, built in the lakes and rivers or in the sea by piling rocks on top of each other. The day ends in Rowardennan, where you can stay in a hotel, a youth hostel, or a castle.

26–27 Loch Lomond with Balloch Castle. Balloch Castle Country Park, recognized as a national park in 1980, has 200 acres (80 ha) of walled gardens, nature walks, and guided walks.
27 top Another spectacular view of Loch Lomond, the largest lake in Great Britain, where you can go on a boat or kayak trip or windsurf.
27 bottom Panoramic view of Butter Bridge over Kinglas Water in Loch Lomond National Park.

28 *Castle Stalker, a 14th-century castle on Loch Linnhe. Loch Linnhe is an Atlantic sea loch in the Highlands region of northwest Scotland.*

29 top *Bridge of Orchy on a beautiful fall day with Beinn Dorain in the background. This section is for canoeists and rafters in search of pure adrenaline.*

29 bottom *The view from Ben Nevis of Glen Nevis and the Mamores is an excellent reward for the effort of climbing it. It is the highest mountain in Great Britain.*

DAY 3: Rowardennan–Inverarnan

Today you walk mainly through the woods on the banks of Loch Lomond, which is dotted with islets and surrounded in this area by woodland. You reach the small hamlet of Inversnaid, and after 3.7 miles (6 km), you leave Loch Lomond behind you. You climb for about 2.5 miles (4 km) to the Beinglas Farm campsite at Inverarnan. Here, those looking for a pub or a room for the night can walk less than a mile further to the Drovers Inn at Inverarnan.

Day 4: Inverarnan–Tyndrum

In the morning you set out on a slight climb that leads from Inverarnan to Glen Falloch, with a breathtaking view of the surrounding mountains. After passing the midpoint of the walk near the village of Crianlarich, the trail leads to the ruins of St Fillan's Priory and the small village of Tyndrum, where you stay for the night.

DAY 5: Tyndrum–Bridge of Orchy

The trail from Tyndrum leads through a beautiful valley to Bridge of Orchy, where you leave civilization behind you and enter the wildest part of the trail. The panoramas over Mam Carraigh and Loch Tulla are fantastic. You stop for the night at Bridge of Orchy, a village on the Orchy River, a well-known destination for canoeists.

DAY 6: Bridge of Orchy–Kingshouse

This stage is the most pleasing of the trail and includes the iconic Rannoch Moor, a boggy moorland of considerable environmental importance for the preservation of some species of plants and animals, and one of the last great wild areas of Europe. When the sun shines, the view on the surrounding mountains and the peaks of Blackmount is stupendous. In case of rain, however, there is nowhere to take shelter and the hike can become quite challenging. In any case, it will be a memorable journey. After the descent, you are welcomed by the Kingshouse Hotel and Bunkhouse.

DAY 7: Kingshouse–Kinlochleven

The most iconic part of this stage is the Devil's Staircase, a zig-zag climb that leads to the highest point of the Highlands (1,800 feet [550 m]). As the name suggests, it is hard on the legs but not impossible. The panorama over Ben Nevis is an excellent reward for your efforts. You descend toward Kinlochleven, which has numerous bars and a well-supplied shop, and you stop here for the night.

DAY 8: Kinlochleven–Fort William

After breakfast you face a steep climb from Kinlochleven: as always, the spectacular landscape is rewarding. After this initial effort, an old military road wanders through the magnificent Glen Nevis and you suddenly find yourself before the highest peak in Scotland and Great Britain, Ben Nevis. You descend through the glen, a long, narrow valley typical of the Highlands, toward the town of Fort William, the outdoor sports capital of the United Kingdom. The trail ends in Gordon Square, with its monument dedicated to hikers.

ECO-TIPS

IN SCOTLAND, THERE IS "RIGHT OF PASSAGE," AND IT IS POSSIBLE TO CAMP ALMOST ANYWHERE IN THE COUNTRY, PROVIDING YOU ADOPT RESPONSIBLE BEHAVIOR AND DO NOT LEAVE TRASH BEHIND. THERE ARE SOME RESTRICTIONS ON CAMPING BETWEEN MARCH 1 AND OCTOBER 31 EACH YEAR NEAR EAST LOCH LOMOND. IN ANY CASE, YOU ARE NOT ALLOWED TO STAY FOR MORE THAN TWO OR THREE NIGHTS. DO NOT DISTURB THE LOCAL WILDLIFE AND AVOID DAMAGING THE ENVIRONMENT. THIS IS ESPECIALLY IMPORTANT DURING CERTAIN PERIODS OF THE YEAR, FOR EXAMPLE, BETWEEN APRIL AND EARLY MAY, WHEN IT'S LAMBING TIME.

Useful Websites
www.visitbritain.com/us/en/scotland
kingshousehotel.co.uk
droversinn.co.uk
beinglascampsite.co.uk

Hadrian's Wall Path

The island of Great Britain comprises three countries, each with its own character. England is vast and diverse, with large cities, villages, country landscapes, steep mountains, wild moors, ancient forests, and lonely windswept cliffs. The panoramas of Scotland, many of which are wild and picturesque, are the ideal destination for losing one's sense of time and place, in perfect harmony with nature. Wales, on the other hand, is particularly famous for its beautiful nature, its renowned coastal resorts, and its silent countryside with unspoiled valleys, rolling hills, and craggy mountains.

Hadrian's Wall is a UNESCO World Heritage Site, a spectacular testimony of the Roman invasion, dating from the late 2nd century AD. It was a stone fortified wall that separated the Roman province of Britannia from Caledonia, a territory corresponding more or less to present-day Scotland. Situated in one of the most beautiful and least tamed areas of the country, with its extraordinary wildlife, the wall runs coast to coast below the border between Scotland and England, and includes regularly spaced turrets and milecastles. The National Trail follows the wall from Wallsend on the east coast of England to Bowness-on-Solway on the west coast. The signposting of the path is impeccable: just follow the acorn signs.

Start: Wallsend
Finish: Bowness-on-Solway
Distance: 84 mi (135 km)
Time: 6 days
Difficulty: easy/medium
Accommodation: B&Bs

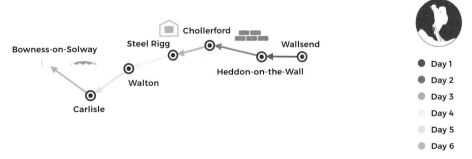

Bowness-on-Solway

Steel Rigg

Chollerford

Wallsend

Heddon-on-the-Wall

Walton

Carlisle

- Day 1
- Day 2
- Day 3
- Day 4
- Day 5
- Day 6

30–31 The UNESCO World Heritage Site in the splendid Northumberland National Park. The fortification was ordered by Hadrian, a Roman emperor in the first half of the 2nd century.

Eco because: This trail across wild and solitary moors is open only to hikers: bicycles and horses would damage the grassy trail.

DAY 1: Wallsend–Heddon-on-the-Wall

The trail starts at Wallsend, the ancient Segedunum on the outskirts of Newcastle-upon-Tyne. Here you can visit the Museum of Segedunum and the Roman fort. The trail runs beside the River Tyne: between the 13th and the late 20th century, coal barges traveled the river and Tyneside was the heart of the British shipbuilding industry. You pass Wylam Waggonway, the historical road heading for Heddon-on-the-Wall, where you will stay for the night.

DAY 2: Heddon-on-the-Wall–Chollerford

This part of the trail is not difficult and runs near cultivated land. The landscape was proclaimed a UNESCO World Heritage Site, and the trail apparently does not run beside the wall. In fact, the wall now lies below the military road B6318, built on the orders of General Wade in the 18th century as a defense against the Jacobite Rebellion. In some points, you can see stones from the Roman era, nestled among farms and wildlife. You spend the night at Chollerford.

DAY 3: Chollerford–Steel Rigg

During today's stage, the panorama begins to change: the grazing land is higher and wilder, and the horizon is vaster. You can see the Roman wall and the northern moat. From milecastle 35 onward, you come across the characteristic winding road: it is more challenging than it seems. On fine days, there is little protection from the sun, but in springtime (the best season for this trail), you can smell the wild thyme that grows on the stones of the wall. The trail allows you time to consider the skill of the Roman engineers and builders, and also that of the Victorians, who were determined to preserve Hadrian's Wall. You spend the night at Steel Rigg.

DAY 4: Steel Rigg–Walton

About halfway along the trail, at Walltown Crags, you can see southern Scotland and the northern Pennines, and also the end of the trail in Bowness-on-Solway, in the distance. The Great Whin Sill escarpment—the rocky crags characteristic of the northern Pennines—reaches its highest point at Windshields Crags, just 1,131 feet (345 m) above sea level. The crags form a sort of natural threshold that the builders of Hadrian's Wall used strategically. The villages of Greenhead and Gilsland offer a break on this stage. The last part of the wall, to the west, is at Hare Hill. You spend the night at Walton.

DAY 5: Walton–Carlisle

In this stage, the remains of the wall are not visible, but you can see the earthworks that bear witness to its ancient presence. Since you are close to sea level, the gradients are not particularly challenging, the climate is mild, and the woodland is a pleasant change from the more open landscape of Northumberland. The whole of this stage is very calm and seems to prepare you for your arrival on the estuary of the Solway Firth, beyond Carlisle, where you spend the night.

DAY 6: Carlisle–Bowness-on-Solway (Maia Roman Fort)

Today, as you walk, you can enjoy the vast Scottish landscapes. Except for the singing of the birds, the estuary marshes of the River Eden in Solway Firth offer peace and solitude and an opportunity to think about the trail as you come to the end. From Segedunum to Maia, from fort to fort, a Roman odyssey. Here the trail that follows Hadrian's Wall ends. The coast of Solway Firth—between Dykesfield and Drumburgh and between Port Carlisle and Bowness-on-Solway—is at sea level, so it is therefore necessary to consult the tide tables. The UK Hydrographic Office provides a free information service about tide predictions on its website.

When to go: The best time is from May to October, when the weather is drier. It is advisable to book accommodation in advance because it is very busy, particularly at weekends.

How to get there: Newcastle has an international airport with services to many domestic and foreign destinations. From here, you travel to Wallsend, about half an hour by car. In any case, it is easy to reach the Hadrian's Wall Path by public transport: both the extremities (Carlisle in the west and Newcastle-upon-Tyne in the east) have urban railway links and National Express coach services.

What to pack: We advise taking a map or guidebook. If you remain on the trail, it is a good idea to have a checkbook because not all accommodation facilities accept credit cards. In summer, you will need insect repellent for the midges, sunscreen—there are long stretches with no shade—and anti-blister bandages. A well-charged mobile phone (and a spare battery) is useful if you have to agree on arrival times with the accommodation facilities. Many of the sights along the trail are owned and managed by English Heritage or the National Trust, so members should take their membership card with them. In addition to food, hikers should carry a good quantity of water. Hiking boots, garments that cover the arms and the legs, hat, sunglasses, sunscreen. Windbreaker, waterproof cape, waterproof coverings for cameras and video equipment. The book *Memoirs of Hadrian* by Marguerite Yourcenar would be a good traveling companion.

32 *The ruins of Milecastle 39, one of the fortifications placed at intervals of about one Roman mile along various important frontiers, like Hadrian's Wall.*

33 top *The sunset illuminates the wall, Highshield Crags, and Crag Lough, a lake inside the southern boundary of the Northumberland National Park.*

33 bottom *The ruins of Chesters Roman Fort, one of the numerous Roman outposts built to protect Hadrian's Wall near the Scottish border.*

GERMANY

Start: Titisee/Saig
Finish: Titisee/Saig
Distance: 70 mi (113 km)
Time: 6 days
Difficulty: difficult
Accommodation: shelters, inns, hostels (it is best to book a couple of days ahead)

34–35 A cuckoo clock painted on the side of a building at Titisee: it belongs to a company that today specializes in cuckoo clocks and elegant wristwatch models.

Eco because: Considered one of the best hikes in Germany, this trail winds through dirt roads, mountain trails, and forests. There are very few paved sections.

Hiking in the Black Forest

One of the most environmentally aware countries of the old continent, Germany offers not only natural beauty but also quality infrastructures: all the destinations are easily reached thanks to an efficient network of public transport. In particular, you can hire bicycles at any station of the major cities and in tourist resorts (some centers also hire e-bikes). Many hotels manage resources and waste disposal responsibly, and they welcome guests that are knowledgeable about a sustainable economy.

Germany safeguards its artistic and natural heritage through farsighted strategies; it has forty-two UNESCO World Heritage Sites and fifteen biosphere reserves, sixteen national parks, and more than one hundred nature parks.

The Black Forest is the largest nature park in the country and has always been a destination for hikers. The hike we propose here is a circular route that comprises magnificent landscapes, woods, lakes, and wide valleys. The trail is generally well-maintained, but be careful on the rocky sections, which may be wet and slippery.

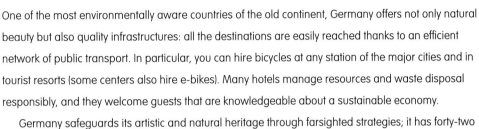

Hinterzarten

Titisee/Saig

Feldberg

Todtnauberg

Schluchsee

Bernau im Schwarzwald

- Day 1
- Day 2
- Day 3
- Day 4
- Day 5
- Day 6

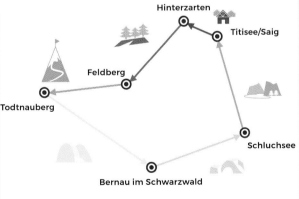

35 *View of the lake, Titisee, and the mountain, the Feldberg, which reaches a height of 4,898 feet (1,493 m). It is the highest mountain in the Black Forest.*

36 *The Gertelbach Falls begin from a spring horizon west of the main road of the Black Forest and end after only 1.5 miles (2.5 km).*

37 left *Summer view of the Schluchsee, a reservoir lake in Baden-Württemberg: around it, there are hills, forests, and meadows.*

37 right *Trekker near the Schluchsee, which the Dreiseenbahn (Three Lakes Railway) reaches. It is so called because it passes by the three lakes: Titisee, Windgfällweiher, and Schluchsee.*

DAY 1: Titisee/Saig–Hinterzarten

The itinerary starts at Lake Titisee, near Saig, and the first stretch heads southeast toward the forest of the Rotmeer nature reserve. The trail then passes through Bärenthal, where the hills are dotted with the traditional houses of the Black Forest, to reach the Seebach waterfalls. From here you climb rapidly toward the West Trail, which leads past a number of small lakes to Hinterzarten, the Baden-Württemberg ski resort, where you stop for dinner and for the night.

DAY 2: Hinterzarten–Feldberg

Having left Hinterzarten, you walk toward Lake Feldsee. At present, it is forbidden to swim in the lake, in order to protect a rare water fern that grows in waters 3 to 6 feet (1–2 m) deep. This species is found only in the German lakes of Feldsee and Titisee. You continue along a narrow path, climbing toward Seehalde. In the last section, you pass a small ski resort and reach the shelter on Mount Feldberg, where you stay the night.

DAY 3: Feldberg–Todtnauberg

Today you climb to the peak of Mount Feldberg, which, at 4,898 feet (1,493 m), is the highest peak in the Black Forest. The trail climbs sharply to the peak of the mountain, from which there is a magnificent panorama of the Alps to the south. After a short break, you continue along the West Trail, and you pass through quiet forests, descending gradually. The last destination for the day is Todtnauberg, a ski resort named after the mountain of the same name.

DAY 4: Todtnauberg–Bernau im Schwarzwald

From the mountains, you descend into the Todtnau valley, where you take the cable car to Hasenhorn, a 3,789-foot (1,155 m) mountain to the southeast of the town. After a brief detour toward the peak, you pass the Prägbach waterfall and arrive at the Bernau valley, with dozens of scattered villages and hamlets, one of the most beautiful places in the Black Forest. The valley offers quality accommodation.

When to go: The best time is in summer.

How to get there: You arrive at the EuroAirport Basel-Mulhouse-Freiburg (the only airport shared by three countries: Switzerland, France, and Germany), which is about 62 miles (100 km) from Lake Titisee. From here you can take a bus or a train.

What to pack: Food supplies, water, hiking boots, garments that cover the arms and the legs, hat, sunscreen, sunglasses, and bathing suit. First-aid kit, anti-blister bandages, insect repellent, walking stick, headlamp. Windbreaker and waterproof cape.

DAY 5: Bernau im Schwarzwald–Schluchsee

This is one of the most exciting stages of the hike. After setting out from Bernau, you pass by an abandoned silver mine and continue along the Schluchtensteig trail, which leads to the Krummenkreuz shelter. From here you descend along forest tracks to Schluchsee, the end of today's hike, which stands on the lake by the same name. These waters, navigable with electric boats, are surrounded by a cycle path.

DAY 6: Schluchsee–Titisee/Saig

On the last day of your hike, you walk for a time along the banks of Lake Schluchsee, leaving it to head north toward the small community of Falkau. Another climb takes you back to the north of Lake Titisee, your starting point, where you stay the night. Lake Titisee, originating from the waters of the Feldberg glacier, is one of the most beautiful lakes in the Black Forest: you can either walk or cycle around it, exploring the dense forest of tall, impenetrable trees. Or you can organize a boat ride. Only electric boats are allowed, to respect the environment.

ECO-TIPS

IT IS NOT THE HIKE IN ITSELF THAT IS BENEFICIAL; IT IS THE TIME SPENT IN NATURE THAT REFRESHES THE BODY AND THE SPIRIT. IT IS THEREFORE NECESSARY TO RESPECT THE NATURAL ENVIRONMENT YOU ARE WALKING THROUGH. IF YOU PICNIC IN THE BLACK FOREST, YOUR TRASH MUST BE DISPOSED OF CORRECTLY, EITHER BY TAKING IT BACK TO THE NIGHT'S ACCOMMODATION OR PLACING IT IN THE BINS PROVIDED. IT IS NECESSARY TO AVOID MAKING A LOT OF NOISE BECAUSE THE WILDLIFE REQUIRES SILENCE.

Useful Websites
germany.travel/en
schwarzwald-tourismus.info

SWITZERLAND

Start: Dielsdorf
Finish: Nyon
Distance: 199 mi (320 km)
Time: 16 days
Difficulty: easy
Accommodation: inns (*métairies*), B&Bs, shelters

38–39 Regensberg, a district of Dielsdorf, is considered to be the smallest city in Switzerland. You reach it during the first stage of the itinerary, after an ascent through vineyards.

Eco because: Far from mass tourism and holiday-makers, this itinerary is ideal for relaxing in the mountains and recharging one's batteries. It is also an opportunity to explore the culture of the Jura, stopping at the *métairies*, mountain inns where the owners are farmers and offer typical local menus.

Jura Crest Trail

In Switzerland everything appears perfect; the villages are well-kept and harmonize with the landscape, the major cities are tidy and ecologically aware. Its natural beauty, with peaceful valleys and magnificent mountains to explore, attract a number of tourists. More than 40,389 miles (65,000 km) of marked trails through some of the most beautiful landscapes in Europe make it a paradise for anyone who loves walking and losing themself in the infiniteness of the mountain roads. With a capillary network of transport, ski lifts, and cable cars, it is easy to reach the most panoramic peaks, just as it is easy to reach the starting points of the main trails, thanks to trains, buses, and boats. The combination of walking and public transport is a feather in the cap of the Swiss tourist industry, with ecological benefits.

The Jura Crest Trail, inaugurated in 1905, is one of the least challenging hikes in the country and follows the oldest long-distance trail in Switzerland, linking Zurich and Geneva in a sweeping arc. The panoramas are unforgettable: woods and pastures, towns and lakes accompany the views of the Alps, of the Black Forest, and of the Vosges mountains. Along the way, you enjoy the traditional Helvetic mountain hospitality.

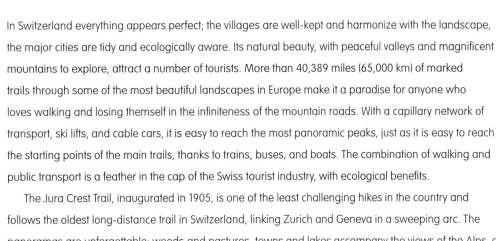

- Day 1
- Day 2
- Day 3
- Day 4
- Day 5
- Day 6
- Day 7
- Day 8
- Day 9
- Day 10
- Day 11
- Day 12
- Day 13
- Day 14
- Day 15
- Day 16

Dielsdorf
Brugg
Staffelegg
Unterer Hauenstein
Balsthal
Weissenstein
Frinvillier
Chasseral
Vue des Alpes
Noiraigue
Les Rochats
Ste-Croix
Vallorbe
Le Pont
Col du Marchairuz
St-Cergue
Nyon

39 *The small village of Boppelsen, in the Dielsdorf district. Here, every family originating from the village has the responsibility for the maintenance of public goods within the boundaries of the municipality.*

40 *Vineyards in autumnal colors slope down to Lake Biel. In front, there is St. Peter's Island; in the background, you see Ligerz, in the canton of Bern.*

41 top *The historic center of Brugg, in the canton of Aargau, and the Aare River, the longest and the most important of those that flow solely through Switzerland.*

41 bottom *Old buildings in Brugg. In the surrounding area, you can go hiking in the protected river park and cycle along marked trails.*

DAY 1: Dielsdorf–Brugg

You start from Dielsdorf station, climbing through the vineyards to Regensberg and Lägern, one of the peaks of the Jura, and continue to Baden and the Gebenstorfer Horn, from which you have a splendid view of the moated castle and the Jura chain. Three rivers join below Gebenstorfer Horn: the Reuss, the Limmat, and the Aare, known as Switzerland's "water castle." The trail passes through Gebenstorfer and heads for Brugg, where you spend the night.

DAY 2: Brugg–Staffelegg

After passing through Brugg's old town, you take a path that leads to the Linner Linde (linden tree), one of the oldest in Switzerland, planted 800 years ago, the starting point for many excursions. You walk through beech woods to Staffelegg, where you stop for the night.

DAY 3: Staffelegg–Unterer Hauenstein

Today's stage crosses five mountain passes: Staffelegg, Bänkerjoch, Salhöhe, where you stop for a break, and Schafmatt. The fifth and last of the day is the Unterer Hauenstein pass, where you spend the night.

DAY 4: Unterer Hauenstein–Balsthal

This morning the path climbs, and along the way you see stones with coats of arms, graffiti, and old bunkers from the Second World War. The trail then continues through woods and reaches Bärenwil, where it is a good idea to fill up with water at the village fountain. After Tiefmatt, you climb up a path with about 100 steps to Roggenschnarz, and after another effort, you reach the Roggenflue peak at almost 3,280 feet (1,000 m), which offers a wonderful panorama over the plateau. In the valley bottom, Balsthal and its castle await you: this is the end of the day's stage.

DAY 5: Balsthal–Balmberg

The first destination of this stage is the peak of the Höllchöpfli, which can be reached by a steep climb through woods and pastures. The last ascent of the day leads to the Weissenstein peak (4,213 feet [1,284 m]), a natural belvedere on Canton Soletta. You spend the night at Balmberg near the mountain.

DAY 6: Balmberg–Frinvillier

Today you conquer Mount Hasenmatt, the highest point of the stage (4,740 feet [1,445 m]), while in the valley you see Lake Biel. You reach Plagne, the first settlement beyond the linguistic frontier between German-speaking Switzerland and the French-speaking sector. From here, it is about another hour's walk to Frinvillier, where you can eat and sleep.

DAY 7: Frinvillier–Chasseral

The trail climbs steeply to Les Coperies and continues above Lake Biel to the highest point of the Bernese Jura, the Chasseral peak at 5,269 feet (1,606 m). Along the way there are several *métairies*, more and more frequent in the French part: you will be spoiled for choice when it comes to accommodation. From Chasseral, you can enjoy a spectacular view of the Three Lakes Region and, if the sky is clear, of the Alps from Mont Blanc to Säntis.

DAY 8: Chasseral–Vue des Alpes

From Chasseral, you begin the long descent to Le Pâquier, a winter sport resort. After passing through the resort, you climb again to the peak of Mont d'Amin, just a little above Vue des Alpes, the end of today's stage, where you stop for the night.

When to go: The best time for walking is from April to October.

How to get there: The nearest international airport is Zurich, then you take a train (about half an hour) or a car (about twenty minutes) to Dielsdorf..

What to pack: We recommend hiking boots with good ankle support and a rubber hiking sole. It is necessary to have protection from the sun and the rain as well as warm clothes: in the mountains the weather can be severe and change suddenly. First-aid kid, isothermal blanket and mobile phone for emergencies. Canteen and energy bars. An up-to-date map can be useful.

DAY 9: Vue des Alpes–Noiraigue

The first peak of the day is Mont Racine (4,593 feet [1,400 m]), which is followed by Tête de Ran. Descending you will come to the Grand Sagneule *métairie*, which has a restaurant adjacent to the paddocks for horses. You continue toward Col de la Tourne, then follow the path through the woods of Rochers de Tablettes, which offer a marvelous view of Lake Neuchâtel. A final, steep descent takes you to Noiraigue, the destination for this stage.

DAY 10: Noiraigue–Les Rochats

Today you will face the climb to Creux du Van: in the early morning there is a marvelous atmosphere as the first rays of the sun pierce the mist. This mountain, with its picturesque semicircular formation, looks like an amphitheater of vertical rock, almost 1 mile (1.6 km) wide and 1,640 feet (500 m) deep. It is one of the most important and exciting stages in the trail. You cross the pastures to Les Rochats, where you will find the restaurant and your accommodation.

DAY 11: Les Rochats–Sainte-Croix From Les Rochats the trail proceeds through woods and fields to the peak of the Chasseron, from which there is one of the most spectacular views of the Canton Vaud. From this natural terrace you can admire Lake Neuchâtel. You then arrive at Sainte-Croix, the world capital of music boxes, where you will stay the night.

DAY 12: Sainte-Croix–Vallorbe

The trail plunges into unspoiled nature and reaches Chalet de Grange-Neuve. You continue through the woods, enjoying wonderful views under the peak of Le Suchet: to the north you will see Lake Neuchâtel, to the south Lake Geneva. You follow the descent to Ballaigues, walking beside the Orbe River, crossing the Le Day viaduct, and climbing to the station of Vallorbe, an important railway and road junction on the border between Switzerland and France. You stay here for the night.

DAY 13: Vallorbe–Le Pont

In the morning you leave Vallorbe on the trail that climbs to Dent de Vaulion. At your feet lies Lac de Joux, and at its upper tip stands Le Pont, your destination, where there is a fine promenade beside the lake. You stop here for dinner and for the night.

DAY 14: Le Pont–Col du Marchairuz

Continuing along the same path as yesterday, you reach Mont Tendre, with a wonderful view of Lake Geneva ranging as far as Mont Blanc, the Alps, and the Vosges. You begin the descent toward Col du Marchairuz, the pass that links Lac de Joux with the winegrowing regions of Lake Geneva. At the bottom of the valley you can already glimpse Nyon, the end of your trail.

DAY 15: Col du Marchairuz–Saint-Cergue

The Col du Marchairuz links the Vallée de Joux to Lake Geneva with a climb that is rewarded by an all-round view of the Crêt de la Neuve. There follows a descent toward Saint-Cergue, where you stay the night, accompanied by fantastic views of the Alps, Lake Geneva, and Mont Blanc.

DAY 16: Saint-Cergue–Nyon

The first destination of today's walk is the rock bastions of Dôle: if you are lucky, you may see some chamois. You reach Col de Porte and the observatory. After Chalet de la Dôle, you take the forest path, cross the Bonmont golf course and the surrounding farmland, to arrive at Nyon on Lake Geneva, the end of your hike.

PORTUGAL

Fishermen's Trail

On the extreme southwestern tip of Europe, Portugal in ancient times was known as *finis terrae*, or "the end of the world," the exact point at which the known land ended and the infinite ocean began. This legendary past is matched by 497 miles (800 km) of coastline overlooking the Atlantic, historical villages, wonderful architecture, music, food, and wine: a combination that today attracts all kinds of traveler.

Thanks to the great variety of landscapes and climate, tourism makes a good contribution to the country's economy, and ecotourism is one of the fastest growing sectors. There are walks, riding trails, and cycle paths, and tours to discover the country's history, culture, and natural beauty—something for everyone. Numerous national parks protect the natural and man-made landscapes: the Parque Natural do Sudoeste Alentejano e Costa Vicentina is one of the best preserved stretches of European coastline.

Along this coastline, the Fishermen's Trail (Trilho dos Pescadores) is part of the Rota Vicentina, the historical trail that crosses the Alentejo and Algarve regions for about 249 miles (400 km). The hiking trails follow the coast and lead to beaches and fishing villages: the section that runs from Porto Covo to Odeceixe is the one that offers the most exciting views from the high Atlantic cliffs. Although there are no major ups and downs, this trek requires physical fitness because you often walk on sand. Fishing villages, dishes based on local products, and a wild maritime landscape with dunes, vast beaches, and small bays will charm visitors.

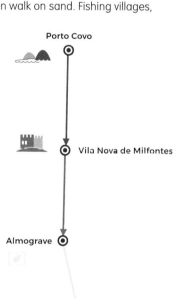

44 Sines has the largest Portuguese port and is considered to be the main logistic coastal center in the country.

Porto Covo

Vila Nova de Milfontes

Almograve

Zambujeira do Mar

Odeceixe

- Day 1
- Day 2
- Day 3
- Day 4

44

Start: Porto Covo
Finish: Odeceixe
Distance: 47 mi (75 km)
Time: 4 days
Difficulty: easy but requires fitness
Accommodation: tents, hostels, rented rooms

44–45 The ocean waters along the Trilho dos Pescadores (Fishermen's Trail) are dotted with rocks emerging from the waves.

Eco because: Along the route you sometimes catch glimpses of unusual natural attractions, such as otters or storks nesting on the cliffs (a unique sight in the world).

When to go: From September to May, in the low season.

How to get there: From the Lisbon-Portela airport you reach Porto Covo by bus, about 106 miles (170 km) away.

What to pack: Tent and sleeping bag. Lightweight clothing, with long pants for protection against the undergrowth, overpants, and trail shoes with good ankle support. We recommend wearing gaiters to avoid filling your shoes with sand; hiking poles are useful. Earmuffs and muffler for protection from the wind. Hat, sunglasses, and sunscreen. Canteen (at least half a gallon of water in winter, more in summer) because there is no drinking water available along the trail. First-aid kit, anti-blister bandages, insect repellent, painkillers and disinfectant for minor wounds. Waterproof bags for cameras and video equipment. Maps and guides in your own language.

DAY 1: Porto Covo–Vila Nova de Milfontes

You start from Porto Covo, a fishing village with whitewashed houses, then head southward following the green-blue signposts. On this first day, you walk along the beaches and on the vast sand dunes of Ilha do Pessegueiro, Aivados, and Praia do Malhão. It is a tiring stage, both because of the distance and the sandy ground, but it reveals surprising discoveries of deserted coves. In the evening, you arrive at Vila Nova de Milfontes, where you camp for the night.

DAY 2: Vila Nova de Milfontes–Almograve

The following day, in the first part of the walk, you enjoy the panorama of Vila Nova de Milfontes and its 16th-century fortress. Here the Mira River, which runs from south to north, flows into the Atlantic Ocean, after passing through the Parque Natural do Sudoeste Alentejano e Costa Vicentina. You again walk on the sand, and at the end of the day, you reach Almograve, where you spend the night in a hostel or in a previously booked room.

DAY 3: Almograve–Zambujeira do Mar

Almograve is a quiet place to visit without haste and has a beautiful beach, which is part of the natural park. On the walk you encounter small fishing harbors, jagged rocky coasts, and red sand dunes that look like Martian landscapes. You can also see storks unusually nesting on the cliffs. You reach Zambujeira do Mar, where you prepare for the night in tents.

DAY 4: Zambujeira do Mar–Odeceixe

The itinerary for this day is less challenging than the previous ones: you cross the beaches of Alteirinhos, Carvalhal, Machados, and Amalia on the way to Azenhas do Mar. You enjoy the extraordinary landscape all along the route. Odeceixe, at the end of your walk, has one of the most beautiful beaches on this coast, on the mouth of the Seixe River, a popular canoeing destination. It is the ideal place to rest after the efforts of your hike.

▶ ECO-TIPS

AVOID DAMAGING OR GATHERING SAMPLES OF PLANTS OR ROCKS, OR LEAVING TRASH OR OTHER SIGNS OF YOUR PASSAGE ALONG THE TRAIL (FOR EXAMPLE, PAPER TISSUES DROPPED ON THE GROUND TAKE A LONG TIME TO DECOMPOSE). ONLY WALK ON THE TRAIL AND DO NOT DAMAGE OR ALTER THE SIGNPOSTS. DO NOT LIGHT FIRES OR DROP CIGARETTE BUTTS. LEAVE GATES AND DOORS OPEN OR CLOSED, AS YOU FOUND THEM. ALWAYS RESPECT PRIVATE PROPERTY AND THE HOSPITALITY OF THE LOCAL PEOPLE.

Useful Websites
visitportugal.com/en
portuguesetrails.com/en
pousadasjuventude.pt/pt/pousadas
/almograve

46 top Many of the bays along the trail have a half-moon shape. During the trek, you walk a lot in the sand, so it is better to be prepared.
46 bottom Zambujeira do Mar: this little fishing village on the cliff seems suspended over the sea. It is one of the most beautiful spots on the Alentejo coast.
46–47 Odeceixe beach, protected by cliffs and Mediterranean scrub, is a surfer's paradise about 2 miles (3.5 km) away from the village of the same name.

Sentiero del Brigante Trail

Start: Gambarie
Finish: Stilo/Bivongi or Serra San Bruno
Distance: 87 mi (140 km)
Time: 7 days
Difficulty: easy/medium
Accommodation: refuges, hostels, guest houses, farm holiday

At the southern tip of Italy, Calabria is surrounded by the waters of the Ionian Sea and the Tyrrhenian Sea: this enchanting land has many emerald coasts and a mountainous core, with the chains of the Lucanian and Calabrian Apennines and the plateaus of Serra, Aspromonte, and Sila. This rocky treasure is all to be discovered: it preserves a number of woods greatly exceeding that of the other Southern regions, and its hinterland, harsh and wild, with many water courses, is still partly dedicated to pastoral activities.

One way to discover Calabria is to follow the Sentiero del Brigante trail, identified and marked by the GEA (the Aspromonte Trekkers' Group), and included in the Parco dell'Aspromonte plan as a thematic path. The reason for its unusual name ("Brigand's Path") lies in place names evoking the figures of rebels and brigands who in the past found refuge in these mountains. The itinerary travels along the ridge between the Parco Nazionale dell'Aspromonte, marked by great biodiversity, and the Parco Naturale Regionale delle Serre, a protected nature area.

48 top The state forest in Alto Aspromonte. It is notable for its tree species, of considerable size and many centuries old.
48 bottom In the distance, beyond the Strait of Sicily, you can see the city of Messina on the coast: it can be reached by ferry from Villa San Giovanni.
49 The Amendolea falls (known as Maesano) are three tiers, which each end in a hollow dug out by the incessant action of water on the rock. They are an impressive sight.

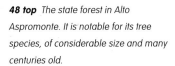

● Day 1
● Day 2
● Day 3
● Day 4
● Day 5
● Day 6
● Day 7

Eco because: It is a trail in the footsteps of rebels, brigands, and fugitives of every era, through areas of great natural interest. This land has a strong identity and authenticity: an unexpected welcome awaits you in these mountains that for too long have been considered hostile and impenetrable.

When to go: Preferably between April and October.

How to get there: The nearest airport is Reggio Calabria. From there you reach Gambarie by car, about 19 miles (30 km) away.

What to pack: Sleeping bag, hiking boots, garments that cover the arms and the legs, hat and sunglasses, sunscreen, and first-aid kit. Painkillers and disinfectant for minor injuries, headlamp, mineral supplements, and insect repellent. Canteen and food supplies.

50 top *The olive groves near San Lorenzo, one of the Greek villages in Calabria, between the streams of Melito and Amandolea.*
50 bottom *Stilo, a town included in the circuit of the most beautiful villages in Italy, lies at the foot of Monte Consolino. The Stilo wood is typical of the woods on the Calabrian Serre.*
51 *The Cattolica di Stilo, a small square-plan Byzantine church from the 10th century, bears witness to Byzantine rule, which lasted until the 11th century.*

DAY 1: Gambarie–Piani di Carmelia

The trail starts in Gambarie, a tourist resort where you can ski at 5,905 feet (1,800 m) above sea level, enjoying a magnificent view over the Strait of Messina. Gambarie is the headquarters of the Parco Nazionale dell'Aspromonte. You walk in the forest, alternating steep ascents and descents, and follow the path leading to Sant'Eufemia d'Aspromonte, where a mausoleum celebrates Giuseppe Garibaldi: here on these mountains, the hero of the two worlds, returning from his Sicilian expedition and moving northward to Rome, was wounded by the Piedmontese troops. You continue through the beech woods as far as Masso Grosso. You spend the night in Il Biancospino refuge, in Piani di Carmelia.

DAY 2: Piani di Carmelia–Zervò

In the morning you leave Piani di Carmelia and head for Zervò, a former sanatorium built in the 1920s for tuberculosis patients. Today, it is a hostel and guest house for trekkers.

DAY 3: Zervò–Canolo Nuova

During this stage you enter Valle dell'Uomo Morto ("Valley of the Dead Man"), a remote and inaccessible place in Aspromonte. This is one of numerous places whose names recall the centuries-long conflictual relationship between local people and their mountains. After the so-called Spartacus' Walls, Roman remains dating from 72–71 BC, you reach the Mercante pass, a crossroads on the ridge where roads from the south and north, the Ionian Sea, and the Tyrrhenian Sea converge. A little more than a mile (1.6 km) further you reach Canolo Nuova. This town was rebuilt in the mountains: its history is the opposite of that of many mountain villages, which were abandoned and then reconstructed by the sea. Here you stop for the night.

DAY 4: Canolo Nuova–Limina Pass

This stage takes you from Canolo Nuova to the Limina pass (2,697 feet [822 m]), which marks the boundary between Aspromonte and the Calabrian Serre mountains. On the plateau you can find the sanctuary of San Nicodemo. It is a place of pilgrimage all through the year. At a short distance, the three crosses on Monte Kellarana dominate the Ionian Sea, the Tyrrhenian Sea, and the sanctuary. You stay the night at the San Nicodemo farm.

DAY 5: Limina Pass–Croce Ferrata Pass

Today you walk on the ridge: to the east you see the Ionian coast and to the west the Tyrrhenian coast and the plains of Gioia Tauro. You walk through the great, luxuriant beech woods of the Calabrian Serre mountains and reach the Croce Ferrata pass, a mountain crossroads, where you find accommodation for the night.

DAY 6: Croce Ferrata Pass–Mongiana

The trail continues through the Parco Naturale Regionale delle Serre Calabresi, in a peculiar rural landscape teeming with little bridges, mills, fields of corn, hens, and stone farms (*pagghiari*). You reach Fabrizia, a small mountain town at 3,281 feet (1,000 m), where you can taste local food products, like mushrooms, corn bread (*pizzata*), and cured meats. Then you stop in Mongiana, once an important industry center thanks to the presence of iron, soapstone, plentiful water, and forests of beech and chestnut trees necessary for the ironworks. There is a traditional job here that is now disappearing because it is very tiring and wearing: that of the *carbonari*, miners of precious, high-quality charcoal, produced from healthy, scented trees, never subject to acid rain, and sold to high-end Italian and Russian restaurants. Near Mongiana, the Riserva Naturale Cropani-Micone protects a very important area of woodland.

DAY 7: Mongiana–Stilo/Bivongi

From Mongiana you head for Ferdinandea, a former foundry founded around 1800 by Ferdinand II, King of the Two Sicilies. Next to it, there is the Gran Bosco di Stilo ("Great Forest of Stilo"), comprising mainly beech and fir trees, heather, and holly. Then, in a holm oak wood, you find the megaliths of Nardodipace, lesser-known, gigantic constructions from 6,000 years ago, an Italian Stonehenge discovered by chance in the early years of the last decade. According to recent studies, these megaliths seem to be a natural phenomenon. You then approach Stilo and see La Cattolica, a little church near the town at the foot of Monte Consolino: it is a beautiful testimony to the glorious Byzantine past of Italy. Other significant sights in the town are the Norman castle from the year 1000 and the Sanctuary of Santa Maria della Grotta. The final stage of the trek is Bivongi, a town in the hills famous for its wine and for its view on the Ionian Sea.

OPTIONAL

DAY 7: Mongiana–Serra San Bruno

Instead of heading for Stilo and the Ionian coast, you can move into the hinterland. From Mongiana, you cross the Archiforo woods with its majestic silver fir trees and ancient beech trees to reach your final destination, Serra San Bruno, where you find one of the most important charterhouses in Italy.

ECO-TIPS

DURING THIS MOUNTAIN TREK, IT IS GOOD PRACTICE TO CARRY YOUR TRASH WITH YOU AND THEN, WHEN YOU CAN, LEAVE IT IN THE APPROPRIATE CONTAINERS.

Useful Websites
italia.it/en
turiscalabria.it
sentierodelbrigante.it
rifugioilbiancospino.it
tenutasannicodemo.com
zervo.jimdo.com
museocertosa.org

Gozo Coastal Walk

Gozo is part of the Maltese archipelago, comprised of three main islands in the Mediterranean Sea (Gozo, Malta, and Comino) between southern Europe and Africa.

The country's history dates back to the fifth millennium BC, as demonstrated by Ġgantija, the megalithic temple complex from the Neolithic period, a UNESCO World Heritage Site.

Gozo is a verdant island surrounded by a sparkling sea, ideal for diving and snorkeling. In order to protect these natural wonders, the government follows a "green" philosophy, keeping the land and the sea clean, developing new methods for the collection and conservation of rainwater, and using renewable energy.

The Gozo Coastal Walk is an itinerary that offers breathtaking landscapes and glimpses of rare beauty, in addition to archaeological and cultural treasures. This circular trail wanders along the coast and is perfectly safe: it can be undertaken by anyone who is reasonably fit in their own time.

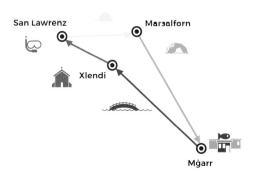

San Lawrenz
Marsalforn
Xlendi
Mġarr

52 *Old mill between Nadur and Qala. There are thirteen mills on the island, generally built with a square or rectangular base and a cylindrical central body.*

● Day 1
● Day 2
○ Day 3
● Day 4

Start: Mġarr
Finish: Mġarr
Distance: 31 mi (50 km)
Time: 4 days
Difficulty: medium
Accommodation: farmhouses, hotels, B&Bs, hostels

52–53 The tower on the rocky bay of Dweira was also used to prevent unauthorized individuals from having access to Fungus Rock and picking the Malta Fungus, to which exceptional qualities were attributed.

Eco because: The Gozo Coastal Walk was organized by the Maltese government as part of the Eco-Gozo project, a sustainability program to protect the attractions and promote the island as an ecotourism destination. Eco-Gozo allows visitors to encounter local culture and understand it through meeting the residents.

54 A small watchtower surrounded by yellow stone walls near the village of Xlendi. It is one of the Lascaris towers built by the Order of Saint John in Malta and dates from 1650.

55 left The Blue Hole, the iconic sub-aqua site on Gozo, is an abrupt drop into the sea created by thousands of years of wind and waves. At the bottom, a great grotto, which is a spectacular sight.

55 right The San Blas valley, which opens onto San Blas beach, is a particular red-orange color. It can be reached only on foot, and therefore it is fairly quiet.

DAY 1: Mġarr–Xlendi

The walk starts in front of the ferry terminus of Mġarr. You follow the trail parallel to the coast, which is dominated by the imposing Fort Chambray, and reach a viewpoint from which it is possible to enjoy the view over the little island of Comino. The trail along the coast leads to ancient salt flats in the little inlet of ix-Xatt l-Aħmar. Just a little further on you come to the fougasse, a kind of rock-hewn mortar designed by the Knights of Malta to fire large quantities of stone onto approaching enemy ships. The clear waters in this area are ideal for scuba diving. You walk along the beautiful inlet of Mġarr ix-Xini, then take the path down to the beach, where you can swim and relax in the shade of the tamarisk trees. This isolated gorge is home to a wide variety of flora and fauna. Continuing along the trail, you pass a promontory where you take one of the minor paths along the cliffs, toward the tower of Xlendi. You cross a small stone bridge to reach the picturesque fishing village of Xlendi, popular for its fine beach, caves, and scuba diving. You stay here for the night.

DAY 2: Xlendi–San Lawrenz

From Xlendi you take the road that leads toward Victoria, the capital of Gozo. After about a half mile, you take the steep and winding path that leads to the edge of the village of Kerċem, passing through the abundant vegetation of the valley of Wied il-Lunzjata. You reach the town of Santa Luċija and then the freshwater pool Ta 'Sarraflu. To rejoin the coast at Wardija Point, you take a pleasant path along the cliffs. Here stands the Punic sanctuary, or Nympheum, sculpted in the yellow limestone about 2,500 years ago and said to have been dedicated to the goddess Tanit. Along the trail, there are spectacular views over the bay of Dweira and the Fungus Rock. The area of Dweira has numerous sinkholes, the largest of which is the Inland Sea, a briny pool that formed many thousands of years ago, linked to the sea by a 230-feet-long (70 m) tunnel that

TRAVEL TIPS

When to go: From mid-September to mid-June.

How to get there: By plane to Malta and then by ferry to Ċirkewwa (17 miles [27 km] from the airport) and to Mġarr (Gozo). Or by ferry from the main Mediterranean ports.

What to pack: Walking shoes and comfortable clothing. Bathing suit, sunhat, sunglasses, sunscreen. A canteen for water. First-aid kit, anti-blister bandages, painkillers and disinfectant for small wounds, insect repellent. Maps in your own language.

passes through the steep cliff. Here you can have a refreshing swim. You then take the trail along the coast to reach the best spot for admiring the picturesque Blue Hole, the ideal place for scuba diving. It is 50 feet (15 m) deep and 33 feet (10 m) wide, linked to the open sea by a tunnel. The trail climbs through endemic plants, the most characteristic being the Helichrysum, which grows only on the western cliffs of Gozo and in the Fungus Rock Nature Reserve. The trail passes through quarries before climbing toward the village of San Lawrenz and its parish church.

DAY 3: San Lawrenz–Marsalforn

This part of the walk begins at the church of San Lawrenz and moves in the direction of the nearby village of Gharb and the Il-Madonna Taż-Żejt chapel. You walk inland, passing some refurbished farmhouses and well-cared-for little fields. Beside the trail appears the imposing lighthouse of Ta' Ġordan, perched on a hill, and a little further ahead, the chapel of San Dimitri. The trail rejoins the coast with its rocks sculpted by the wind and leads to the wonderful valley of Wied il-Mielaħ.

It then winds eastward, and you can admire spectacular cliffs and large caves. Later the trail approaches a valley that ends in the magnificent Wied il-Għasri gorge. You continue along the coast to reach a stretch of ancient salt marshes. This vast complex of artificial basins, cisterns, and canals was dug by hand from limestone platforms, and some of the cisterns are still used for the production of sea salt. You finally arrive at the bay of Xwejni and the coastal city of Marsalforn, where you stop for the night.

DAY 4: Marsalforn–Mġarr

This is the longest and most challenging section of the walk. You set out toward the cave of Calypso, the cavern home to the nymph Calypso, mentioned by Homer in the *Odyssey*. The panorama from the platform above the cave and from its mouth, looking out over the sea, is amazing. Ramla Bay, with its red sand, is also an impressive sight: at the back of the beach, there are sand dunes, the best example remaining in Gozo and Malta of this particular habitat. From here, you turn inland. The gigantic reeds that you encounter along the way are used by farmers to create shade and form a windbreak around the fields. From the top of the hills, there are splendid views over the fertile valley of San Blas. The trail descends through lush citrus orchards, then climbs again to the panoramic viewpoint near the village of Nadur. As you approach the coast, you can see the tower of San Blas, built in

1667 as part of the coastal defenses around Gozo and Malta. The path winds around the great rocks and through verdant vegetation, under the magnificent cliffs to reach Daħlet Qorrot. This little bay is used by fishermen who have dug storerooms into the limestone cliffs. Once you reach the village of Qala, you see the chapel of the Immaculate Conception, the ancient walls of which bear historical graffiti. The road curves beyond another ancient chapel to reach Ħondoq Bay, with a splendid view over the sea. From the beach you take the path westward along the coast to return to Mġarr, a little more than a mile away. In this last stage, it is possible to admire little inlets, the island of Comino, and its Blue Lagoon.

Andros Route

58–59 A view of Chora, Andros. The oldest area of the town is on the narrow peninsula extending into the center of the bay. At the end, there is an island with the ruins of a Venetian castle.

59 A kamara, or arch, linking the island to the mainland. Beyond it a lighthouse is perched on a rock in the sea.

Greece comprises three main geographical areas: the mainland, the Peloponnese peninsula, and about 6,000 islands and islets scattered through the Aegean and the Ionian Seas. Among the Hellenic archipelagos, one of the most important is the Cyclades, of which Andros is the most northern island: it is a mainly mountainous land, surrounded by beaches, with valleys, waterways, and beautiful scenery, and far away from mass tourism. It is the ideal destination for hikers, offering a variety of trails, including the Andros Route, which the European Ramblers' Association awarded the title of "Leading Quality Trail–Best of Europe" in October 2015. From north to south, among natural landscapes and important monuments, this hike will evoke great emotion. This itinerary avoids two of the traditional stages, so that walkers do not visit the same place twice. Given the considerable number of paths on the island, it is possible to plan a personal itinerary.

Start: Frousei
Finish: Dipotamata
Distance: 45 mi (72 km)
Time: 8 days
Difficulty: medium/difficult
Accommodation: B&Bs or studios
(single rooms with cooking facilities)

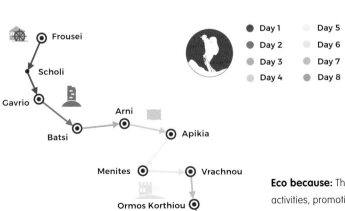

● Day 1	○ Day 5
● Day 2	● Day 6
● Day 3	● Day 7
● Day 4	● Day 8

Frousei
Scholi
Gavrio
Batsi
Arni
Apikia
Menites
Vrachnou
Ormos Korthiou
Dipotamata

Eco because: The Andros Route combines research and environmental activities, promoting the local culture and sustainable tourism on the island. The main objective is to record, preserve, and improve the old hiking trails that cross Andros. Almost half of them are located in important nature reserves, where many rare, endemic species of flora and fauna can be found.

When to go: The walk can be undertaken throughout the year, but not in July and August.

How to get there: From the Athens international airport, you continue by bus or taxi to Rafina on the coast (18.5 miles [30 km]). Then you take the ferry to Gavrio (42 miles [26 km] by sea) and from there you can take a taxi to Frousei, about 5 miles (8 km) away.

What to pack: As for most hikes, it is best to choose comfortable, layered clothing. We advise waterproof hiking boots for crossing streams, canteen, hat, sunglasses, sunscreen, bathing suit, first-aid kit, anti-blister bandages, painkillers and disinfectant for minor wounds, insect repellent. Maps and guides to the island.

▶ ECO-TIPS

ALONG THE ROUTE, YOU WILL ENCOUNTER TEMPORARY GATES OR METAL GRILLS USED TO FENCE IN THE LAND OR GOATS: THEY SHOULD BE OPENED AND CLOSED AGAIN AFTER PASSING THROUGH. THERE ARE NUMEROUS SPRINGS AND RIVERS WITH DRINKABLE WATER ALONG THE ROADS OF ANDROS, AND THEY ARE CLEARLY MARKED.

Useful Websites
visitgreece.gr
andros.gr/en

DAY 1: Frousei–Scholi–Gavrio

The hike begins with the exploration of the northern part of Andros, starting from the old village of Frousei. You walk through varied landscapes, with splendid panoramas, chapels, wooded ravines, centuries-old olive trees, stone buildings, and watermills. You arrive at Scholi and continue for another half hour to Gavrio, the port of Andros, well protected in the bay, where you stay the night.

DAY 2: Gavrio–Batsi

From Gavrio you return to Scholi. Today you start and end on the west coast, with a detour into the internal highlands. Along the way, you reach the pretty village of Agios Petros with its imposing Hellenistic tower. From here you see the islets of Gavrio, the historical fortified monastery of Agia, one of the oldest in the Cyclades, and the splendid bays of Kypri and Batsi. The road that leads out of Agios Petros and descends toward Batsi, your destination for this stage, is exposed to the wind.

DAY 3: Batsi–Katakilos–Arni

During today's stage, you move from the coast to the mountainous hinterland. The trail runs through impressive changes of scenery, with verdant vegetation and ravines along the wooded valley of Andros. You come to the village of Katakilos, and before you reach Arni, where you stop for the night, you have to carefully cross three beautiful ravines.

DAY 4: Arni–Apikia

The next morning, you set out for one of the most exciting paths on Andros, which partly follows the ridge of the highest peak on the island, Mount Kouvara (3,264 feet [995 m]). From the Arni valley, you walk east toward the villages of Vourkoti, Katakalei, and Apikia. The woods, the villages, the views along the coast, and the mountainous territory of Andros offer ever-changing scenarios: an unforgettable path, but it is better to avoid it when cloudy or windy. At the end of the walk, you stop at Apikia for the night.

DAY 5: Apikia–Menites

This stage follows another attractive path that explores the verdant villages around Chora, the capital of Andros. You encounter the farming villages of Ypsilou and Lamyra, passing through flourishing orchards on cobbled paths and coming across numerous springs that make the walk refreshing and pleasant all year round. The final stop is in Menites, a village on Mount Petalo, rich in springs.

DAY 6: Menites–Vrachnou

In the morning, you start out from Menites and come across a series of fine watermills before you reach Mesaria, an attractive medieval village. The walk continues toward the second highest mountain chain on Andros, Gerakonas (2,362 feet [720 m]). Along the way, you

pass the arched bridge of Steichiomeni and the fortified monastery of Panachradou, from which there are enchanting views over the valley of the Big River. Finally, you arrive at the village of Vrachnou, the end of today's stage.

DAY 7: Vrachnou–Ormos Korthiou

Today you walk through the central and southern part of the island, with its important agricultural heritage and the rich biodiversity of the mountain chains of Gerakonas and Rachi. The path descends to the coastal village of Ormos Korthiou, where you stay for the night. From here, there is a beautiful view over the bay of Mylos.

DAY 8: Ormos Korthiou–Dipotamata

In this last stage of the walk, you set out again from Ormos Korthiou and, passing through the rural hinterland, which extends to the southern part of Andros, you reach Dipotamata. The valley you walk along is crossed by an old cobbled road that, until the 1960s, linked the village of Korthi with Chora. At the point where the road meets the river, there is the delightful arched stone bridge of Dipotamata. Here you will also find small chapels, stables, threshed fields, and windmills. Dipotamata is an EU official ecological site that can be crossed only on foot. At Dipotamata, your walk along the Andros Route ends.

60 top A small waterfall on the island. Andros is considered to be the greenest island in all the archipelago.

60 bottom left A lookout tower on Andros, the northernmost island in the Cyclades and the second largest after Naxos.

60 bottom left Trekker walking along the trail. Andros can be enjoyed in all its splendor, which is "non-tourist" and unspoiled: up to now, it has avoided the tourism of the other Aegean islands.

61 The village of Ormos Korthiou on the coast. The nearby valley of Dipotamata is also worth a visit: it is a natural area transformed into an ecological museum of hydroelectric energy.

MOROCCO

Start: Chefchaouen
Finish: Bab Taza
Distance: 35 mi (56 km)
Time: 5 days
Difficulty: medium
Accommodation: *gîtes* and tents

62–63 Chefchaouen rests in a small valley. The oldest part of the town rises toward the top of the mountain: at the highest point, you find the sources of the Ras al-Ma waterfalls.

Eco because: The itinerary presented here is one of the best introductions to the Rif mountains. It allows direct contact with the local people, who host hikers in their simple homes for the night.

From Chefchaouen to Bab Taza

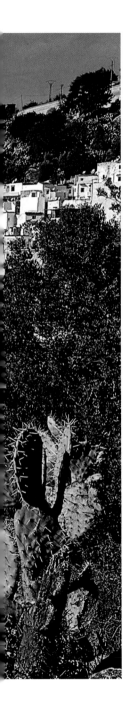

The beauty of the Moroccan landscape is peerless: Africa, Europe, and the Middle East blend here in a fascinating combination. Lapped by the waters of the Mediterranean and the Atlantic, this African country is the meeting point of multiple influences: a magical place, in which diversity matches a commitment toward the environment. The Moroccan Responsible Tourism Charter and the Moroccan Sustainable Tourism Awards have been established here to guarantee the sustainability of the tourist industry, according to precise standards. In this favorable context, a growing number of companies and tourist destinations have been recognized for their environmental responsibility. Local organizations, supported by the government, set up structures for rural tourism (like the gîtes, basic apartments, and hostels) and manage the routes and training for guides.

Among the regions of this country, Tangier-Tétouan-Alhoceima proposes several zero-impact trips, profiting from its natural landscapes and the protection of its biodiversity. It is a haven for marine and terrestrial fauna and migratory birds, with beaches, waterfalls, canyons, and snow-capped mountains. The coast lies between the Atlantic and the Mediterranean, near the Rif, the greenest mountains in Morocco: springtime, with the blaze of wildflowers, is one of the most pleasant times to walk here. An irresistible attraction for anyone who loves hiking.

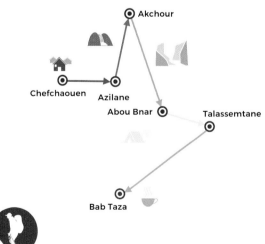

- ● Day 1
- ● Day 2
- ● Day 3
- ○ Day 4
- ● Day 5

63 *This blue town was founded in 1471 by Andalusian and Muslim exiles: for this reason, the old part recalls Andalusian towns, with uneven narrow streets.*

When to go: Spring and autumn are the best times.

How to get there: You arrive at the Tangier Ibn Battuta airport, and from there, you take a bus to Chefchaouen, about 7.5 miles (12 km) away.

What to pack: Tent, sleeping bag, food, canteen. Hiking boots, clothes that cover the arms and the legs, hat, sunglasses, sunscreen. Painkillers and disinfectant for minor wounds. Medicines for sunstroke and intestinal problems.

64 left A visitor during a mountain trek. It is better to be accompanied by an experienced guide to reach destinations in time.
64 right A footbridge crosses the Akchour Falls, a UNESCO biosphere reserve. The route to reach them goes through the Parc National de Talassemtane.
65 At the end, the Akchour Falls have some natural pools where you can swim, although the water is very cold.

DAY 1: Chefchaouen–Azilane or Afeska

The first day of the walk starts with a climb from Chefchaouen. Flanking the southern slopes of Jebel El Kelaa, the path follows a stream that runs through the village of Aïm Tissimlane, then veers toward the Sfiha Telj pass. It is a challenging climb, but on clear days you can see the Mediterranean from here. You continue to the village of Azilane: here you can stay for the night with a family or in an apartment. Alternatively, you can continue for another hour along a more level path to Afeska, where similar accommodation is available.

DAY 2: Azilane or Afeska–Akchour

In the morning, you set out through oak and pinewoods to Sidi Meftah. Here you descend toward Imizzar on the banks of the Oued Farda River and continue northward along the mule track that leads to Pont Farda. Here, near Ouslaf, the trail leaves the river and arrives in the suburbs of Akchour, on the Oued Kelaâ River. An unforgettable trek of 2 miles (3 km) takes you from Akchour to Pont de Dieu, a red stone arch, 82 feet

(25 m) high: for thousands of years the river has eroded the rock, creating the sculpture you see today. You can also visit the Akchour waterfalls, a UNESCO biosphere reserve. The trail to the waterfalls is well marked: as you draw nearer, the trail becomes less straightforward but the landscape is even more beautiful. The waterfalls grow until you reach the highest one, where the water has patiently carved capricious forms in the limestone. You reach Akchour, where you spend the night.

DAY 3: Akchour–Abou Bnar

Early in the morning, you leave Akchour heading north, crossing the bridge over the Oued Kelaâ River and then taking the trail for Izrafene. The village is the mid-point on the day's walk. From Izrafene, the dirt road follows a narrow valley, gradually turning east on a ridge. At the fork in the trail, you look out for the path toward Abou Bnar, then you continue along the river through an open landscape until you reach the marabout (sanctuary) of Sidi Jil. This is a lovely place to camp, but if you walk on for a further thirty minutes, you reach a large meadow near the El Ma Souka wellspring, where you camp for the night.

DAY 4: Abou Bnar–Talassemtane

From the Abou Bnar campsite, you return to the main path, cross the river, and walk south toward the pinewoods. Then the trail begins to climb. You continue along the main trail: to the west Jebel Lakraa dominates the countryside. In the late morning, you reach the village of Talassemtane, in the national park by the same name. The park is a paradise for those who love hiking, and there is time to explore the area, observing the wildlife, in particular the Barbary apes.

DAY 5: Talassemtane–Bab Taza

On the last day you walk along the main trail down a steep slope. You cross a large meadow and walk into the Jebel Setsou cork oak forest before arriving at Bab Taza, a village that offers some cafés and hotels along the main street. The walk ends here.

66–67 *The last stage of the trek is downhill through fields of crops and large grazing areas.*

ECO-TIPS

IT IS A WISE CHOICE TO HIRE AN EXPERT LOCAL GUIDE WHO CAN FACILITATE ACCESS TO A SERIES OF SERVICES, SUCH AS THE HIRING OF MULES AND ACCOMMODATION (THE HIKERS' MAPS FOR THE AREA ARE NOT ALWAYS PRECISE).

Useful Websites
visitmorocco.com
gitetalassemtane.com/en
ecologie.ma/parc-national-de-talassemtane

Sinai Trail *(Darb Sina)*

Egypt is a proud and independent country with more than six thousand years of civilization behind it. It attracts the explorer in us with its immense treasures: the pyramids, the secret tombs of the pharaohs, the treasures in the Egyptian Museum in Cairo, the Red Sea, rich vegetation and fauna, and the vast expanses of desert with verdant oases populated by fascinating and mysterious Bedouin tribes.

The Sinai Trail was the first long-distance hiking trail in the country, and it is officially recognized by the Egyptian Ministry of Tourism. Opened in 2015, it was 137 miles (220 km) and involved three Bedouin tribes in its organization. Originally it ran from the Gulf of Aqaba to the peak of Jebel Katherina—the highest mountain in Egypt—and in 2016 it was voted best tourist project in the world by BGTW Tourism Awards. The three tribes initially involved in the trail have worked to extend it to others: now the Sinai Trail is 342 miles (550 km) long and links the Gulf of Aqaba and the Gulf of Suez through a 54-day circular hike, involving eight tribes in its management.

The itinerary that we recommend goes from Ras Shetan on the coast of the Gulf of Aqaba to Ein Kidd, an enchanting oasis with palm trees and bamboo groves. The trail crosses wadis, sandy deserts, and oases in the territory of the Tarabin and Mueina tribes.

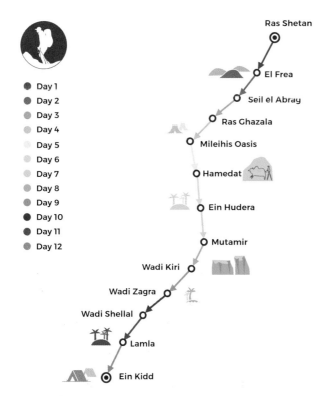

Day 1
Day 2
Day 3
Day 4
Day 5
Day 6
Day 7
Day 8
Day 9
Day 10
Day 11
Day 12

Ras Shetan
El Frea
Seil el Abray
Ras Ghazala
Mileihis Oasis
Hamedat
Ein Hudera
Mutamir
Wadi Kiri
Wadi Zagra
Wadi Shellal
Lamla
Ein Kidd

68–69 A Bedouin camp near Ras Shetan, the starting point of the Sinai Trail, which ends at Ein Kidd.

Start: Ras Shetan (Gulf of Aqaba)
Finish: Ein Kidd (oasis)
Distance: 112 mi (180 km)

Time: 12 days
Difficulty: medium
Accommodation: Bedouin tents

Eco because: This trail is a community project that aims to support the region by creating a sustainable tourist economy in which jobs with fair wages are made available to the Bedouin communities in remote and marginalized areas. Nowadays, the trail offers regular work to almost fifty nomads, who work as guides, camel drivers, hosts, and cooks, and at the same time contributes to safeguarding the Bedouin heritage of the Sinai, in danger of extinction. The hike is made exclusively accompanied by one of the guides from the local tribes. A visit is made to the Bedouin camps and it is possible to meet the women and children who sell handmade goods; the trade helps to preserve the traditional crafts and is a source of income for the people who live here. The food eaten during the hike is supplied by local producers. The Sinai Trail is developing a range of traditional craft products, mountain honey, and olive oil that can be purchased at the end of the journey. The local people receive a fair wage for the production and sale of the products, and the profits go to the Sinai Trail Bedouin Cooperative, allowing them to continue with their work in developing the trail and supporting the Bedouin communities involved.

When to go: Spring and autumn are the best seasons, because the weather is not too hot.

How to get there: The nearest international airport is Sharm el-Sheik; from here you travel by car to Ras Shetan, about 102 miles (165 km) away.

What to pack: A small backpack with water, snacks, batteries, and a waterproof jacket. A larger bag will be carried by camel, just for clothing. A tent, mattress, and sleeping bag must be carried separately. It is essential to seal the sleeping bag and clothes in dry bags, in case of rain. Hiking boots, long-sleeved sweater, fleece sweater, waterproof jacket, long pants, sunhat, sunglasses, first-aid kit, water purification tablets, insect repellent, sunscreen, army knife, lighter, headlamp.

ECO-TIPS

THESE ARE REMOTE PLACES, AND THE HIKE PASSES THROUGH UNCONTAMINATED ENVIRONMENTS. DURING THIS EXPERIENCE, HIKERS INTERACT WITH THE LOCAL COMMUNITY, AND THEREFORE THEY SHOULD DRESS IN ACCORDANCE WITH LOCAL CUSTOMS, WEARING LONG PANTS TO COVER THE LEGS, AS THE BEDOUINS DO. YOU HAVE TO ASK FOR PERMISSION BEFORE TAKING PHOTOGRAPHS OF THE PEOPLE, IN PARTICULAR WOMEN.

Useful Websites
egypt.travel
sinaitrail.net

DAY 1: Ras Shetan–El Frea

The hike begins listening to ancient Bedouin stories during the walk toward the palm oasis of Ein Malha, continuing over colored rocks toward areas with palm trees, fig trees, and bamboo at the foot of the mountain.

DAY 2: El Frea–Seil el Abrag

In the morning you take an excursion in the harsh coastal mountains, passing a small oasis and climbing upward. You pass through the Colored Canyon, one of the natural wonders of the Sinai, a labyrinth of sandstone rock colored yellow, purple, red, magenta, and gold, that rises to 131 feet (40 m). You continue through the wadi to the evening camp.

DAY 3: Seil el Abrag–Ras Ghazala

You walk along the winding wadi, beyond the oasis of Ein Furtaga, through the gorges, away from the coastal mountains toward the sandstone desert.

DAY 4: Ras Ghazala–Mileihis Oasis

You walk through wild, rocky gorges in the sandstone valleys of Umm Hadabat. Once you have passed Umm Hadabat, you camp in the Moiyet el Mileihis oasis.

DAY 5: Mileihis Oasis–Hamedat

It is possible to climb Jebel Milehis, the first real peak of the Sinai Trail. On clear days, from the peak, it is possible to see the Hejaz region in Arabia and the highlands of St Katherine, where the Sinai Trail ends, although they are still a week's hike away. Then you cross the sandstone pass to Hamedat, where the rocks are decorated with graffiti left by pilgrims over the centuries.

DAY 6: Hamedat–Ein Hudera

You reach the Ein Hudera oasis, which, according to legend, hides an immense treasure. A number of Bedouin families live here, and it is a staging post for guides and camels.

DAY 7: Ein Hudera–Mutamir

You pass the prehistoric tombs of Nawamis and walk to Jebel Mutamir. From the top of these hills, there is a vast panoramic view of the desert. The camp is set up nearby.

DAY 8: Mutamir–Wadi Kiri

You walk through the windswept desert, passing the peaks of Jebel Makharumm, "the mountain with a hole." You can see Jebel Barga clearly from here, a high and solitary peak standing in a wide plain.

DAY 9: Wadi Kiri–Wadi Zagra

You reach Wadi Zagra through a narrow wadi, where there is an old water well, and you camp here for the night.

DAY 10: Wadi Zagra–Wadi Shellal

You continue along the long and winding wadi toward Wadi Shellal.

DAY 11: Wadi Shellal–Lamla

The hike proceeds along other wadis and various passes to Lamla.

DAY 12: Lamla–Ein Kidd

Finally, you reach Ein Kidd, where the excursion ends. The overnight camp can be set up in the oasis or near the village.

70 top The Sinai Trail was the first long-distance trekking trail in Egypt, 143 miles (230 km) from the Gulf of Aqaba to the summit of the highest mountain of the Sinai range.

70 bottom left During the trek across the Sinai desert with the Tarabin tribe, you will see a brightly colored canyon. This is one of the most iconic deserts in the Middle East.

70 bottom right Lunch in the Wadi Hudera, with unleavened Bedouin bread baked in the hot ashes. Today, not many Bedouins or farmers still know the ancient baking technique dating from about 2,000 BC.

71 Trekkers guided by a Bedouin. The three tribes that opened the trail have worked with others to extend it. Today the itinerary is 342 miles (550 km) long, takes 54 days, and involves eight tribes.

Israel National Trail

Seas, deserts and oases, green uplands, streams, and parks: Israel, even though it is small, is a surprisingly varied land. Moreover, in regard to ecology and sustainable development, the country is in the vanguard, including in areas such as water administration, the increase in renewable energy, and agriculture 4.0. If you want to get to know this extraordinary land, there is no better way than covering it from north to south, on foot.

The Israel National Trail (INT), which was opened in 1995, starts at Tel Dan in the far north and crosses the entire length of the country, as far as Eilat, in the far south. The trail was conceived in order to give a complete vision of all the possible environments and landscapes in the country. The INT goes through many villages and small towns, and has many options and opportunities: for example, you can stay near civilization or be at one with the desert. There are no real destinations and there is not a network of accommodations, as in the other great European trails. However, there are trail angels, volunteers who live nearby and make travelers' journeys much easier by finding them accommodation or emergency services, like water supplies. You can cover the trail in part. Here we give a list of all the stages, with a description only of the places that are interesting from a natural or historical point of view.

● Day 1	● Day 24
● Day 2	○ Day 25
● Day 3	○ Day 26
● Day 4	● Day 27
○ Day 5	● Day 28
○ Day 6	● Day 29
○ Day 7	● Day 30
○ Day 8	● Day 31
○ Day 9	● Day 32
○ Day 10	● Day 33
● Day 11	● Day 34
● Day 12	● Day 35
● Day 13	● Day 36
● Day 14	● Day 37
● Day 15	● Day 38
● Day 16	● Day 39
● Day 17	● Day 40
● Day 18	● Day 41
● Day 19	● Day 42
● Day 20	● Day 43
● Day 21	● Day 44
● Day 22	● Day 45
● Day 23	● Day 46

Map labels (north to south): Tel Dan, Tel Hai, Yesha Fort, Dishon, Mount Meron, Migdal, Safed, Hanezirim Mill, Kibbutz Kinneret, Mount Carmel, Kfar Kisch, Nahal Me'arot, Mesh'had (Nazareth), Zikhron Ya'Lamed Heh, Hadera, Netanya (Poleg), Tel Aviv (Old Jaffa), Tel Afek, Gimzo, Messilat Zion, Even Sapir (Jerusalem), Netiv Ha' Lamed Neh, Tel Keshet, Beit Guvrin, Kibbutz Dvir, Meitar, Amasa, Arad (Dead Sea), Be'er Efe, Makhtesh Katan, Meizad Tamar, Oron, Akev (nca)-Midreshet Ben Gurion, Mador (nca), Miztpe Ramon, Hava (nca), Gevanim (nca), Zofar, Gev Holit (nca), Barak (nca), Zihor, Shizafon, Shaharut, Elifaz (Timna Park), Raham-Etek (nca), Yehoram (nca), Almon/Eilat

Start: Tel Dan
Finish: Eilat
Distance: 680 mi (1100 km)
Time: 46 days
Difficulty: from easy to difficult
Accommodation: private homes, kibbutzim, B&Bs, tents

72–73 The country near Safed, the highest city in the Holy Land, situated in the pinewoods of Upper Galilee, with a view of Tiberias and the Sea of Galilee.

Eco because: INT travelers experience the extraordinary variety of natural landscapes and human experiences. It is enjoyable to meet the trail angels, to discover less well-known communities, and above all to share stories of people along the Shvil Yisrael, the Hebrew name of the trail.

When to go: The best times are from October to November and from February to May.

How to get there: You land at Tel Aviv international airport, and from there you take the train or the bus: after about 6–7 hours traveling you can reach Dan.

What to pack: If possible, you need to try to take everything necessary, while trying to reduce the weight of the backpack as much as possible. Tent, sleeping bag, food, water bottle, boots, clothes covering arms and legs, hat, sunglasses, and sunscreen. Energy bars, nuts, and dried fruit. First-aid kit, anti-blister bandages, binoculars, flashlight, maps, insect repellent, spare batteries.

DAY 1: Tel Dan–Tel Hai

The trail begins at Dan, near the Lebanese border. On this first stage, you find the nature reserve of the River Hasbani (Nahal Snir Nature Reserve), the longest tributary of the River Jordan, which flows through a forest of plane trees and travertine rocks: it is the natural habitat for various animal species. Further on, Hurshat Tal, near Kibbutz Dafna, is a national park that preserves 240 Mount Tabor ancient oaks and various animal and plant species. The travertine rocks are the natural habitat of 13 species of orchid.

DAY 2: Tel Hai–Yesha Fort

Nahal Kadesh is another interesting nature reserve. You walk among canyons.

DAY 3: Yesha Fort–Dishon
DAY 4: Dishon–Mount Meron

The Monte Meron Nature Reserve, with its 28,500 acres (11,500 ha), is the largest in Israel: here you can find scores of paths to discover flowers and rare trees, as well as a wide variety of wild animals. Around the mountain, there are many tombs of the *tzadikim* ("the righteous"), as well as sacred tombs of figures in the Druze religious community.

DAY 5: Mount Meron–Safed

Safed is not only one of the most sacred cities in Israel, but it is also one of the highest cities in the Holy Land, famous for being the place where the kabbala, the esoteric knowledge of the Jews, originated.

DAY 6: Safed–Migdal

You see many Christian sites and three springs: Ein Seter, Ein Amud, and Ein Nun.

DAY 7: Midgal–Kibbutz Kinneret

On the River Jordan, you find Yardenit, a baptism site visited by pilgrims, which is indicated as the place where Jesus Christ was baptized.

DAY 8: Kibbutz Kinneret–Kfar Kisch
DAY 9: Kfar Kisch–Mesh'had (Nazareth)

Nazareth is the cradle of Christianity, where the Angel Gabriel announced to Mary that she would conceive thanks to the power of the Holy Spirit, and the place where Jesus spent his youth and childhood. In March the irises are in full bloom, which is a sight not to be missed!

DAY 10: Mesh'had (Nazareth)–Hanezirim Mill

Along the trail you find the site of the ancient center of Tzipori, known in ancient times as Sepphoris or Diocaesarea, with archaeological traces from various eras and some of the most beautiful mosaics in the country.

DAY 11: Hanezirim Mill–Mount Carmel/Isfiya
DAY 12: Mount Carmel/Isfiya–Nahal Me'arot

Mount Carmel, despite its modest height (1,724 feet [525 m]), offers an interesting change of scenario from the coast. From its summit, you can take in the coast and the valleys of the Alona and Jezreel in Galilee.

DAY 13: Nahal Me'arot–Zikhron Ya'Lamed Heh

In this stage, you find the Nahal Me'arot Nature Reserve, an extraordinary complex of caves. Further on, you reach Ramat Hanadiv, splendid botanical gardens with incredible views and many quiet corners. A visitors' center tells the story of Ramat Hanadiv and of the building itself, which was the first certified ecological structure in Israel.

DAY 14: Zikhron Ya'Lamed Heh–Hadera

Caesarea, with its splendid beaches, is a port dating back thousands of years. Many objects and some ruins are under the water, so with a wetsuit and scuba tank, you can follow an expert guide from the Caesarea Dive Club and discover these undersea marvels.

74 left The Old City of Safed. It was originally built by Spanish Jews, who settled after being expelled from Spain in 1492. Today, it is also famous for its paved streets.

74 right The Basilica of the Annunciation in Nazareth is the most important Roman Catholic church in the city. The dome dominates the grotto traditionally believed to be the dwelling of the Virgin Mary.

75 The amphitheater in Caesarea, a city in Palestine on the shores of the Mediterranean. It was built by Herod the Great from 25 to 13 BC to show his loyalty to Caesar Augustus.

DAY 15: Hadera–Netanya (Poleg)

DAY 16: Netanya (Poleg)–Tel Aviv (Old Jaffa)

Ganei Yehoshua Park in Tel Aviv is the largest park in the city; it includes extensive lawns and botanical gardens.

DAY 17: Tel Aviv (Old Jaffa)–Tel Afek

DAY 18: Tel Afek–Gimzo

DAY 19: Gimzo–Messilat Zion

DAY 20: Messilat Zion–Even Sapir (Jerusalem)

Even Sapir is on the edge of Jerusalem, the holy city. For over 3,000 years, this symbol of spirituality has been a religious center and witnessed important changes. The heart of old Jerusalem is the Old City with its four quarters. The Christian Quarter developed around the Church of the Holy Sepulcher, which contains the last five stations of the Via Dolorosa. The symbol of the Muslim Quarter

is the Dome of the Rock. One of the focal points of its daily life is the *shuk*, the market in Ottoman style, full of life, flavors, and colors. The Jewish Quarter, reconstructed in 1967, is, together with the Western Wall, the symbol of the bond of the Jewish people with its past. The Western Wall is a place that is worth visiting, like the tunnels and the City of David just outside the walls, the Israel Museum housing the Dead Sea Scrolls, and the Yad Vashem, the memorial to the six million Jews killed in the Holocaust.

76–77 *Panoramic view from the Mount of Olives in the Old City of Jerusalem, with the Temple Mount, Dome of the Rock, and Al Aqsa Mosque.*

78 *The Dead Sea is situated in the deepest depression on Earth. It has been produced by the evaporation of water over millennia.*
79 left *The Makhtesh Katan. The* makhtesh *is a kind of crater typical of the Negev Desert with steep rocky walls surrounding a deep closed valley. It contains a variety of rocks of different colors.*
79 right *The Timna Park. From the high points, you enjoy a colorful view, with shades ranging from red to yellow, depending on light reflections and the composition of the terrain.*

DAY 21: Even Sapir–Netiv Ha'Lamed Heh

DAY 22: Netiv Ha'Lamed Heh–Beit Guvrin

DAY 23: Beit Guvrin–Tel Keshet

DAY 24: Tel Keshet–Kibbutz Dvir

On the edge of the Negev Desert, you find the Pura Nature Reserve, where a river flows and there are various types of flowers, paths, and a small lake.

DAY 25: Kibbutz Dvir–Meitar

DAY 26: Meitar–Amasa

In this stage, you reach Yatir, the largest natural forest in Israel, created by the Keren Kayemeth LeIsrael (KKL), the oldest ecological organization in the world. Founded in 1901, it works for the reclamation and reforesting of the land in Israel and develops technologies and skills in various sectors, from agriculture to scientific research, to the struggle with desertification.

DAY 27: Amasa–Arad (Dead Sea)

Arad is the entrance to the Dead Sea, the salt lake in the deepest depression on Earth, 1,388 feet (400 m) below sea level. One can float with no effort because of its high salinity, and swimming in it is considered therapeutic, as is its mud. From Arad you enter the Negev Desert.

DAY 28: Arad–Be'er Efe

Rosh Zohar is a good panoramic look-out point over the Dead Sea.

DAY 29: Be'er Efe–Meizad Tamar

DAY 30: Meizad Tamar–Summit of Makhtesh Katan

You have a spectacular view from Makhtesh Katan; makhtesh are river basins of varying size..

DAY 31: Makhtesh Katan–Oron

DAY 32: Oron–Mador (night camping area)

The fittest can climb Mount Karbolet for a spectacular view.

DAY 41: Zihor–Shizafon

DAY 42: Shizafon–Shaharut

DAY 43: Shaharut–Elifaz (Timna Park)

Timna Park is an area of archaeological value in the Negev Desert, where there are copper mines that operated from the sixth millennium BC to the Middle Ages.

DAY 44: Elifaz–Raham-Etek (nca)

On this stage, you encounter the spectacular Pillars of Solomon, limestone formations up to 160 feet (50 m) high.

DAY 45: Raham-Etek (nca)–Yehoram (nca)

DAY 46: Yehoram (nca)–Almon/Eilat

On the last day of the trail, you climb Mount Shelomo for a breathtaking view of Eilat and the Red Sea. You have arrived at the end of your journey in Israel!

DAY 33: Mador (nca)–Akev (nca)-Midreshet Ben Gurion

Ben Gurion's tomb is the place where the Israeli statesman is buried, but also the center of the environmental research and enhancement of the desert desired by him.

DAY 34: Akev (nca)–Hava (nca)

Today you reach Ein Shabiv, a real oasis with many shady trees.

DAY 35: Hava (nca)–Miztpe Ramon

DAY 36: Miztpe Ramon–Gevanim (nca)

DAY 37: Gevanim (nca)–Gev Holit (nca)

DAY 38: Gev Holit (nca)–Zofar

DAY 39: Zofar–Barak (nca)

DAY 40: Barak (nca)–Zihor

ECO-TIPS

IN ISRAEL, TOO, THE RULE IN SUSTAINABLE TRAVELING IS *LEAVE NO TRACE*. FOR EXAMPLE, IT IS ALWAYS BETTER TO TAKE A BAG TO COLLECT TRASH, TO BE PUT WHERE POSSIBLE IN THE CORRECT CONTAINER. DO NOT PICK WILD FLOWERS OR BRANCHES TO MAKE CAMPFIRES, WHICH CAN ONLY BE LIT IN THE SPACES ASSIGNED. IT IS FORBIDDEN TO PITCH A TENT OUTSIDE THE SPACES ALLOWED.

Useful Websites
info.goisrael.com
israeltrail.net

LA RÉUNION
(FRANCE)

Start: Col des Bœufs
Finish: Cilaos
Distance: 20 mi (32 km)
Time: 3 days
Difficulty: medium
Accommodation: *Gîtes d'étape* (rest houses)

80–81 Mount Cimandef, 7,303 feet (2,225 m) high, seen from Col des Bœufs.

Eco because: There are no roads to the Mafate villages. It is like an island on an island, and the trek is a plunge into the heart of nature.

Cirque de Mafate

La Réunion, an overseas region of France, is a mountainous island of volcanic origin in the Indian Ocean. Surrounded by a wild coast with white or black sand and crystal-clear seas protected by a coral barrier reef, the island has an extraordinary wealth of landscapes, and in just 965 square miles (2,500 sq km), it comprises the variety of environments of a continent. The most unusual features are the volcanoes Piton des Neiges (10,070 feet [3,070 m]), the highest mountain in the Indian Ocean, and Piton de la Fournaise (8,635 feet [2,630 m]), one of the most active volcanoes on the planet. Its distinctive calderas—Mafate, Cilaos, Salazie—dot the mountainous interior of the island (Les Hauts). The land between the two volcanic mountains, together with the three calderas, form the Parc National de La Réunion, a UNESCO World Heritage Site.

The Cirque de Mafate is a caldera, the core of a collapsed shield volcano, inaccessible and remote. It is a geological environment marked by steep bastions, accessible only on foot along narrow mountain paths or by helicopter. Its wild landscape made it an ideal refuge for Maroon slaves and later poor white laborers. Today, the inhabitants treasure their isolation and their small farms, continuing the traditions and growing fruit, cereals, and corn. Far from the chaos of modern life, the 700 inhabitants, divided into ten îlets, welcome excursionists with courtesy and kindness. Some of these "islets" are well-organized villages, with schools, solar-powered electricity, and grocery stores mainly supplied by helicopter.

When trekking in the Cirque de Mafate, it is advisable to take a local guide.

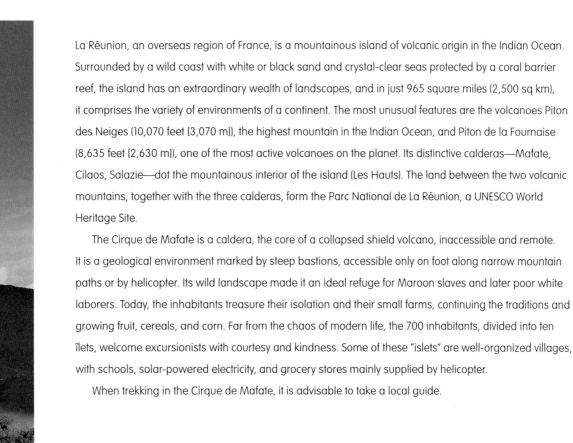

81 Some trekkers on Col des Bœufs, the most traveled access to Mafate, an easy path for La Nouvelle, the main village.

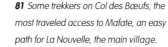

● Day 1
● Day 2
● Day 3

82 *The Cirque de Cilaos, the great volcanic caldera, is a deep depression surrounded by high walls. In the background, the beaches of the south coast.*

83 top *A young trekker climbs the Piton des Neiges through the rain forest, in the Cirque de Cilaos caldera.*

83 bottom left *A trekker crosses the caldera of the Cirque de Mafate at La Nouvelle.*

83 bottom right *The hamlet of Marla is the highest in the cirque, at 5,397 feet (1,645 m). Its name derives from the Malagasy word* marolahy *which means "many people."*

DAY 1: Col des Bœufs–La Nouvelle You start from Col des Bœufs, at 5,900 feet (1,800 m) above sea level, on the ridge between the two calderas Salazie and Mafate, from which there is a magnificent view. You begin walking down into the Cirque de Mafate, crossing the Plaine des Tamarins: this is a highland dense with a tamarind forest, often wrapped in a mist that gives it a mysterious appearance. Here you can rest and eat. You take the path toward La Dècouverte, and after about an hour along a gentle descent through the tamarind forest, you arrive in La Nouvelle. In this small village, the most important in Mafate, you have dinner and stay overnight at a *gite d'étape*. It is advisable to book in advance.

TRAVEL TIPS

When to go: The best time is the dry season, which runs from May to November (the Southern Hemisphere's winter), when it rains only occasionally and the temperatures are pleasant.

How to get there: From the international airport of Saint-Denis, you take a taxi for 40 miles (65 km) to Col des Bœufs.

What to pack: Water and food supplies. Hiking boots, windbreaker, and headlamp. Waterproof cape. Sunglasses and sunscreen. First-aid kit and insect repellent. Protective waterproof cases for cameras and video equipment. Spare batteries and a map.

DAY 2: La Nouvelle–Marla

In the morning, you set out in the direction of Marla, stopping on the way for a picnic and a swim in the Rivière des Galets. In the afternoon, you reach Marla, an îlet in the highest part of the Mafate, dominated by Trois Salazes, the rocky peaks of the Piton des Neiges. You stay here for the night.

DAY 3: Marla–Taïbit–Cilaos

In the morning, you leave the village of Marla to reach Cilaos, crossing the Taïbit hill. After a steep climb, you plunge into an acacia forest. You arrive at a viewpoint from which it is possible to admire almost all the Cirque de Mafate and the village of Marla. Once you reach the Taïbit hill, there is a wonderful panorama of Cirque de Cilaos and Mafate. You descend by Plaine des Fraises to Îlet des Salazes. From here you continue to the small town of Cilaos, a settlement with shops, a hotel, and a spa, where you can relax after the trek.

ECO-TIPS

CAMPING AND BIVOUACKING IS FORBIDDEN ALMOST ALL OVER THE ISLAND. IN THE AREAS WHERE IT IS PERMITTED, IT IS NECESSARY TO FOLLOW THE RULES SET BY THE PARK AUTHORITIES. EXCURSIONISTS ARE ASKED TO TAKE THEIR TRASH AWAY WITH THEM; THE INHABITANTS' TRASH IS TAKEN BY HELICOPTER TO THE MAIN DUMPS ON THE ISLAND. AVOID BRIGHT OR FLUORESCENT CLOTHING IN THE AREAS INHABITED BY ANIMALS. WEAR LONG PANTS AND SHIRTS OR SWEATERS WITH LONG SLEEVES. ALWAYS ASK FOR PERMISSION BEFORE TAKING PHOTOGRAPHS OF PLACES OR PEOPLE.

Useful Websites
reunion.fr
www.reunion-parcnational.fr
www.reunion-mafate.com

Lost Coast Trail

Start: Mattole Beach
Finish: Shelter Cove
Distance: 25 mi (40 km)
Time: 3–4 days
Difficulty: medium
Accommodation: tents

The most carefully safeguarded national parks on the planet are to be found in the United States, where the first to be founded was Yellowstone National Park, in 1872. In 1968, the National Scenic Trails trekking network was founded here. California is a state in which ecotourism is well-established, and an environmentally friendly attitude is widespread. The state has nine national parks, which boast a surprising variety of landscapes, from the granite peaks of Yosemite to the magnificent redwood trees and the vast Death Valley desert.

More than 620 miles (1,000 km) of Californian coast are flanked from north to south by the legendary State Route 1, from Orange County to Leggett in Mendocino County. At the northern tip, it meets with US Route 101, but the coastline continues, curving west just north of Fort Bragg.

There are no main access roads to this region, lapped by the ocean and known as the Lost Coast, and it is one of the most rugged and remote areas of the US coastline. It can be explored on foot by crossing the King Range National Conservation Area. Here the signposting is minimal, in order to limit the presence of visitors. If you intend to visit the area, it is essential to acquire precise and updated information on the tides, which cover beaches and trails: waves can suddenly create dangerous situations.

● Day 1   ○ Day 3
● Day 2   ○ Day 4

Mattole Beach

◉ **Sea Lion Gulch**

◉ **Spanish Flat**

◉ **Big Flat Creek**

◉ **Shelter Cove**

84 top A sea lion at Punta Gorda. The California sea lion is a very intelligent, strong, and agile animal. The male can weigh up to 661 pounds (300 kg) and reach 6.5 feet (2 m) in length.

84 bottom The old lighthouse at Punta Gorda, now abandoned, is an attraction as well as being a place for trekkers to pause and shelter.

85 A meadow of Angelica californica at Mattole Beach.

Eco because: Reaching this stretch of coast, which is without cars, roads, or telephone lines, will already be an adventure. You might see white sharks in the ocean waters, or bears and moose along the road. At night you will be able to admire the starry skies without light pollution. The resources of this area must be preserved in the exact same state they were found in, as the Leave No Trace signs constantly remind visitors.

When to go: The high season, from mid-May to mid-September, generally enjoys good weather; during the rest of the year the weather is variable, but there are less tourists. It is necessary to plan the journey carefully, taking into account the tides.

How to get there: The nearest international airport is San Francisco; from here you can take a bus or a car for about 250 miles (400 km) to Mattole Beach.

What to pack: A tent, a sleeping bag, provisions, canteen, and water purification tablets. Hiking boots, a hat, sunglasses, and sunscreen. Headlamp, windbreaker, waterproof cape, and groundsheet for protection from the damp at night. Spare batteries and first-aid kit.

DAY 1: Mattole Beach–Sea Lion Gulch

An excursion along the Lost Coast is an art: there is no trail—except for the flat areas—and along the beach, finding the right place to walk could be challenging. The trail begins in soft, dry sand, littered with driftwood, seaweed, and all sorts of shells. Soon, however, the sand gives way to smooth pebbles and rocks. The Punta Gorda lighthouse appears, built in 1910 following a series of fatal shipwrecks on the rocks just off the coast. It was operative until 1961, when new technologies made it obsolete. The trail continues to Sea Lion Gulch, where there are sea lions and seals swimming just off the coast. Camp here overnight.

ECO-TIPS

IF YOU APPLY FOR PERMITS FOR THE KING RANGE IN TIME, YOU CAN CAMP ANYWHERE. HOWEVER, WHEN POSSIBLE, IT IS BETTER TO USE EXISTING CAMPSITES, IN ORDER TO REDUCE THE ENVIRONMENTAL IMPACT. EVEN BUILDING SMALL SHELTERS USING DRIFTWOOD FOUND ON THE BEACH IS A PRACTICE DISAPPROVED OF BY THE RANGERS, BECAUSE IT IS IN CONTRAST WITH THE LEAVE NO TRACE PHILOSOPHY. DUE TO THE PRESENCE OF BEARS ALONG THE LOST COAST, IT IS NECESSARY TO RENT FROM THE RANGERS STRONG METAL CONTAINERS IN WHICH TO KEEP FOOD AND SUNSCREEN (WHICH CONTAINS PERFUME).

Useful Websites
visitcalifornia.com
visittheusa.com
www.blm.gov/visit

DAY 2: Sea Lion Gulch–Spanish Flat

The trail continues over large, rounded stones, and you should walk slowly and carefully. After a while, the trail turns inland because it is impossible to continue along the coast. Then, you return to the beach of cobbles and black sand, until you reach Randall Creek, which marks the northern limit of Spanish Flat, the area bounded on the south by the Spanish Creek and the campsite for the night.

DAY 3: Spanish Flat–Big Flat Creek

On the third day, you walk through a wood, crossing Kinsey Creek to return to the beach and reach Big Creek. The trail climbs to a plateau: this is the northern limit of Big Flat, the highest point of the trail—although it is less than 100 feet (30 m) above sea level—which is reached through dense and crooked pinewoods. From here, you continue through the grassy meadows to Big Flat Creek, a river with numerous welcoming campsites on both banks.

DAY 4: Big Flat Creek–Shelter Cove

The following morning, you continue southward, crossing Miller Flat. The trail descends toward the beach, where you walk to Gitchell Creek. Here the trail descends steeply toward the sand, which is partially covered during high tide. The surrounding wooded hills are home to deer, bears, and other animals, whose tracks can often be spotted in the sand. Beyond Gitchell Creek, the trail shows considerable erosion—a sign that the sea is continually eating away at the coast. At this point, the beach widens (the characteristic Black Sands Beach) and you can see houses on the cliffs of Shelter Cove, two miles away, the final stage of the trek.

86 left *Aerial view of a stretch of the Lost Coast Trail. With pebbles and black sand, it is a challenge to find the right surface for walking.*
86 right *An area of poppies in California near Shelter Cove.*
87 *The lighthouse at Shelter Cove actually came from Mendocino: it was dismantled in 1998 and restored, with new glass, painted, and installed on its new site.*

COSTA RICA

Start: Puerto Jiménez
Finish: Puerto Jiménez
Distance: variable for the first day, dedicated to a walk in the jungle near the lodge; about 31 miles (50 km) altogether for days two and three.

Time: 3 days
Difficulty: medium
Accommodation: eco-lodge

88–89 Danta Corcovado Lodge, on the Península de Osa, in Parque Corcovado, is an eco-lodge that participates in a program gradually improving the environmental and social impact of tourism.

Eco because: Ecotourism in Costa Rica has a lengthy history: in fact, the Reserva Natural Absoluta Cabo Blanco was founded in 1963. Corcovado is considered one of the most biologically rich places on the planet thanks to its incredible biodiversity, which is preserved thanks to the remote location of the park and the limited presence of human beings. Ecological tourism generates more income for the country than the traditional export products, like bananas, pineapples, and coffee.

Parque Nacional Corcovado

When mentioning ecotourism, Costa Rica immediately springs to mind. In the strip of land that separates the Pacific Ocean from the Caribbean Sea, in an area of just 20 square miles (51 sq km), there is a variety of landscapes and micro-climates sufficient to meet the tastes of each and every traveler. The country is home to 5% of the world's biodiversity, and the lush flora is a national resource for ecotourism and for the national energy sector, which makes use of resources such as water, geothermal energy, solar, and wind power. The policies against pollution are central to government strategies, and the initiatives aimed at significantly reducing the levels of CO_2 emissions, such as the development of sustainable mobility and electric vehicles, are constantly increasing.

Given the numerous waterfalls, volcanoes, and beaches that Costa Rica has to offer, it is difficult to know what to visit, but to enjoy the most spectacular variety of flora and fauna in the country, one of the best places is the Parque Nacional Corcovado. Situated on the Península de Osa, in the southwest of Costa Rica, the park covers more than 98,000 acres (40,000 ha) and can be visited only on foot. This incredible naturalistic treasure chest protects eight different habitats (from forests to marshes) and is home to more than 400 bird species and 140 species of mammal. The flora and fauna of Corcovado is unforgettable but challenging, and it is essential to visit it with an authorized guide.

- Day 1
- Day 2
- Day 3

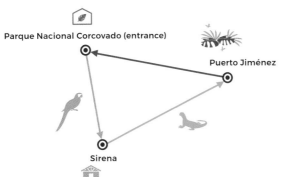

Parque Nacional Corcovado (entrance)

Puerto Jiménez

Sirena

89 *A view of the Rio Sierpe flanked by dense mangroves. Boats are used both by local people and tourists.*

When to go: The best time is during the dry season, from December to April.

How to get there: The nearest airport to the Parque Nacional Corcovado is in Puerto Jiménez.

What to pack: A medium-sized backpack, rubber boots, insect repellent, headlamp with extra batteries, long distance camera lens, portable battery for recharging the devices. It is essential to take trash bags, sunglasses, a hat, a canteen, and binoculars. Given the high levels of humidity in the park, it is also necessary to take waterproof coverings for cameras and video equipment, a waterproof bag, microfiber towels, and clothing that will dry out very quickly.

DAY 1: Puerto Jiménez–Parque Nacional Corcovado (entrance)

On the first day, after purchasing the tickets for excursions in the park from one of the agencies in Puerto Jiménez, you follow the park guide to one of the eco-lodges on the edge of the Corcovado, where you will stay the night. Once you have settled in, it is possible to take a walk around the area looking for frogs, howler monkeys, lizards, leaf-cutter ants, and rubber plant thickets. The bravest can also go out at night with the guide: in the dark, the jungle looks different and intriguing.

DAY 2: Parque Nacional Corcovado (entrance)–Sirena

At dawn the forest explodes in a cacophony of sound. Woken by these noises in the early morning, you walk less than 1 mile (1.6 km) to Los Patos, the first rangers' station on the edge of the park, where you pick up a supply of water. Accompanied by the guide, you take the trail, crossing streams and encountering rivers. During the trek, you will see butterflies, coatis, iguanas, and great green macaws (*Ara ambiguus*), which are at risk of extinction. And then there are palm trees, cocoa

trees, banana trees, etc. For about 15 miles (24 km), the trail continues over ground that is often damp and slippery: try to stay on your feet. Finally, you reach the Sirena rangers' station, where you have dinner and sleep.

DAY 3: Estación Sirena–Carate–Puerto Jiménez

The third day, you walk toward the ocean and follow the coastline. The trail alternates between jungle and soft sand. Forest and palm trees overlook the pristine beach and the turquoise water: a heavenly sight. During the trek, you may encounter a Baird's tapir (*Tapirus bairdii*) the largest mammal in Costa Rica, in danger of extinction. There are also anteaters, vultures, hawks, herons, and colorful crabs, and on the beach, if you are lucky, you may see the paw prints of an ocelot. Finally, you reach Leona, the last rangers' station before you leave the park. From here you go to Carate and return by car (just less than two hours) to Puerto Jiménez, where this marvelous experience ends.

> **ECO-TIPS**

MARSHES, MANGROVE SWAMPS, RIVERS, SANDY COASTS—THE CORCOVADO RAIN FOREST HAS A SPECTACULAR CONCENTRATION OF FLORA AND FAUNA. EVERYONE HAS TO RESPECT IT. IT IS FORBIDDEN TO BRING FOOD INTO THE PARK, BUT YOU CAN PICK UP A FRESH WATER SUPPLY AT THE RANGERS' STATIONS.

Useful Websites
visitcostarica.com
osawildtravel.com
www.sinac.go.cr/EN-US/ac/acosa/pnc
www.explorelatarde.com/index.html
www.dantalodge.com

90 top One of the many rivers and streams crisscrossing the park.
90 bottom In Costa Rica, there are about 1,500 species of flower, of various colors, shapes, and sizes.
90–91 The roots form a buttress for a banyan fig (Ficus subgenus Urostigma) at Sirena. The park protects the largest primary forest in Central America, a tropical rain forest.

PERU

Start: Cusco
Finish: Cusco
Distance: 43 mi (70 km)
Time: 5 days
Difficulty: medium, but it is necessary to acclimatize before starting the trek
Accommodation: lodges (*tambos*)

92–93 Vinicunca, also called Montaña de Siete Colores, is 17,060 feet (5,200 m) high and characterized by stripes of seven colors, due to various minerals that have been successively laid down over the years.

Eco because: This trek is part of a program of ecotourism organized with the local communities of Josefina and Chillca, who actively take part and offer hospitality in their comfortable eco-lodges. The participants are accompanied by pack llamas belonging to local shepherds from the Chillca community, who are proud to share their land and the spirit of their world with travelers.

Apu Ausangate Trek

In Peru, nature expresses an incredible variety of ecoregions (11) and habitats (84). It is a paradise for anyone who loves adventure and wants to undertake a trek: thanks to the many trails and snow-capped peaks, excursionists can choose from more than 932 miles (1,500 km) of highland, with mountains, lakes, volcanoes, canyons, and gorges. These natural wonders are also combined with the archaeological remains of pre-Columbian civilizations.

Among the many treks in the Cordillera de Vilcanota, the one we propose here is the five-day circular trek of Camino del Apu Ausangate, in the vicinity of the highest sacred mountain of the Cusco region. Snowy peaks, wide valleys, wonderful lakes add to the opportunity to understand the shepherd's way of life and to explore one of the least polluted mountain ecosystems in the world. The trail lies at more than 16,404 feet (5,000 m) above sea level and is generally not very busy, passing through shepherds' villages. In addition to the llamas, excursionists can see alpacas, vicunas, spur-winged geese, and, if they are lucky, the incredible Andean condor. The colorful spectacle of the hills is priceless: the mineral layers of rock show red stripes from the oxidized iron, yellow from the ferrous sulfide, purple brown produced by goethite or oxidized limonite, and green created by chlorite. Baggage is carried by llamas, and the itinerary ends with two sections on horseback for those who do not wish (or cannot) walk. During the trek, daily meals are provided at the *tambos* (Andean lodges), prepared by expert cooks who will introduce you to a variety of delicious dishes and Peruvian products.

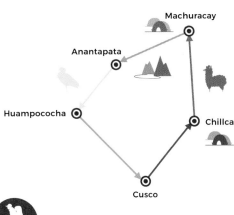

93 In the past, Cusco, situated in the Peruvian Andes, was the capital of the Inca Empire. Today, it is famous for its archaeological ruins and Spanish colonial architecture.

- ● Day 1
- ● Day 2
- ● Day 3
- ○ Day 4
- ● Day 5

When to go: From March to November.

How to get there: You arrive at the international airport of Cusco, and from there, in five minutes by taxi, you reach Cusco. You travel to Chillca by bus (about 51 miles [82 km]).

What to pack: A padded jacket, hiking boots, clothing for the mountains, thermal underwear for sleeping, woolen hat, gloves and scarf, a hat for the sun. Waterproof jacket and pants or a rainproof poncho. Comfortable sandals to wear in the lodge. Small towel. Canteen, headlamp (there is little light in the lodges, only candlelight). Anti-blister bandages, energy bars for high altitude, first-aid kit, diarrhea tablets, spare batteries for cameras.

DAY 1: Cusco–Chillca

Since you will be trekking at a high altitude, we recommend you spend a preliminary acclimatization period in Cusco (three to four days at 9,843 feet [3,000 m]), so that your body can react better during the trek. From Cusco, a UNESCO World Heritage Site, you take the bus along the Vilcanota River to visit the temple of Checacupe, then cross the high valley of Pitumarca to arrive at Japura, where the trek begins: with a short walk you arrive at Chillca. At the first Andean lodge (*tambo* in the Quechua language), you are greeted by locals and musicians playing Andean instruments while sipping coca tea. The lodge is eco-sustainable and was built by the local community. Hot showers, baths, and eight double rooms are available here. The local cuisine is tasty and nutritious (for example, alpaca meat), but there are also vegetarian options like quinoa soup.

ECO-TIPS

DO NOT LEAVE TRASH BEHIND ON THE TREK. BRING IT WITH YOU TO THE DESIGNATED DISPOSAL POINTS. BEFORE ARRIVING, YOU SHOULD GATHER INFORMATION ON THE COUNTRY YOU ARE VISITING AND FIND OUT ABOUT THE LOCAL PEOPLE SO THAT YOU CAN FIT IN WITH THEM, AND NOT THE OTHER WAY ROUND.

Useful Websites
peru.travel/en
andeanlodges.com/en

DAY 2: Chillca–Machuracay

After breakfast you walk along the Chillcapampa valley, encountering herds of grazing llamas and alpacas. When you reach the end of the valley, the shepherd guides who precede the trekkers will set up temporary tents and prepare a hot soup, a welcomed treat in case of rain. Then you begin the climb toward the great mountains. You flank lakes and lagoons at the foot of the shiny glaciers until you reach Machuracay Tambo. The baggage carried on the pack llamas has already arrived, and the family of the lodge managers will welcome you with a steaming *mate de coca* to help you bear the effects of the altitude.

DAY 3: Machuracay–Anantapata

In this stage you reach the first mountain pass at more than 16,404 feet (5,000 m) above sea level, with its spectacular panoramic views (Palomani pass). You descend beside the glaciers and walk toward Lake Ausangate (*cocha* is the local word for "lake"), then you plunge into the sediment formations of red sandstone, a wonderful experience and the reason why these mountains were considered magical and worshiped as a divinity. Here it is easy to see condors and vicunas coming to drink. At the end of the day, you reach the third Andean lodge, where you can relax with a hot shower.

DAY 4: Anantapata–Huampococha

After breakfast you set out on the most exciting stage of the trek. The contrast between the white glaciers and the ochre stripes caused by mineral content makes this an electrifying experience. The most surprising colors are in the sediments of Yauricunca. The fourth Andean lodge is on the banks of a lake that is home to dozens of Andean geese. This big white and black bird nests on the cliffs of Anta and on the ferrous formations of Apu Labrayani near the lodge, where you spend the last night of the Apu Ausangate Trek.

DAY 5: Huampococha–Cusco

A last brief but steep climb allows you to admire the glaciers, including the Nevado del Inca and, in the distance, the Nevado Ausangate. You begin the descent toward the valley, dotted with flocks and stone pens built by the shepherds. The trail ends near the village of Trapiche. From here you return by bus to Cusco.

94 left A particular rock formation found along the Camino del Apu Ausangate. It is about 230 feet (70 m) long at a high altitude.

94 right Ascending toward Mount Vinicunca: the terrain is tinged with red from iron oxide.

95 A Quechua woman using natural dyeing techniques to dye alpaca wool to make fabrics.

Torres del Paine W Trek

96–97 *The Paine Grande campsite and refuge at Torres del Paine, Patagonia. It is a strategic place in the park, which is accessible only from the lake or by trekking paths.*

Long and narrow, it starts in the heart of South America and reaches the most southern lip: Chile, with its vast and spectacular variety of landscapes—from deserts to glaciers, from verdant valleys to volcanoes, from forests to fjords—is nature at its finest. Along the 2,485 miles (4,000 km) from the tropics to Tierra del Fuego, extraordinary landscapes abound, ideal destinations for anyone who wants to lose themselves in compelling natural adventures.

The Parque Nacional Torres del Paine lies in Patagonia, the kingdom of excursionists, about 1,243 miles (2,000 km) south of the capital Santiago. In the park, the W Trek, the shorter version of the famous O Circuit Torres del Paine, allows close-up views of Las Torres, the iconic rock formations for which the park is famous. It is a route that offers spectacular panoramas of immense glaciers and imposing granite peaks, up to 9,514 feet (2,900 m) high, and it snakes through pristine landscape. This exciting walk demands a certain level of physical preparation: there are steep sections, and some parts of the route are challenging. However you don't have to be a professional athlete to complete it.

Start: Refugio Paine Grande
Finish: Hotel Las Torres
Distance: 37 mi (60 km)
Time: 5 days
Difficulty: medium
Accommodation: tents and shelters

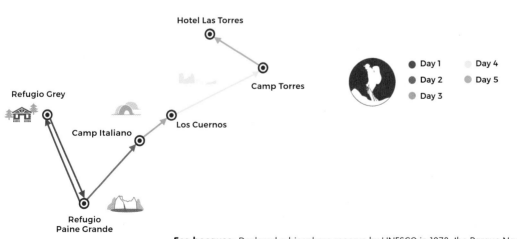

Hotel Las Torres

Refugio Grey

Camp Italiano

Camp Torres

Los Cuernos

Refugio
Paine Grande

● Day 1   ○ Day 4
● Day 2   ● Day 5
● Day 3

Eco because: Declared a biosphere reserve by UNESCO in 1978, the Parque Nacional Torres del Paine is the ideal habitat for more than one hundred species that populate the various ecosystems in the area. The trails snake through well-preserved and monitored natural areas. The park receives a limited number of tourists each year, which allows visitors to enjoy it in complete tranquility.

DAY 1: Refugio Paine Grande–Refugio Grey

You start out from Refugio Paine Grande for the Mirador Grey, the perfect viewpoint for admiring the Grey Glacier, which is more than 98 feet (30 m) high and extends for almost 4 miles (6 km). From the belvedere you are overcome by the spectacle of the blocks of ice that tumble into the waters of the lake. You walk for another half mile toward Refugio Grey, where there are other viewpoints from which to admire the glacier. You can spend the night at the refugio (book in advance) or in the adjacent campsite.

DAY 2: Refugio Grey–Camp Italiano

The next morning, you leave from Refugio Grey and, following the same trail as the previous day, return to Refugio Paine Grande, walking for a further 4.6 miles (7.5 km) to Camp Italiano, one of the two free campsites on the trail. You can spend the second night here.

When to go: In Chile, like all countries below the equator, the seasons are reversed with respect to our hemisphere. This is a well-known excursion, and therefore, in the summer months between December and March, the trails are crowded and the weather is sunny and mild. Spring is also a good time to enjoy the reawakening of nature, but it is windy and nighttime temperatures can fall to 33°F (1°C). In winter, from June to September, the trek is more challenging and can be undertaken with the support of a guide, but not all the services are open. It is less windy, but the temperature can fall below zero and daylight hours are shorter.

How to get there: Punta Arenas is the nearest city: from here it is possible to go by taxi or bus to Puerto Natales (about 155 miles [250 km]) and to the entrance to the Parque Nacional, which is a further 50 miles (80 km) away.

What to pack: At Torres del Paine, it is very important to bring clothing that adapts to both hot and cold weather and protection against wind, rain, and snow. Lip sunscreen and sunglasses. Tent, sleeping bag, insulation mat, food, canteen, first-aid kit. Hiking boots and change of shoes. Blister bandages. Painkillers and disinfectant for minor wounds. Headlamp and spare batteries for the headlamp and your camera. Mineral salts and energy bars.

DAY 3: Camp Italiano–Los Cuernos

Today you leave the heavier equipment at the camp and take only a light knapsack for the excursion. From Camp Italiano you make a day's round-trip hike of 6.8 miles (11 km) to contemplate the spectacular Valle del Francés, with beech woods and the Francés glacier. After picking up your backpack at the base camp, you walk a further 3.4 miles (5.5 km) to Los Cuernos, where you stay overnight. There are a number of accommodation options: Refugio Los Cuernos, Camp Los Cuernos, or the more luxurious Los Cuernos Cabanas.

98–99 The vicuna is a wild camelid that lives in the Andes. It thrives at high altitudes because of the high concentration of hemoglobin in its bloodstream.
99 top Trekkers in the Valle del Frances. In the background, from left to right, are the peaks of Cerro Espada, Cerro Hoja, Cerro Mascara, and the great Cuerno Norte.
99 bottom Lake Pehoe, situated near Los Cuernos.

DAY 4: Los Cuernos–Camp Torres

After breakfast you leave from Los Cuernos and walk about 6.8 miles (11 km) toward Camp Torres, at the base of the famous Las Torres peaks, three gigantic granite monoliths, of which Torre Central is the highest. From here you take a half-mile excursion to Mirador Torres to admire the peaks from the nearest and very picturesque viewpoint. You return to Camp Torres for the night.

DAY 5: Camp Torres–Hotel Las Torres

On the last day, it is worth getting up very early to go to Mirador again so you can see the Torres in the light of dawn. After this unforgettable spectacle, you return to Camp Torres and walk back toward Hotel Las Torres, about 5 miles (8 km) away and the last stage of the trail.

100 top Dome tents mounted on wooden platforms. They are easy to carry on your shoulders, give protection in extreme conditions, and have a light aluminum frame.

100 bottom You reach the Hotel Las Torres on the last day of the trek. Situated in the heart of the park, it has an organic kitchen garden that helps the restaurant offer traditional dishes.

100-101 Panoramic view of the mountains with the peaks of Los Cuernos and Lake Pehoe in the Parque Nacional Torres del Paine.

ECO-TIPS

IT IS COMPULSORY TO TAKE ALL TRASH AND CONTAMINATING SUBSTANCES OUT OF THE PARK, SINCE THE WIND CAN EASILY SCATTER IT. BATTERIES CONTAIN SUBSTANCES THAT ARE HARMFUL TO THE ENVIRONMENT AND MUST BE TAKEN BACK TO THE NEAREST CITY AND DISPOSED OF IN THE SPECIFIC CONTAINERS. ORGANIC OR BIODEGRADABLE WASTE (FOOD SCRAPS, FRUIT PEEL, EGGS, ETC.) SHOULD NOT BE LEFT BEHIND BECAUSE THEY DO NOT BELONG TO THE ENVIRONMENT YOU ARE VISITING: THEY ROT SLOWLY AND ARE A POTENTIAL SOURCE OF INFECTIONS, THEY ATTRACT WILDLIFE, AND THEY DESPOIL THE ENVIRONMENT. NEVER THROW SEEDS ON THE GROUND BECAUSE THEY COULD INTRODUCE NEW SPECIES THAT WOULD ALTER THE BALANCE OF THE ECOSYSTEM.

Useful Websites

chile.travel // parquetorresdelpaine.cl // www.conaf.cl/parques // www.verticepatagonia.cl

El Chaltén–Laguna Torre

Argentina: a land of contrasts, an immense nature reserve with wetlands, deserts, glaciers, arid steppes, forests, salt flats, lakes, mountains, etc. These biodiverse ecosystems are home to a vast assortment of flora and fauna.

Numerous sites in the country have been declared protected areas, becoming nature reserves or national parks, while some of the most important natural monuments have been declared UNESCO World Heritage Sites. Argentina also has a number of investment plans to promote eco-sustainable tourism. One example is certainly the Corredor Ecoturístico del Litoral, a project designed to preserve and strengthen the biodiversity and the cultural heritage of a vast territory that includes six different provinces and is home to more than 634,000 people.

Another bastion of Argentinian ecotourism is the village of El Chaltén, the world capital of mountain climbers and the starting point for many excursions. The name of this magical place derives from the Tehuelche language and means "smoking mountain," alluding to the effect produced by the clouds that often float around Monte Fitz Roy (also called Cerro Chaltén).

The trek that we propose covers the northern area of Parque Nacional Los Glaciares, in Patagonia, a UNESCO World Heritage Site since 1981, with the spectacular peaks of Monte Fitz Roy and Cerro Torre, "the Scream of Stone," "the impossible mountain," the legendary mountain with precipitous walls that rise toward an often-stormy sky.

● Day 1
● Day 2

Cerro Torre
Mirador Maestri
Mirador Laguna Torre
El Chaltén
Bridwell Base Camp

102 Monte Fitz Roy—also known as Cerro Chaltén or "the Smoking Mountain"—and the village of El Chaltén in a spectacular photo taken at dawn.

Start: El Chaltén
Finish: El Chaltén
Distance: 9 mi (15 km). If the trek continues
to the Mirador Maestri, a further 12 mi (19 km).
Time: 1 or 2 days
Difficulty: easy
Accommodation: tents

102–103 The entrance to El Chaltén in the Parque Nacional Los Glaciares, in Patagonia, a UNESCO World Heritage Site since 1981. The Argentinian government has made this village the national trekking capital.

Eco because: Argentina is an ecological paradise thanks to the rigorous care and attention reserved for its landscapes. The Parque Nacional Los Glaciares protects a large area of continental ice, the Bosque Andino Patagónico, and Patagonian steppe. For decades the Argentinian government has been active in promoting eco-sustainable tourism, making the little village of El Chaltén the capital of mountain climbing.

104 top *Cerro Torre: its spectacular peak west of Monte Fitz Roy is considered inaccessible, since ascent from any point means climbing at least 2,950 feet (900 m) of granite wall.*

104 bottom *It is estimated that every year hundreds of climbers and trekkers travel to Monte Fitz Roy, attracted by its steep slopes and challenging climate.*

105 *Mirador del Cerro Torre: the sign indicates the names and heights of the iconic peaks.*

106–107 *Monte Fitz Roy and Laguna de Los Tres in the Parque Nacional Los Glaciares. This is the viewpoint nearest to the mountain walls, which can also be reached by amateur hikers.*

DAY 1: El Chaltén–Laguna Torre–El Chaltén

El Chaltén, a border town between Argentina and Chile, is the base camp for climbers and excursionists. It is the starting point of the trek: from here you take the RN23 northward. On reaching the sign that marks the trail, continue west. The trail runs through a marsh, then climbs through the beech woods to Mirador Laguna Torre. From here, after little more than an hour's walk, you see Cerro Torre for the first time.

The trail leads to the bottom of the valley, where it divides into a number of possible routes that, after another 45 minutes, all lead to a signposted junction (this is the meeting point for treks to Cerro Torre and to Monte Fitz Roy). Continue on the descending left-hand trail, walking beside the Rio Fitz Roy and flanking the hill until you reach the Jim Bridwell Base Camp, after about 30–40 minutes.

From the base camp, you climb the moraine to the banks of the lake: Laguna Torre. From here there is a fantastic view of Cerro Torre, 10,550 feet (3,128 m) and more than a half mile of rocky ridge, and the neighboring peaks. To return to El Chatlén, retrace your steps.

DAY 2: Bridwell Base Camp–Mirador Maestri

If you intend to continue the trek, dividing it over two days, it is a good idea to camp at the Bridwell Base Camp, continuing along the trail on the eastern bank of the lake on the second day. From here, take the trail that leads to Mirador Maestri, a name that commemorates Cesare Maestri, the Italian climber who, in 1959, claimed to have climbed Cerro Torre for the first time. This granite face, about 2,950 feet (900 m) high, is considered one of the most difficult climbs in the world. Mirador Maestri is a forty-five-minute walk away, and from the viewpoint there is a spectacularly unique view over the Glaciar Grande and the Glaciar Torre (another of the glaciers making up the Hielo Sur, the third-largest ice sheet in the world), which slopes down to the lake. The mountain chain starts with the looming Cerro Solo and ends with Cerro Torre, in which there are three peaks: Cerro Torre, Torre Egger, and Punta Herron.

TRAVEL TIPS

When to go: The best time is December to March. This trek presents no difficulties if the weather is good, but Patagonia has an unpredictable and changeable climate, with strong winds during the summer. Above all, in the area of El Chaltén, the weather is often cloudy and rainy, and the temperature span between the day and the night is accentuated by the nearby ice sheet.

How to get there: The small town of El Calafate has an airport and is the gateway to the region. From here, continue by bus, taxi, or car to El Chaltén, about 124 miles (200 km) away.

What to pack: Trekking pants are essential, and an extra pants layer may be useful, hiking boots, wind- and waterproof jacket, small backpack (for a change of clothes, some food, and a bottle of water), sunscreen, a flashlight, extra batteries, snowshoes.

Ushuaia and Tierra del Fuego

You are at the end of the world. Ushuaia lies in the Tierra del Fuego archipelago, between the Beagle Channel and the Martial mountain range, bounded by the Atlantic and Pacific Oceans. From its port, ships leave for the Antarctic. Ferdinand Magellan was one of the first Europeans to reach this territory in 1520, finding the Yámana people, who lit bonfires to warm themselves: a custom that gave rise to the name of Tierra del Fumar ("land of smoke"), which later became Tierra del Fuego ("land of fire"). The landscape around Ushuaia, which means "deep bay" in the Yámana language, comprises mountains, forests, sea, and small rivers. The climate is unpredictable and extremely windy, with an average temperature of 41°F (5°C).

In this legendary land, where many winter sports are practiced, there are a number of itineraries for hikers, canoeists, and cyclists. Some one-day excursions, like the trek in the Parque Nacional Tierra del Fuego or the canoe trip in the Beagle Channel, are unforgettable.

108 Ushuaia. This is the southernmost city in the world and the capital of the Argentinian province of Tierra del Fuego. It faces the Beagle Channel and is sheltered from behind by the mountains.

Start: Ushuaia
Finish: Ushuaia
Distance: approximately 124 mi (200 km), by various means of transport
Time: 3 days
Difficulty: medium
Accommodation: hotels

108–109 Sea lions resting on the rocks. They feed on a great variety of fish, which they catch near the coast. In their turn, they are preyed upon by sharks, pumas, and orcas.

Eco because: It is a journey through unspoiled nature and wild landscapes, in the company of sea lions, birds, foxes, and penguins.

When to go: From November to March (summer in Argentina).

How to get there: Ushuaia airport, then by car to the city, about 4 miles (7 km) away.

What to pack: It is recommended to bring thermal underwear, T-shirts, and other warm clothing to wear in layers. Windbreaker and waterproof jacket, hat, waterproof gloves, hiking boots, waterproof backpack cover, first-aid kit, energy bars, mineral salts, canteen. Plastic resealable bags as extra protection for cameras and spare batteries. For the canoe trips: waterproof jacket and fleece jacket, waterproof sneakers, hat or cap, sunglasses. An extra pair of socks, to change into after the canoe trip. Rubber boots, technical pants, and life jacket for the trip are supplied by the organizers.

DAY 1: Ushuaia

Ushuaia, with its 60,000 inhabitants, is the southernmost city in the world and the starting point for countless exciting excursions. Lively and teeming with bars, restaurants, and B&Bs, it stands near the 55th parallel, it has long summer days, and in December the sun never sets completely. A visit to El Museo del Fin del Mundo on the seafront in Ushuaia is a must: visitors are introduced to the history of the city, the local bird and animal life, and the customs of the local people. With the same ticket, you can visit the Antigua Casa de Gobierno (the governor's palace) with a display of photographs and relics from the shipwreck of the *Monte Cervantes* in 1930.

DAY 2: Ushuaia–Parque Nacional–Lapataia–Ushuaia

You start out in the direction of Ruta 3 (the 2,193-mile [3,530 km] road that crosses Argentina from Buenos Aires to Ushuaia), and after about 5 miles (8 km), you reach the Parque Nacional Tierra del Fuego, with rivers, ponds and peat bogs, and an exceptional marine ecosystem along the 3.7 miles (6 km) of the coast. It is precisely the Costera itinerary, which follows the banks of the Beagle Channel for about 5 miles (8 km), the one chosen among the many offered by the park. The starting point is in Bahia Ensenada Zaratiegui: all around you can see luxuriant vegetation of *lengas, ñires, cohiues, orchideas, canelos*, and *notros* (Chilean firetree). Along the rivers of Patagonia, you can encounter foxes and ducks, Andean condors, and Magellanic woodpeckers. You stop for lunch at Lake Roca, on the Argentinian side. Here, equipped with rubber boots, pants, and life jacket, you set out from the banks of the lake in an inflatable canoe, following the slow Lapataia River, passing Laguna Verde, and paddling along the Ovanda River. For about an hour, you explore the natural environment that shifts from freshwater to seawater in Lapataia Bay, your destination. Here you have the opportunity to see otherwise inaccessible places. When you reach the bay, you leave the canoe near the end of Ruta 3 and return to Ushuaia by bus.

DAY 3: Ushuaia–Martillo–Gable–Ushuaia

This day is dedicated to a ride by motorboat: not very ecological, it is true, but on the other hand, why go to Tierra del Fuego if you don't get to see the penguins? You start out from Ushuaia by bus, traveling east on Ruta 3, and then take Ruta J. When you arrive at the Lasifashaj River, you get into an inflatable canoe and paddle to the Beagle Channel. Along the way, you see a fine variety of birds and sea lions. You reach Estancia Haberton, the oldest estate in

Tierra del Fuego, home to the Museo Acatushún de Aves y Mamíferos Marinos Australes, dedicated to the marine mammals and birds of the Southern Hemisphere. From here you take a motorboat toward Isla Martillo: you don't get off on the island, but you can easily see the rookeries of Magellanic and Gentoo penguins that nest here every year from the beginning of November to the end of March. The motorboat then takes you toward Isla Gable, where you explore the forest and the marine coast. You return to the boat, which takes you back to Puerto Haberton, where you take the bus to Ushuaia. Back to the end of the world.

▶ ECO-TIPS

THE PEAT BOGS OF TIERRA DEL FUEGO HAVE GROWN BY A FEW MILLIMETERS IN THOUSANDS OF YEARS, AND THE FOREST IS THE SAME THAT HAS BEEN HOME TO THE YÁMANA PEOPLE AND THE FIRST EUROPEAN COLONIZERS FOR THE LAST SEVEN THOUSAND YEARS. IT IS THEREFORE THE DUTY OF VISITORS TO LEAVE THIS AREA TO POSTERITY INTACT, WITHOUT LEAVING ANY TRACE OF THEIR PASSAGE.

Useful Websites
argentina.travel
findelmundo.tur.ar/es/ushuaia
/recomendaciones/como-llegar-a-tdf/1012
canalfun.com/en/
argentina.gob.ar/parquesnacionales
estanciaharberton.com

110 top The Les Eclaireurs lighthouse in the Beagle Channel.
110 bottom and 111 The Tierra del Fuego landscape. Peat bogs are a combination of vegetation and water that creates colorful mosaics.

Trekking in the Altai Mountains

Straddling two continents—Europe and Asia—Russia is the largest country in the world, and more than half of its territory is uninhabited. Vast plains and plateaus make up most of its landscape, while the mountainous areas extend toward the southern borders and the eastern tip of the country. Almost half of the country is covered in forests, a fifth of all those on the planet: among these, the Russian taiga is considered the largest in the world.

From a naturalistic standpoint, Russia has it all: there is plenty of exciting activities for adventure lovers. The trek through the Altai mountains runs along the border with Kazakhstan, Mongolia, and China. Part of the region is a UNESCO World Heritage Site, because "the Altai region represents an important and original center of biodiversity of montane plant and animal species in northern Asia, a number of which are rare and endemic."

112 top and bottom A suspension bridge crosses a water course along the trail. The region is traversed by a network of rivers fed by melting snows and summer rains.

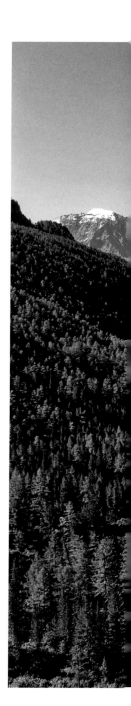

Start: Tiungur
Finish: Tiungur
Distance: approximately 105 mi (170 km)
Time: 10 days
Difficulty: medium
Accommodation: tents

112–113 Lake Kucherla. Together with Lake Teletskoye, Mount Belukha, and the Ukok plateau, it constitutes a UNESCO World Heritage Site called the "Golden Mountains of Altai."

Eco because: The trek takes place in a wild environment and makes use of the assistance and skills of local people. It is unlikely to meet anyone on the trail: in these areas you walk in almost total solitude, accompanied by the pure enjoyment of the unexplored.

When to go: In July and August, when the meadows are in bloom and the temperatures are mild.

How to get there: You land at Moscow-Domodedovo international airport, and from here you take a flight to Barnaul airport. You then travel 466 miles (750 km) to reach the Vysotnik base camp.

What to pack: You will need equipment to keep you warm, dry, and protected from the sun. You should be able to walk efficiently on the mountain trails and be comfortable in the evening and at night. Sleeping bag, waterproof hiking boots, flip-flops, gloves, hat, first-aid kit, biodegradable products for washing. Canteen and energy bars.

DAY 1: Tiungur–Oroktoy

You start from the Vysotnik base camp (2,789 feet [850 m] above sea level), on the banks of the Katun River near the village of Tiungur. You pass Kucherla, the last populated place on the road to the mountains, and you walk through the forest. Once you have crossed the Kuzuyak pass, you camp in a meadow on the banks of the Oroktoy stream.

DAY 2: Oroktoy–Tukhman River

As you climb beside the Oroktoy stream to the Tukhman River, the landscape changes from taiga to alpine meadows. You reach a campsite with a vast panorama over Mount Belukha, the highest mountain in Siberia, and the surrounding peaks.

DAY 3: Tukhman River-Lake Kulduairy

Along the trail to Lake Kulduairy, where you camp for the night, you may encounter Caspian red deer, one of the largest species of deer.

DAY 4: Lake Kulduairy–Tekeliu River

Today's trek starts with a moderate climb to reach a plateau with rocks and stones of unusual shapes. After a brief but steep descent, you reach the campsite on the banks of the Tekeliu River. In the afternoon you can walk 2.5 miles (4 km) further along the river to see two waterfalls.

DAY 5: Tekeliu River–Ak-kem River

Today you cross the Tekeliu River and the Sarybel pass. After a long walk along the ridge and a steep descent, you arrive in the Yarlu valley, where you cross the Ak-kem River. Shortly afterward, you reach the campsite, where you have dinner and stay for the night. The view of the snow-capped Mount Belukha is enchanting.

DAY 6: Ak-kem River–Ak-Ojouk Valley or Yarlu Valley–Ak-kem River

In the morning, you set out on a trip in the Ak-Ojouk valley, famous for its seven lakes, all of a different hue. Alternatively, you continue along the Yarlu valley—a place of high spiritual energy with a "stone city" created by those who come here to meditate.

DAY 7: Ak-Kem River–Talus

The second part of your trek starts here: you climb toward the Karatiurek pass (10,039 feet [3,060 m]), from which you descend on steep paths toward Talus, where you camp in the cedar forest.

DAY 8: Talus–Lake Kucherla

Today, after a brief climb to a plateau, you descend through the taiga toward the wonderful Lake Kucherla, surrounded by snow-capped peaks and teeming with fish. You camp for the night on the banks of the lake.

DAYS 9–10: Lake Kucherla–Tiungur

You begin with the gradual descent along the Kucherla River, one of the most beautiful of the Katunsky ridges, camping for the night along the way. Then you start out again, admiring the ancient rock carvings, and you return to the Vysotnik base camp at Tiungur, your starting point and the end of the trek.

> ## ECO-TIPS
>
> THE PEOPLE OF THE NORTHERN ASIAN STEPPE HAVE ANCIENT AND WELL-ESTABLISHED TRADITIONS. FOR EXAMPLE, THEY STRONGLY BELIEVE IN SHAMANISM AND LIVE AS THEY DID CENTURIES AGO, DESPITE THE ARRIVAL OF SOLAR PANELS AND MOBILE PHONES. THE PLACES TOUCHED BY THIS TRAIL ARE NOT ON THE USUAL TOURIST ROUTES, AND THEY MUST BE RESPECTED AND PRESERVED IN THEIR ORIGINAL INTEGRITY.
>
> ### Useful Websites
> europe.russia.travel/
> www.nhpfund.org/nominations/altai.html
> whc.unesco.org/en/list/768
> www.altzapovednik.ru/en.aspx

114 top Tent for camping on the grassy bank of a mountain stream. Trekking in the Altai mountains includes the mountains along the borders that separate Russia, Kazakhstan, Mongolia, and China.

114 bottom The landscape offers views of steppe, small taiga woods, mountain subdeserts, snow-covered peaks, and tundra: there is a great variety of landscapes.

115 Mount Belukha, 14,783 feet (4,505 m) high, is the highest peak in the Altai mountains in Russia. The trek to approach it crosses a wonderful valley with alpine meadows.

Shin-etsu Trail

Japan is a timeless land, where ancient traditions mingle with modernity. Densely populated, futuristic cities that dictate trends in architecture and fashion coexist with elegant and charming gardens and temples, imperial palaces, and thousands of sanctuaries that exude culture and spirituality. Visitors will be enchanted by the cherry blossoms, the mountains, and the immense and spectacular national parks.

There are also trails for enthusiastic hikers. Among them is the Shin-etsu Trail, opened in 2008, the first hiking trail that allows visitors to experience the extraordinary beauty of the *satoyama* landscape (where the interaction between man and nature is preserved) and to participate in the local culture and hospitality. It runs along the border between the prefectures of Nagano and Niigata, following the Sekida mountain ridge, at an average height of 3,280 feet (1,000 m) above sea level. Modeled after the Appalachian Trail in the United States, its itinerary links small towns and villages in a network that allows hikers to visit attractions and communities and rest in traditional accommodations. Although it was long used for commerce and travel (it is one of the oldest trails in Japan), it remains one of the least known in the country.

Day 1   Day 4
Day 2   Day 5
Day 3   Day 6

Busuno Pass

Sekita Pass

Mount Amamizu

Hotokegamine
Tozanguchi

Akaike Pond

Wakui

Mount Madarao

116 *The blossoming of the cherry trees is a much-awaited event. There is the custom of having a picnic with a blue tablecloth, sheltered by the blossoming trees, watching the falling blossoms (sakura), which symbolize the cycle of life.*

Start: Mount Madarao
Finish: Mount Amamizu
Distance: 50 mi (80 km)
Time: 6 days
Difficulty: easy

Accommodation: tents or lodges (book the transport service for the lodges in advance because they are not on the trail)

116–117 A view of Mount Myoko, about 9,200 feet (2,800 m) high, a stratovolcano that was formed about 300,000 years ago. It is located southwest of the city of Myoko, in the Niigata Prefecture.

Eco because: *Satoyama* is the Japanese term for the area between the foothills and the farmland, and it describes the symbiotic interaction between man and nature in the mountainous areas of Japan. The *satoyama* values and practices are used by the local residents to support and improve their lives and in carrying out activities such as agriculture, forestry, and fishing, respecting the balance of the ecosystem: a perfect combination of human well-being and natural biodiversity. Hiking in the *satoyama* region is an immersion in the natural beauty and the mountain culture of Japan.

118 *A boat trip is the perfect way to explore the river and the area near the Shin-etsu Trail. The boatmen use long bamboo poles to steer.*

119 left *Zen gardens in the area around Lake Katsura. The traditional garden offers miniature landscapes, often in an abstract and stylized form.*

119 right *Buddhist temples with Shinto sanctuaries are very important buildings in Japan and share the fundamental characteristics of Japanese architecture.*

DAY 1: Mount Madarao–Akaike Pond

The Shin-etsu Trail starts at the top of Mount Madarao. From here you descend toward the Manzaka Pass, and when you reach the road, the trail continues on the hill, passing through splendid Japanese beech and birch woods. You then reach the wetlands of Hakama, crossing them to climb the mountain of the same name in less than an hour. From here, there is a splendid view of Mount Myoko to the west. You descend to Akaike Pond by a pleasant path.

DAY 2: Akaike Pond–Wakui

From Akaike you walk to a small hill, passing through the beech woods toward the wetlands of Numanohara, which blossom after the spring thaw but are very attractive at any time of the year. Once you have explored the wetlands, you climb toward Lake Nozomi. From the peak, on a clear day, you can see Mount Madarao, the peak of Hakama, and even Mount Myoko. The trail descends through a beautiful forest to arrive

at the jetty on the lake. The climb to the peak of Mount Kenashi lasts about 30–40 minutes and offers a superb view of the Iiyama basin. You descend through a larch forest toward the pond, known as Wakui Shin-ike. From here you walk along the road: it is an easy walk that arrives at Road 292 in the village of Wakui.

DAY 3: Wakui–Hotokegamine Tozanguchi

Today, from Wakui, after a climb through a forest and a cedar plantation, you come to the Tomikura Pass. It is a path partly used by local people seeking mushrooms and mountain herbs. The pass was once a place for trade and commerce between Shinano and Echigo, and you can see the remains of the ancient road where it crosses the Shin-etsu Trail. Soon you come to a historical site called Taishojin, where Kenshin Uesugi

TRAVEL TIPS

When to go: From June to November.

How to get there: From Tokyo airport you travel by train and then by shuttle to Madarao (about 155 miles [250 km] altogether).

What to pack: Maps of Japan and of the trail from your own country, because very few are available in foreign languages once you arrive. Tent, sleeping bag, canteen. Hiking boots, waterproof clothing suitable for the mountains. Headlamp, food, snacks, compass, sunscreen, medicines, first-aid kit, mobile phone or walkie-talkie, spare batteries.

(the 16th-century Echigo warlord) set up a lookout to control the Iiyama and Kita Pass territories. On the crest, above the trail, there is a small sanctuary dedicated to the horses and the cattle that died supporting the Samurai army of Uesugi. The trail continues toward Lake Sobu, with its sanctuary on the water, then toward Mount Kuroiwa. You descend a ravine before arriving at the shelter for lunch. The last—quite challenging—climb up to Mount Kuroiwa is just a little further ahead. The entire mountain is a Japanese natural monument, being a rare habitat for the gifu and hime gifu butterflies, and for the *Rhacophorus arboreus* tree frogs (*moriaogaeru* in Japanese). In the area surrounding Lake Katsura, where the skunk cabbages flower in springtime, there is a natural wellspring called Taro Shimizu. From the Hiramaru Pass, you walk along the western bank of Lake Nakafuruike. You cross the wetlands of Kitafuruike on the forest road, reaching a clearing

where you find the sign for the Shin-etsu Trail. From this point on, the path enters a national forest, where there are many ups and downs. You finally reach the last steep climb to Hotokegamine Tozanguchi. This is the top of one of the slopes in the Togari ski resort and the end of the third stage. Here there is a panoramic view over Nozawa Onsen.

DAY 4: Hotokegamine Tozanguchi–Sekita Pass

From Hotokegamine you come to the Ozawa Pass. If you descend on the Niigata side, you arrive at Lake Yoshihachi; if you choose the Nagano side, you arrive on the Tondaira slopes of the Togari ski resort. In either case, you return to the trail, which leads through a spectacular, centuries-old beech wood, where you stop for lunch. The climb up Mount Nabekura requires much caution, in particular when the weather is poor: it can be tiring, but the effort is rewarded by the view of Mount Myoko and Mount

Hiuchi, and the magnificent Chikuma River. You stop on Mount Kurokura for only a short time; from here you can see the Sea of Japan. Once you have passed the Dogata Pass, you descend to the Sekita Pass. On the Niigata side, there is the Shin-etsu Trail Visitor Center of Green Pal Kogenso, where you can gather information. Near the Sekita Pass, you can visit Chayaike Pond.

DAY 5: Sekita Pass–Busuno Pass

On the fifth day, there are many brief ups and downs, which make it one of the most difficult sections of the trail. However, it rewards hikers with rich natural surroundings. The area is dotted with seasonal flowers, mushrooms, and beech saplings. From the Sekita Pass you reach the Maki Pass, from which, on a clear day, you can see the Sea of Japan and the island of Sado. The pass is also a good place to see the rare golden eagle. From here you make a fairly steep climb along the ridge to Mount Hanadate to enjoy the breathtaking view. After the Utsunomata Pass, you come to Maboroshi-no-ike, the Lake of the Ghost. Surrounded by a beech forest, it is the kingdom of the *Rhacophorus arboreus* tree frog and the Japanese black salamander. As you draw closer to the Busuno Pass, the end of the day's walk, you catch a glimpse of Mount Hishigatake, a reference point for Niigata.

DAY 6: Busuno Pass–Mount Amamizu

This stage of the Shin-etsu Trail leads to Mount Amamizu, the northern tip of the trail. It is also one of the most gratifying. The route is almost completely wrapped in splendid beech woods, with many panoramic views of the Niigata delta. From the Busuno Pass, you reach the Sugawa Pass and then continue toward the Nonoumi Pass. Less than one mile before you reach the pass, you find the wetlands of Nishimado, just off the trail. From Nonoumi, a forest road leads beyond the lake by the same name to the Misaka Pass, which is an excellent stopping place with a wonderful panoramic view. The last two hours of the walk between Misaka and Mount Amamizu lead to Mount Sanpodake (3,734 feet [1,138 m]). The path winds through the beech trees with some fantastic views to the north and the south. When you reach the peak of Mount Amamizu (3,570 feet [1,088 m]), you admire the landscape of Tsunan. This is the end of the trail! There are three options for leaving the Shin-etsu Trail. The nearest hub for transport is at Matsunoyamaguchi to the north, about 45 minutes away, but you can also go toward Tsunan in the east (one hour) or Sakae to the south (two and a half hours).

120 top Nanataki is one of the 100 best waterfalls in Japan, and it is in the city of Myoko, in Niigata Prefecture. It is so powerful that below it the ground resounds.

120 bottom A suspension bridge over the water along the route: an enchanting place in nature.

121 A field of ferns in Ozegahara, a Japanese national park between the prefectures of Niigata, Fukushima, and Gunma. It represents an important natural monument.

ECO-TIPS

THIS TOUR IS MADE POSSIBLE BY THE SHIN-ETSU TRAIL CLUB, AN ORGANIZATION ACCREDITED BY THE PREFECTURE OF NAGANO. ITS MISSION IS TO MANAGE AND MAINTAIN THE BIODIVERSITY OF THE TRAIL, TO SUPPORT AND PROMOTE ITS BEAUTY, AS WELL AS THE LOCAL HISTORY AND THE CULTURAL HERITAGE, AND TO TEACH ABOUT THE NATURAL ENVIRONMENT SURROUNDING THE TRAIL. THIS WALK ALSO ALLOWS HIKERS TO EXPERIENCE THE GENUINE LOCAL HOSPITALITY DURING THE NIGHTS SPENT IN THE MOUNTAIN VILLAGES. ACCESS TO THE WETLANDS IS LIMITED DUE TO THE PRESENCE OF PROTECTED PLANTS.

Useful Websites
s-trail.net/english
japan.travel/en/

 **CHINA**

Tiger Leaping Gorge

Immensely vast, China offers a huge geographical and climatic variety of environments, from the Himalayan peaks to the coastline of the Pacific Ocean. In the environmental field, its numbers are impressive: it is home to one-tenth of the plant species on the planet, while the animal species represent 14%. This heritage is protected in 2,740 nature reserves that occupy one-sixth of the territory.

Of the twenty-two provinces that make up China, Yunnan occupies the extreme southeast of the country and presents a wide cultural and biological diversity, thanks to the many ethnic groups that live here. Much of the territory has preserved its authenticity.

The Tiger Leaping Gorge is situated in this province. It is one of the deepest river canyons in the world—up to 12,795 feet (3,900 m) deep—dug out by the Jinsha River, a tributary of the Yangtze. The gorge is surrounded by snow-capped mountains and crossed by steep winding trails that pass through incredibly beautiful landscapes. Near the mouth of the gorge is Tiger Leap Rock: legend has it that a tiger escaping from hunters leapt across the river at this point, where it is 82 feet (25 m) wide. The gorge is part of the protected area of the Three Parallel Rivers, a UNESCO World Heritage Site, and there is an entrance fee. The three most important waterways in Asia flow through the area: the Yangtze, Mekong, and Salween Rivers. The trail is known as the High Road, and it is a good path, high above the river, with excellent views

122 *The statue of the tiger: legend has it that a tiger escaping from hunters leapt across the river at this point, where it is 82 feet (25 m) wide.*

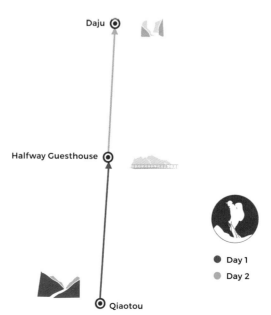

Daju

Halfway Guesthouse

Qiaotou

● Day 1
● Day 2

Start: Qiaotou
Finish: Daju
Distance: 19 mi (30 km)
Time: 2 days
Difficulty: easy
Accommodation: guesthouse

122–123 The powerful Yangtze River has cut one of the deepest gorges in the mountains north of Lijiang. The trek follows a very well-known, well-marked route.

Eco because: Since the beginning of the century, the Chinese government has undertaken a number of projects for the safeguarding and protection of the country's natural resources. The gorge, where tourism has been promoted since 1990, is important for the safeguarding of the wildlife and the course of the three rivers. There is also an unusual number of plant and animal species in the region, some of which are quite rare.

When to go: October, November, and May are the best months; at other times of the year, the rain makes the trail slippery and dangerous.

How to get there: The nearest airport to the start of the trail is in Lijang. From here it is a two-hour bus journey to Quiatou.

What to pack: Non-slip shoes, windbreaker, waterproof cape, clothing for the mountains. Canteen and energy bars, first-aid kit. It is advisable to bring sheets (the guesthouse may not have any clean ones). Spare batteries and waterproof covers for cameras and video equipment, maps and guides in your own language.

DAY 1: Qiaotou–Halfway Guesthouse

You start out from Qiaotou (Hutiaoxia Zhen), the city of Tiger Leaping Gorge, near the upper gorge. You walk for a couple of hours to the Naxi Family Guesthouse, where you can rest and have lunch. Then you continue for another two hours to a sharp bend called "28 Bends." This is the most challenging part of the itinerary: the trail is winding and climbs steeply, but the panorama will repay all the effort. After a short rest, you continue for another two hours to the Halfway Guesthouse, midway along the high road, where you enjoy a splendid view of Jade Dragon Snow Mountain (Yulong Xueshan) and the valley of the Jinsha River, a principal tributary of the Yangtze.

DAY 2: Halfway Guesthouse–Daju

The following day, you encounter wonderful waterfalls and canyons along the trail to Tina's Guesthouse. After a short stay, you continue along a minor track with steep slopes to the banks of the Yangtze, to see the Mantianxing reef section, where the gorge narrows and the view of the rapids is extremely evocative. You continue along the trail to the lower section of the gorge, where you cross the river at Daju, the end of the trek.

124 top Many parts of the trail are winding, and it rapidly ascends toward the top.

124 bottom and 124–125 The path along the rock walls. When it rains, the rocks may be slippery and the path muddy: for this reason, the autumn season is recommended for the trail.

> ## ECO-TIPS

ALL THE TRAILS WERE CREATED AND ARE MAINTAINED BY THE LOCAL PEOPLE, WHO, IN EXCHANGE FOR ACCESS, ASK FOR A SMALL SUM OF MONEY: THEIR PRECIOUS WORK MUST BE RESPECTED.

Useful Websites
whc.unesco.org/en/list/1083
https://www.lijiang-travel.com/Halfway_
Guesthouse

From Ganden to Samye

126–127 The Ganden Monastery on Mount Wangbur, on the south bank of the Lhasa River in Dagzê District, at an altitude of 12,467 feet (3,800 m) above sea level.

Situated on the highest plateau in the world, teeming with monasteries and spectacular panoramas, Tibet has an undoubtable charm. In addition to being an unspoiled and unpolluted country, its culture reflects ancient Buddhist traditions—the ideal place for those seeking spiritual life. The pilgrims who turn the prayer wheels, reciting mantras, the fragrance of incense in the temples, the rituals of tea with butter, holding the cup in both hands to express appreciation: all this, together with the beauty of the landscape, makes a journey through this magical land an unforgettable experience. The trail from Ganden to Samye is one of the best treks in the world. It is a journey into Tibetan Buddhism, exploring lakes, snowy mountain passes, verdant alpine meadows, villages, and ancient sacred places, culminating in the approach to the Samye Monastery.

Do not underestimate the fitness level required for this trek: the altitude presents a serious challenge. In fact, you start at 14,764 feet (4,500 m) above sea level at the Ganden Monastery, and crossing the Shogu-La Pass at 17,224 feet (5,250 m), you descend to 11,614 feet (3,540 m), where you find the Samye Monastery. In order to acclimatize, if you arrive directly from Lhasa, you must spend at least one night in Ganden.

Start: Ganden Monastery
Finish: Samye Monastery
Distance: 50 mi (80 km)
Time: 5 days
Difficulty: medium/difficult
Accommodation: tents

Ganden
Yama Do
Tsotup-chu Valley
Herders' Camp
Yamalung Hermitage
Samye Monastery

● Day 1   ○ Day 4
● Day 2   ● Day 5
● Day 3

Eco because: You walk through magnificent and unforgettable landscapes and have the privilege of meeting the Tibetans, a very tolerant, smiling people, who often share what they have. This itinerary can be undertaken with a horse or a yak.

DAY 1: Ganden Monastery–Yama Do

The trek starts at the Ganden Monastery, where you can hire a yak or a packhorse to accompany you. The monastery is one of the six largest of the Gelupga, the most recent school of Tibetan Buddhism. In addition to the magnificent architecture and its religious importance, it offers a wonderful view on the peak of the Ganden Wangpo hill. Before setting out, we advise making a few brief excursions around the monastery to admire the bird's eye view of the Kichu valley, which lies behind the building. You then set out toward the village of Trubshi, descending toward Hepu, a village of about thirty houses. You walk further until you reach Ani Pagong, where there was once a small nunnery. Then the trail crosses marshy fields to Yama Do, where you can camp.

DAY 2: Yama Do–Tsotup-chu Valley

In the morning you leave the valley, crossing a basin scattered with tussock grass and climb toward the Shogu-La Pass (17,224 feet [5,250 m]). The trail runs through the valley

128 A group of barefoot hikers fords the Tsotup-chu, which flows in the broad valley. Here you meet herds of goats, sheep, and yaks, and so you must watch out for Tibetan mastiffs.

129 left A woman in the tent doorway at Yama Do. The women's situation is not the easiest on the planet, due also to gender discrimination.

129 right The Samye Monastery, dating from around 778 and covering an area of over 265,000 square feet (25,000 sq m), was built according to the description of the universe in Buddhist writings.

and overlooks the lake, the panoramas of which are among the best parts of the itinerary, and then begins to descend. You cross the Tsotup-chu River, which flows through the valley. You will probably encounter flocks of goats or sheep and herds of yak: keep an eye out for the herders' dogs, which may bite. You camp for the night in the valley.

DAY 3: Tsotup-chu Valley–Herders' Camp

The trek starts off again, fording the Tsotup-chu River and following a wide valley that soon curves southward toward the Chitu-La pass (17,093 feet [5,210 m]). A brief descent leads to a basin with three small lakes: the trail runs along the western bank of the first lake and then the eastern banks of the second two. After about an hour's walk, you arrive at a first seasonal herders' camp on the eastern slope of the valley. Here the trail enters a forest of willows and rosebushes. When you leave the wood, after about twenty minutes, you come to another seasonal herders' camp, near the point where the side valley of Gampa-la meets the main valley. Finally, you cross a bridge to the eastern bank, where there are numerous campsites to choose from for the night.

DAY 4: Herders' Camp–Yamalung Hermitage

At the beginning of the day, you take a wide, easy trail along the eastern slope to a river that flows into the adjacent valley. Here you cross a series of woods and meadows. Further on you come to the fork for the Yamalung Hermitage, with a small shop that sells soft drinks, beer, and instant noodles. From here you start the climb to the hermitage. When you return, you stop for the night at the campsite near the shop.

When to go: The best time is between mid-May and mid-October, when the weather is mild.

How to get there: From Lhasa airport, you take a bus t o the Ganden Monastery (40 miles [64 km]).

What to pack: Tent, sleeping bag, hiking boots, warm clothes that cover the arms and the legs, windbreaker. Food, canteen, mineral supplements. Hat, sunglasses, sunscreen, lip balm. First-aid kit, medicines for altitude sickness, anti-blister bandages. Headlamp, spare batteries, waterproof covering for cameras and video equipment. Maps. Insect repellent.

DAY 5: Yamalung Hermitage–Samye Monastery

Now the trail becomes a wide road, suitable for cars, and the valley is much wider. You come to a bridge, where you take the trail along the right-hand side of the valley. You continue walking, and in the center of the valley, you see Hepo Ri, one of the most sacred mountains in Tibet. Along the route you encounter a number of villages, before finally reaching Samye, the first Buddhist monastery to be built in Tibet, around 778 AD: this is the most important tourist destination in the country and the end of the trek.

ECO-TIPS

YOU HAVE THE MORAL OBLIGATION TO RESPECT THE WILDLIFE OF THIS NATURAL PARADISE, AND YOU SHOULD KEEP A SAFE DISTANCE FROM ANY ANIMALS YOU MAY ENCOUNTER. IT IS A GOOD THING TO HELP THE TIBETAN SHOPKEEPERS AND TOUR OPERATORS BY BUYING THEIR GOODS AND SERVICES. ASK FOR PERMISSION BEFORE TAKING PHOTOGRAPHS OF PEOPLE.

Useful Websites
https://tibet.net

NEPAL

Start: Besi Sahar
Finish: Pokhara
Distance: 119 mi (191 km)
Time: 17 days
Difficulty: medium/challenging
Accommodation: lodges or tents

130–131 A man with a horse crossing a suspension bridge over the river Marsyangdi. The river is 93 miles (150 km) long, formed near the village of Manang from the confluence of two streams.

Eco because: The Nepalese trekking and guide organization, with headquarters in Kathmandu, has planned this and other treks in the Himalayas with the aim to explore the territory, while respecting the environment and its values. It has long been working in favor of the population, promoting education, health, preventive hygiene, and projects linked to water supplies and solar power. It has contributed to reconstruction missions following the terrible earthquake of 2015.

Annapurna Circuit

This tiny Himalayan country between Tibet and India, the land of the Sherpa people, yaks, and monasteries, has survived almost completely isolated from the rest of the world thanks to its imposing and unspoiled mountains. Rich in historical and artistic vestiges, with extraordinary landscapes, it has many of the most beautiful trails in the world. The people are as beautiful as the natural environment. Only recently opened to foreigners, Nepal is now easily accessible to the traveler seeking nature and adventure amid the hills, mountains, and jungles of the Himalayas: it is a trekker's paradise.

The region of Annapurna is situated in the north of the country and takes the trekker through villages and forests to the foot of the mountains Annapurna I and Dhaulagiri, two of the famous "eight-thousanders" (mountains above 8,000 m, or 26,247 feet), with a crossing of the Himalayan plateau that is both exciting and satisfying.

● Day 1	● Day 7	● Day 13
● Day 2	● Day 8	○ Day 14
● Day 3	● Day 9	● Day 15
○ Day 4	● Day 10	● Day 16
○ Day 5	● Day 11	● Day 17
● Day 6	● Day 12	

131 top The Krishna Temple and other historic monuments in Patan Durbar Square in the Kathmandu valley, which has been declared a UNESCO World Heritage Site.
131 bottom The stupa is a Buddhist monument that symbolizes an illuminated mind and represents the manifestation of the Buddha, of his law, and of the cosmic universe.

DAY 1: Besi Sahar–Bahundanda

Before starting the excursion, it is wise to spend at least a couple of days exploring the capital Kathmandu in order to acclimatize. The trek starts at Besi Sahar and follows the Marsyangdi River, crossing a long suspension bridge and a fine waterfall that forms a natural swimming pool. At the end of this stage, you arrive at the city of Bahundanda, where there is a hot spring and spectacular views to the north.

DAY 2: Bahundanda–Chamje

The day starts with an exciting experience, the crossing of a cantilever bridge followed by a suspension bridge. You pass some small settlements along the way, and you can see stone houses, less tropical vegetation, and more Tibetan culture. Finally, you arrive in Chamje, the destination for the day.

When to go: September, October, April, and May are the best months. During the monsoon season, there is no rainfall in this area.

How to get there: From the international airport of Kathmandu, you reach Besi Sahar by car or by bus, a distance of 112 miles (180 km) that takes 5 hours.

What to pack: Trekking boots, windproof pants, jacket, and gloves. Thermal underwear, quick-dry T-shirts, polar fleece jacket. Balaclava, neck warmer, sunglasses (100% UV filter), down jacket, trekking poles, dust mask or lightweight scarf. First-aid kit, sunscreen, lip balm, energy bars. Canteen (at least half a gallon). Headlamp, camera, spare batteries, battery charger. Map of the itinerary, pens, binoculars. Ear plugs. Insect repellent.

DAY 3: Chamje–Bagarchap

From Chamje you cross the Manang district, where you meet people from the Bhotia ethnic group, farmers, herders, and trans-Himalayan traders. The trail climbs gradually to the city of Bagarchap, from where you enjoy a fine view of the Annapurna massif and the Lamjung Himal

132–133 Trekker and stones with a painted mantra, along the Annapurna Circuit. A mantra is a sequence of words that makes meditation more effective and brings spiritual benefits.
133 top The city of Chame is the government headquarters of the district of Manang, the most populous in Nepal.
133 bottom A young woman washes kitchen vessels in one of the villages along the trek.

DAY 4: Bagarchap–Chame

After leaving Bagarchap, the valley narrows and is covered in a broadleaf forest. Chame, the destination for this stage, is a government city and the district center of Manang with interesting religious buildings and hot springs.

DAY 5: Chame–Lower Pisang

You continue walking along a valley with pine trees, hemlock, and cedar woods. The trail leads to Lower Pisang: a detour to Upper Pisang, 328 feet (100 m) higher, is essential to enjoy an incredible view of Annapurna II, at 26,247 feet (8,000 m). The men who live here are traders and part-time farmers, the women work in the fields full-time.

134 top *A village in Upper Pisang, from where you have a magnificent view of Annapurna and its 26,000 feet (8,000 m).*
134 bottom left *Wooden bridge along the Annapurna Circuit near Dhikur Pokhari.*
134 bottom right *Panoramic view of Annapurna near Pisang.*
135 *An old Mani prayer wall looking toward Annapurna. There are different types and forms of prayer wheel in Buddhism: from the small Tibetan mani to wheels about 80 feet (2.5 m) high.*

DAY 6: Pisang–Manang

To arrive from Pisang at the next stage, you can choose between two trails: one is lower, and the other is higher and longer, but offers exceptional views of the Annapurna massif. Along this second trail you will meet very few trekkers. Both converge on the large village of Braga, home to the most ancient monastery in the area. Manang is a thirty-minute walk from here.

DAY 7: Manang

You stop for a day in Manang to acclimatize and to reduce the risk of altitude sickness. Manang stands in a spectacular position and offers excursions to lakes, caves, hills, and monasteries.

DAY 8: Manang–Ledar As you leave Manang, the buildings become more scattered and you pass through meadows and birch woods. Here you may see flocks of Helan Shan blue sheep, or bharal, typical of this area. You reach Ledar at 13,779 feet (4,200 m) above sea level.

DAY 9: Ledar–Thorung Phedi

In order to climb gradually, you make a short detour and spend the night at Thorung Phedi, preparing to cross the pass the following day. If you are lucky, at twilight you may see a snow leopard.

DAY 10: Thorung Phedi–Thorung La–Muktinath Temple

This stage begins with a constant climb up the side moraine. The mountain pass of Thorung La is marked by a large mound. It is the highest point of the trek at 17,769 feet (5,416 m) and divides two magnificent Himalayan valleys. You descend in the direction of the Kaligandaki valley toward the Muktinath Temple, one of the highest in the world and a long-time pilgrimage site for Hindus and Buddhists.

DAY 11: Muktinath Temple–Jomsom

Along the trail for the day's stage, near the temple, the people of Mustang (a northern district) gather to sell their handmade products to the pilgrims: among their wares are the Shaligram, seashell fossils that are an iconic symbol of the god Vishnu. Continuing along the trail, the imposing Dhaulagiri mountain appears (26,794 feet [8,167 m]). You pass through the city of Kagbeni and arrive at Jomsom.

> ### ECO-TIPS

FOR ECOLOGICAL REASONS, WE ADVISE USING BIODEGRADABLE SOAP FOR PERSONAL HYGIENE AND WASHING. THERE ARE NO FACILITIES FOR DISPOSAL OF USED BATTERIES IN NEPAL, SO THE VISITOR MUST TAKE THEM OUT OF THE COUNTRY.

Useful Websites
welcomenepal.com
unlimitedninehills.com
/annapurna-circuit

DAY 12: Jomsom–Kalopani

You descend to Marpha, a village of limewashed houses surrounded by fields, and continue along the Kaligandaki River. Along the way, the rain shadow effect (caused by the cloud systems generated by the Himalayas, preventing the rain from falling on the opposite slope) hovers over the coniferous forests. Finally, you reach Kalopani, from where there are spectacular views over Dhaulagiri and the Annapurna massif.

DAY 13: Kalopani–Tatopani

Today's stage foresees a pleasant walk through subtropical vegetation, amid Indian buffalo, banyan trees, and poinsettia. The trail follows the Kaligandaki River, passes through a narrow pass, and crosses a bridge near a spectacular waterfall, before reaching Tatopani. Here the hot springs offer the chance of a relaxing bath.

DAY 14: Tatopani–Ghorepani

The trek continues, leaving behind the terraced fields and passing through a dense forest of rhododendrons to the village of Ghorepani. You camp at the pass and enjoy the spectacle of a sunset on the snow-capped peaks of Dhaulagiri and the Annapurna chain.

DAY 15: Ghorepani–Ghandrung

Today the trail winds through a vast forest of rhododendrons and colonies of orchids to the attractive city of Ghandrung, where the Annapurna chain and the Machapuchare, one of the most spectacular mountains in the world, dominate the panorama. This is the perfect place to see the Lamjung Himal and the Manaslu chain.

DAY 16: Ghandrung–Dhampus

This stage of the trek also offers amazing panoramas, especially on the way to the village of Dhampus.

DAY 17: Dhampus–Pokhara

After the climbs of the previous days, the trail now descends through the forests to the valley bottom, which leads to Pokhara, the end of the trek.

136–137 Trekker and yak near the settlement of Ledar.
137 top The village of Manang: many trekkers stay here to acclimatize, at an altitude of 11,545 feet (3,519 m).
137 bottom Machapuchare and Phewa Tal seen from Pokhara, a city where you find the International Mountain Museum, with exhibits on the history of climbing and the Himalayan people.

Owl Trek

Start: Manchugang
Finish: Monastery of Tharpaling
Distance: 14 mi (22 km)
Time: 3 days
Difficulty: easy
Accommodation: tents

Bhutan, "the land of the thunder dragon," is a Himalayan kingdom where Buddhist culture and tradition blend with increasing globalization. The Bhutanese are very proud of the respect they show to nature: even the constitution states that each of them is an administrator of natural resources and the environment. Tourists immediately perceive this attitude and are led to behave with respect for the environment and the animals, without intruding on the local traditions and culture.

This trek crosses the valleys of the district of Bumthang, the cultural center of the country. It is a journey through forests of blue pine, birch, maple, red pine, juniper, bamboo, and numerous species of rhododendron, nestling in immense spaces and evocative silences. Traditional buildings act as religious, military, bureaucratic, administrative, and social centers, playing a fundamental role in the peculiarities of Bhutanese Buddhism. As you walk along these quiet ridges in the mountains of Bumthang, you can admire the incomparable panoramas of Mount Gangkhar Puensum, the highest peak in the world to remain unclimbed. The avian fauna in this area is varied and contains pleasant surprises, like the beautiful, multicolored western horned tragopan, a pheasant commonly seen during the mating season between April and May. The nights are punctuated by the hooting of the owls that give their name to the tour: The Owl Trek.

138 top Children in typical Bhutanese clothing play near a monastery.

138 bottom The Himalayan monal, a brightly colored pheasant that lives in the forests, is generally extremely shy and elusive. It has a pair of hidden horns on the sides of its head.

139 Fields and terraces used to grow rice. Rice is a subsistence crop for all the country, and only 1% is put on the market. Red rice is unique: it is grown manually without chemical fertilizers or pesticides.

● Day 1
● Day 2
● Day 3

Manchugang

Dhur Village

Schonath

Kitiphu

Monastery of Tharpaling

Eco because: Bhutan is the example of responsible tourism par excellence. The rule for the flow of visitors is clear: small numbers and high income. That is to say, only a limited number of visitors can enter the country each year, and for every day of their stay, they must pay a government tax "for the protection of the nation's culture," of which 37% goes directly to the state for medical welfare and education.

DAY 1: Manchugang–Schonath

The first stage of the trek starts at the base camp of Manchugang. You leave in the direction of the village of Dhur at 9,514 feet (2,900 m) above sea level. The inhabitants of the village are Khep and Brokpa nomads, who speak two distinct dialects, Bumthang Kha and Brokke. Near the river stands a traditional watermill, once a source of income for the population. Leaving the village, the walk continues with a climb through the forests of blue pine toward Schonath, 11,320 feet (3,450 m) above sea level, knee deep in juniper and hemlock. You can camp here.

DAY 2: Schonath–Kitiphu

On the second day of the trek, you pass through forests of red pine with hemlock in the undergrowth and can admire many species of rhododendron, which bloom in the months of April and May. The trail also runs through bamboo thickets, the most common brushwood in this area. After a few hours' walking, you reach the Drangela Pass, 11,810 feet (3,600 m) above sea level, from which, after climbing toward the Kitiphu ridge, you reach the campsite for the night, at about 12,700 feet (3,870 m) above sea level. From here there is a breathtaking view of the snowcapped mountains and the valleys below. On the horizon looms the imposing Gangkhar Puensum (24,836 feet [7,570 m]).

When to go: One of the best times to undertake this trek is late spring, between April and early June, when the rhododendrons are in bloom. In autumn it is sometimes possible to encounter black bears in the Himalayas, so it is necessary to be alert. It could be also interesting to plan the trek during one of the local festivals, in order to take part.

How to get there: The international airport of Paro is the gateway to Bhutan. From here it is possible to take a connecting flight for Bathpalathang and from there to hire a car for an hour's drive to Manchugang.

What to pack: The climate in Bhutan is extremely varied due to the considerable differences in altitude in the country and the influence of the monsoons in northern India. It is necessary to bring a tent, sleeping bag, and warm comfortable clothing, sunscreen, and technical clothing for trekking. Avoid vests, short skirts, and very short shorts.

ECO-TIPS

IT IS ESSENTIAL TO CHOOSE LOCAL GUIDES AND TOUR OPERATORS, REMEMBERING THAT IN ASIA THE ATTITUDE TOWARD TIME AND PUNCTUALITY IS VERY DIFFERENT FROM WESTERN CUSTOMS. IT IS BEST TO USE ORGANIC PRODUCTS FOR DAILY WASHING. IT IS IMPORTANT NOT TO POLLUTE RIVERS AND STREAMS, TO CARRY CANS AND TRASH BACK FOR DISPOSAL, AND TO USE A CANTEEN FOR WATER IN ORDER TO AVOID PLASTIC. YOU CAN TAKE PICTURES AND VIDEOS. HOWEVER, CHECK WITH THE GUIDE BEFORE DOING SO INSIDE THE DZONG, TEMPLES, MONASTERIES, AND RELIGIOUS INSTITUTIONS BECAUSE IN SOME AREAS IT IS FORBIDDEN.

Useful Websites
tourism.gov.bt
www.bhutan.gov.bt
www.bhutan.travel

140 The monastery of Taktsang (also called Tiger's Nest) is a complex of Himalayan Buddhist temples perched on the high peaks of the Paro valley.
141 Prayer flags fly near the Taktsang monastery.

DAY 3: Kitiphu–Monastery of Tharpaling

The last stage involves a descent toward the monasteries of Zambhalha, Chuedak, and Tharpaling, where a visit reveals the daily life and the customs of the monks. The Owl Trek ends here, but the trail continues along the Kikila ridge and follows the Royal Heritage Trail, the traditional route between Trongsa and Bumthang, through panoramic hills and woods. The tour ends with the wonderful view of the Jakar Dzong in the distance. Built in 1549, the Dzong, or "castle of the white bird," played an important role as the fortress of defense of the whole eastern Dzongkhags. It also became the seat of the first king of Bhutan.

"Happiness" Tourism

Traveling in Bhutan is a unique experience, not only for the magical landscape you are thrown into, but also because, as a tourist, you can become part of several projects to support the environment and the population. This Buddhist kingdom, perched in the Himalayas and faithful to its millenary tradition, has in fact decided to provide for the material and spiritual well-being of its citizens by using the income from tourism. The tax visitors have to pay to enter Bhutan, equal to $200–$250 per person per day, is used for the maintenance of the trails and for environmental protection, and also to improve the infrastructures of the country, guaranteeing good standards of health care and free education for all. Some projects of the Tourism Council go further and, with the income from tourism, support children from poor families with daily meals, books, clothes, shoes, and sportswear. This enlightened policy has had excellent results so far. It is no coincidence that Bhutan measures its level of development through the value of Gross National Happiness.

AUSTRALIA

Start: Cape Naturaliste
Finish: Cape Leeuwin
Distance: 78 mi (125 km)
Time: 5 days
Difficulty: medium
Accommodation: tents and resorts

144–145 A gangway at Canal Rocks
near Yallingup in the Leeuwin-
Naturaliste National Park.

Eco because: It is wild, far from the cities, the ideal trail for anyone
wanting to explore the abundant biodiversity and the geomorphology
of this area, providing they respect the seven fundamental principles of the
Leave No Trace outdoor ethic, including the careful planning of the trip,
attention to the choice of camping ground, and respect for the wildlife
and flora.

Cape to Cape Track: From Cape Naturaliste to Cape Leeuwin

Australia boasts a vast and important ecosystem, protected by the government through an extensive network of national parks, nature reserves, and protected areas. In fact, the country has hundreds of protected natural areas covering extremely varied landscapes, twenty World Heritage Sites, and the largest system of marine parks in the world.

Endemic flora and fauna (wombats, koalas, platypuses, quokkas, wallabies, and kangaroos), vast spaces, snowy mountains, forests, savanna, the coral barrier, and unpolluted waters: Australia has unique biodiversity.

The extreme southwestern corner of Australia, along the Leeuwin-Naturaliste Ridge, between the lighthouses of Cape Naturaliste and Cape Leeuwin, offers a spectacular coastal trail. Here you encounter incredible rock formations, spectacular caves, a series of breathtaking panoramas from the top of the cliffs, and long stretches of uncontaminated beaches. At any time of the year, there are good chances of seeing dolphins, and between June and September, humpback whales and southern right whales swim close to the coast, during their annual migration between the Antarctic Ocean and the breeding grounds further north.

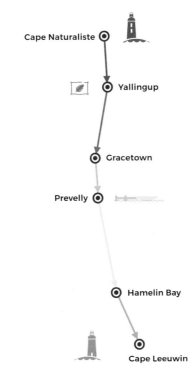

Cape Naturaliste

Yallingup

Gracetown

Prevelly

Hamelin Bay

Cape Leeuwin

Day 1
Day 2
Day 3
Day 4
Day 5

145 Perched on a promontory, the Cape Naturaliste lighthouse, with its unequaled view, is 65 feet (20 m) high and can be visited with a guide.

146 *The Quinninup Falls are in full flow after recent rains. The walk to reach them is rather demanding: do not forget your canteen.*

147 top *Along the way, you find plants of the Agavaceae family, which have adapted well to Australia.*

147 bottom left *Black cockatoos fly over the Leeuwin-Naturaliste National Park. They have many features in common with other parrots, like a curved beak and feet with two claws behind and two in front.*

147 bottom right *Giant karri tree at the entrance to a cave in the Margaret River area. The karri is a eucalyptus that originates from the wetter regions of Australia.*

DAY 1: Cape Naturaliste–Yallingup

The Cape Naturaliste lighthouse (open to visitors), north of the Leeuwin-Naturaliste National Park, is the starting point for the Cape to Cape Track. The first 2.2 miles (3.5 km), from the lighthouse near Sugarloaf Rock, a small island a few hundred feet from the coast, are accessible to all. The trail continues toward Yallingup, where you can stay at the Yallingup Forest Resort, an environmentally friendly accommodation situated among the majestic vineyards of the Margaret River valley.

DAY 2: Yallingup–Gracetown

The high chalk cliffs along the trail are excellent viewpoints from which to sight whales and dolphins in the sea below. A brief deviation of less than 1,000 feet (300 m) inland leads to the Quininup Falls, which are most enjoyable in winter and spring. The area was once an important settlement of the Noongar, the indigenous people of this territory. The imposing Wilyabrup Cliffs are formed of granitic rock, a paradise for climbers and a magnificent scenario. You can camp for the night in Gracetown.

TRAVEL TIPS

When to go: Spring and autumn are the best times, but you can visit Western Australia throughout the year. Bear in mind that the trail runs along the coast and is often subject to sudden changes in the weather.

How to get there: The nearest airport to the start of the track is Perth, where you can rent a car to reach Cape Naturaliste, a drive of about 162 miles (260 km).

What to pack: Tent and sleeping bag. Food, water, and water purification tablets. A comfortable backpack, clothing and boots for trekking, wind- and waterproof jacket, change of clothing. Sunscreen, sunglasses, and sunhat. Flashlight with extra batteries and first-aid kit.

DAY 3: Gracetown–Prevelly

During the third day's walk, you come to the Meekadarabee Falls, a verdant oasis in a stark landscape. The falls tumble down a tufa spur into a small cave below. The waterfall can be reached through the Ellensbrook Homestead. Ellensbrook was built by Alfred and Ellen Bussell in 1850 and became the first European settlement along this coast. The Bussell family lived here for seven years, growing vegetables and producing butter and cheese from the milk of their cattle. It is possible to visit the house, managed by the National Trust of Australia, the organization that safeguards and promotes the natural and historical heritage of the nation. Overlooking one of the beautiful beaches along the trail is the characteristic chalk cliff called Joey's Nose, because it looks like a baby kangaroo (a joey) peeking from its mother's pouch.

Then you come to Margaret River, the largest navigable waterway in the region, which flows into the sea along the coast of the Cape to Cape Track. In summer it is easy to cross on a sandbank, but in winter it can be difficult and a deviation may be necessary. Continuing along the trail, you come to the Frank Mouritz Bridge, which spans the Boodjidup Creek. The materials used to build this bridge were all carried to the site by a group of young volunteers from the Green Corps, who also created much of the trail, under the supervision of the Department of Environment and Conservation. It is possible to stay overnight at the Prevelly Park Beach Resort, less than 1,000 feet (300 m) from the beach.

> ## ECO-TIPS

TREKKERS MUST NOT LEAVE TRASH BEHIND OR ALTER THE ENVIRONMENT IN ANY WAY ALONG THE TRAIL: EVEN A SIMPLE WET WIPE LEFT IN THE BUSH CAUSES POLLUTION. NEVER PICK PLANTS OR FLOWERS, OR TAKE ROCKS OR OTHER NATURAL ELEMENTS.

Useful Websites
tourism.australia.com
www.nationaltrust.org.au/places/ellensbrook
parks.dpaw.wa.gov.au/park/leeuwin-naturaliste
www.yallingupforestresort.com.au

DAY 4: Prevelly–Hamelin Bay

One of the most panoramic sections of the Cape to Cape Track runs through the heath along the cliffs overlooking Contos Beach. In spring, wildflowers abound and it is impossible to miss the kangaroos living in this area. You reach the surprising Boranup Forest, where the shadow of the karri trees (Australian eucalyptus) on the leeward side of the crest contrasts with the windswept cliffs and beaches. Much of this forest was cut down in 1890, when the timber industry flourished in the area. One hundred years of regrowth have resulted in a fine variety of trees, shrubs, and grasses. The Boranup Beach extends for about 5 miles (8 km) north of Hamelin Bay and can be a real challenge for excursionists because it is extremely soft. Finally, you come to the ruins of the Hamelin Bay harbor, built in 1882 to serve the timber exporters and abandoned after a number of momentous shipwrecks.

DAY 5: Hamelin Bay–Cape Leeuwin

The trek continues to the rocky clearing to the south of Cosy Corner, which has numerous holes eroded in the limestone from which jets of seawater shoot in stormy weather. The erosion continues and periodically the rocks crumble into the sea. When you reach Quarry Bay, you cross a low tufa cliff and proceed toward what remains of the Leeuwin Water Wheel, which once pumped water to the homes of the lighthouse keepers. This is the official end of the trek, although the majority of the end-to-end walkers consider the lighthouse door the true starting and finishing point. The Cape Leeuwin lighthouse was built in 1896 from stone quarried in the nearby Quarry Bay. Perched on a low promontory, it is 128 feet (39 m) tall, much taller than the Cape Naturaliste lighthouse. It holds a number of records: it marks the meeting point between the Indian Ocean and the Antarctic Ocean, and it is the most south-western point of Australia.

148 top left *The Eucalyptus diversicolor is a eucalyptus originating from the wettest regions of Australia.*
148 top right *Hamelin Bay with the ruins of the pier built in 1882 to facilitate timber exports.*
148 bottom left *The Leeuwin Waterwheel at Cape Leeuwin, which was used to pump water to the lighthouse keepers' houses, is no longer in use.*
148 bottom right *The Cape Leeuwin lighthouse marks the border between the Indian and Southern Oceans, marking the most southwesterly mainland point of Australia.*
149 *Rock formations along one of the beaches of the marine reserve.*

Canoe and Kayak Itineraries

Wonderful beaches. Breathtaking rapids. Calm lagoons. Harmony, balance, and rhythm. Sliding over the water, exploring bays, inlets, and caves. Or battling with seething currents to make your heart beat faster in your throat, an adrenaline rush for an exciting experience. Always in contact with nature, which surrounds, welcomes—and sometimes submerges—incautious canoeists. And at the end of the day, it's time to socialize or to enjoy solitude, according to your own needs, under a starry sky that seems so close.

On a river, on a lake, or in the midst of the sea, canoeing is a safe and swift way of experiencing the water. The Pesse canoe, from the Mesolithic era (8040–7510 BC), is made from Scottish pine and is the oldest boat known to have existed.

Born to link the two banks of a river, to transport, for fishing, or as a bridge, canoeing in the mid-19th century became a simple and accessible tourist and sporting activity, one that brought about unique emotions.

But be ready for a dunking at any time: to safely enjoy breathtaking trips and explore wonderful landscapes from a new perspective, you should definitely have at least some technical preparation, be fit, and—of course—know how to swim.

For example, you can circumnavigate Elba in the sanctuary for marine mammals, through crystal-clear waters full of sea life. Or you can discover harbors and nature reserves in parks with limited access to preserve the surrounding nature, as in New Zealand. Or Sweden, where you can spend an eco-friendly night in sustainable glass cabins, enjoying complete isolation and silence!

Birdwatchers in Florida will find a paradise in a unique ecosystem. The bravest ones will choose the rapids of the Ardèche River and those who want to understand local customs will paddle through the villages of Poland, along a network of lakes and rivers on one of the most beautiful routes in Europe.

Canoeists are also somehow "guardians" for the rivers and the seas. If they find plastic, trash, dead fish, or spills, they must report them to the authorities: those who take to the water must demand, and leave, clean waters.

151 *Many kayak excursions are suitable for everyone, including small children. Here, a family is kayaking on one of the many rivers in Florida.*

Canoeing Around Dalsland

Design, cuisine, traditions—all important resources—but in Sweden it is nature that reigns. Scattered among the lakes, mountains, moors, forests, and parks, the infrastructures are well distributed and very discreet, the numerous trails are well marked, the accommodation structures are built with sustainable structures, and the towns have a virtuous environmental approach. Rich in natural resources, Sweden holds the world record for public parks per inhabitant, and all its territory—whether state-owned or private—allows public access, guaranteeing the right to move about freely and easily. In this country, every effort is made to keep the environment as intact as possible, thanks to the culture of respect and laws that are rigorously obeyed.

Dalsland, in the west of the country, two hours northeast of Gothenburg, is a region that offers extremely varied natural environments, from the mountains to the dense boreal forests, from the plains to the crystal-clear lakes. It has a lake system that has long been one of the most popular destinations for canoeists in Europe: you can glide through lakes that are 328 feet (100 m) deep, stopping in one of the many coves, or paddle along the Dalsland Canal, which links the navigable lakes for 149 miles (240 km). Adventure lovers can also consider the idea of paddling toward Norway and continuing along the Halden Canal.

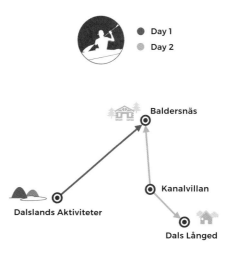

152 Dalsland is a historic province in southwestern Sweden and is part of Västra Götaland County.

Start: Dalslands Aktiviteter
Finish: Baldersnäs
Time: 72 hours (maximum stay)
Difficulty: easy

Accommodation: glass houses with simple and practical design, inspired by the shape of local barns. All the materials come from local suppliers, and the cabins are built on pillars so that they do not leave a permanent mark on the environment.

152–153 Morning mist on a lake near Ed. In this locality, there are about 400 lakes for swimming, canoeing, fishing, and boat trips.

Eco because: The campsites are supported by the purchase of a *naturvårdskort*—a nature conservation card—to be used at the sites. This card contributes to sustainable tourism and shows that the purchaser accepts responsibility for the communal resources.

When to go: From June to September (the midnight sun is in July).

How to get there: Although Sweden can be reached by train, the nearest airport is Gothenburg. From here to Dalsland, continue by train, bus, or car (about 93 miles [150 km]).

What to pack: Anyone who stays in the glass houses will find everything they need for eating, drinking, and sleeping. In any case, we recommend taking a headlamp, kayaking glasses, a hat, biodegradable soap, insect repellent, and a small, lightweight backpack.

72 HOURS IN THE MIDST OF NATURE

An experiment was carried out in Dalsland: five people spent three entire days immersed in nature, enjoying the starry night sky through the transparent roof of the special glass house in which they were staying. The participants lit fires, paddled, swam, and fished. After this experience they were monitored by the researchers to see how their stay in these conditions had affected their well-being. The participants' stress levels had fallen by 70%, their blood pressure was down, their anxiety levels were back to normal, and their creativity had increased. You can enjoy the same unique experience at Dalslands Aktiviteter and at Baldersnäs Herrgård. There are five more glass cabins on the private island of Henriksholm in Lake Ånimmen, which is completely uninhabited. Canoeists will find a hammock, a row boat, a fishing rod, a canoe, a kayak, and a sauna. The organization also provides breakfast, a packed lunch. and dinner. That is all. Note that it is only possible to book a stay of 72 hours—the utmost in ecotourism. The itinerary recommended here is a two-day tour, touching on the main eco-friendly points of Dalsland.

DAY 1: Dalslands Aktiviteter

At Dalslands Aktiviteter, the glass house stands on Lake Iväg. You paddle down the banks of the lake, with sandy beaches where you can stop for a swim, rocks, forests, and cultivated fields. In the middle of the lake, a very quiet environment, is the large, wooded island of Skuggetorpsön, and a number of smaller islands. From the lake, you can see the Stenebynäs estate, with its idyllic, traditional wooden summer homes.

DAY 2: Baldersnäs

The following day, you walk to Baldersnäs, about 6 miles (10 km) away, to stay in a second glass house, or at the Baldersnäs Herrgård estate. To the right of the hotel, there is a small harbor, from which you can take a canoe to paddle around the peninsula, a nature reserve, returning to the hotel on the left-hand side. This route is about 3 miles (5 km) long, and from the water you can see woods, meadows, and small pebble beaches on which to halt for a relaxing pause. You continue paddling southward along the peninsula for about 3 miles (5 km), until you reach Kanalvillan, a hostel. You pass a number of small beaches: there are no places of entertainment, bars, or restaurants, only nature. From Kanalvillan, expert canoeists can enter the Dalslands Canal through a lock, the first of many, to reach Dals Långed. You paddle a little further to return to Baldersnäs Herrgård. The hotel prepares picnic baskets for anyone staying out all day.

154 top Father and son canoeing on a lake on the Kroppefjäll, a plateau and nature reserve founded in 1997 and covering 2,780 acres (1,125 ha) of lakes, marshes, and forests.

154 bottom A cabin of eco-sustainable glass houses a few fortunate tourists. Like a stilt house, it rests on wooden feet made of local timber.

155 These special glass cabins are located on the islands of Baldersnäs Herrgård and Dalslands Aktiviteter, and on the private island of Henriksholm on Lake Ånimmen.

156–157 Spartan and isolated from the rest of the world, these wood and glass cabins enable you to experience total contact with nature.

ECO-TIPS

IF PLANNING THROUGH A SWEDISH TOUR OPERATOR SPECIALIZED IN ECOTOURISM, NATURE'S BEST IS THE LEADING STANDARD FOR ECOLOGICAL QUALITY IN EUROPE, GUARANTEEING RESPECT OF A RIGOROUS CODE OF CONDUCT AND A POSITIVE CONTRIBUTION TO THE ENVIRONMENT IN WHICH THE TOUR TAKES PLACE.

Useful Websites
visitsweden.com
naturesbestsweden.com/en
dalslandnordmarken.se/en/nature-conservation-card
dalslandsaktiviteter.com
baldersnas.eu

Canoeing on the Krutynia River

Poland occupies a slice of Europe that runs from the Baltic Sea to the Carpathian Mountains and boasts a thousand years' history, proven by the hundreds of monuments and wild nature comprising sea, lakes, rivers, woods, and mountains. It is no coincidence that the country boasts sixteen World Heritage Sites and eleven UNESCO biosphere reserves. Its territory lends itself to outdoor activities: hiking, cycling, cross-country skiing, fishing, riding, and canoeing. The Krutynia River is one of the most beautiful canoe routes in Europe: it starts in the Morag region and flows through a series of lakes linked by waterways with a variety of names (usually that of the lake from which they flow). It winds through the moraine hills, the Piska forest, and the Masurian Landscape Park. In addition to the beauty of the landscape and nature, it is the well-equipped tourist infrastructure that attracts canoeists. Along the river, there are places to sleep and eat run by PTTK (Polish Tourist and Sightseeing Society), a non-governmental organization with 312 branches throughout the country—one of the oldest tourist associations in Europe, serving modern explorers.

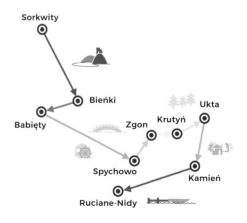

158 *Aerial view of Krutynia, a river in the Masurian Lake District in Poland. It flows into Lake Bełdany, which is linked to Lake Roś by numerous canals and lakes.*

Day 1
Day 2
Day 3
Day 4
Day 5
Day 6
Day 7
Day 8

Start: Sorkwity
Finish: Ruciane-Nidy
Distance: 63 mi (102 km)
Time: 8 days
Difficulty: easy
Accommodation: houses and campsites

158–159 Canoes and kayaks on the Jezioro Mokre (Wet Lake), in the Masurian Lakes Biosphere Reserve, a UNESCO World Heritage Site, near the village of Krutyń.

Eco because: Along the route and nearby, there are eight nature reserves and four natural and landscape parks. More than half of the itinerary runs through the Masurian Landscape Park. At the Krutynia shelters, you can also enjoy local cuisine in small restaurants.

160 *A mallard pair, male and female, are among the fauna of Krutynia. It is the most widespread of the wild duck species: it is estimated that there are over 9 million in Europe.*

161 top *The Krutynia River is 25 inches (65 cm) deep on average. The river bed is covered with algae and water lilies, and the banks are sandy and easy to reach.*

161 bottom left *A gray heron, the species of heron that lives furthest to the north, well beyond the Arctic Circle. It eats a large quantity of fish but can be seen in the fields searching for rodents.*

161 bottom right *An old 19th-century water mill on the Krutynia, which has been transformed into a hydroelectric power station near the village of Krutyński Piecek.*

DAY 1: Sorkwity–Bieńki

The itinerary begins at Sorkwity, on the northern bank of Lake Lampackie, which you cross to reach Lake Lampasz, through a brief pass called Łapinóżka. Subsequently, you enter the small Sobiepanka River: at some points you have to drag your canoe, walking on the river bed. When you have passed the Sobiepanka River, you reach Lake Kujno, passing the village of Grabowo on the left. You move from Lake Kujno to Lake Dłużec by the waters of the Grabówka River. On the left is the town of Dłużec. The itinerary continues along the short Chmielówka River and leads to the waters of Lake Białe. On the right bank is the way station of Bieńki, where you sleep either in a bungalow or in a tent.

DAY 2: Bieńk–Babięty

Continuing south, you enter the Dąbrówka stream, which leads to Lake Gant, and you head for Lake Gancka Struga, which, once joined by the waters of the Tejsówka River, becomes the Babięcka Struga River. After a stretch of about 2 miles (3 km), you reach the Babięty way station, where you stop for the night.

When to go: From June to August, summer in Poland.

How to get there: The nearest airport is Warsaw. To reach Sorkwity, the start of the itinerary, take a train or a bus for an overall distance of about 143 miles (230 km).

What to pack: Kayaking glasses, life jacket, T-shirts, shorts, sandals, hat, sunscreen, bathing suit, towel. Biodegradable soap, insect repellent, first-aid kit, canteen, sandwiches, and vitamin bars.
.

DAY 3: Babięty–Zyzdrój–Spychowo

At the beginning of this stage, after paddling for about 1,640 feet (500 m), you come to a water mill where you have to get out of your canoe and continue on foot on a tarmac road. You return to the clear waters and continue for another 2 miles (3 km), enjoying the spectacle of nature until you reach Lake Zyzdrój Wielki. Continuing southward, you pass the towns of Zyzdrój Wielki on the left and Zyzdrojowa Wola on the right. In the central part of the lake, you paddle around a woody islet, then you enter a smaller lake, Zyzdrój Mały. At the end of this lake, near a lock, you have to carry your canoe again (for the longest section of the entire itinerary, 262 feet [80 m]). Once you return to the water, you continue along the Zyzdrój River toward the end of the stage. On the left is the Spychowo way station.

DAY 4: Spychowo–Zgon

After a hearty breakfast, you put your canoe in the water. You reach the Spychowskie River, passing under a bridge, and then enter Spychowska Struga. You pass the village of Spychowo, the mouth of a small river that leaves to Lake Kierwik, and the village of Koczek, finally arriving on the Zdrużno River. After a few hundred feet, you proceed along the right-hand bank to the bridge, behind which Lake Uplik starts, surrounded by woods. The next destination is Lake Mokre, one of the deepest lakes in the Masurian Landscape Park. You stay for the night at the village of Zgon. It is a good idea to keep an eye on the weather forecast during the trip. In case of strong winds, it is better to stop: high waves can be, to say the least, a nuisance.

DAY 5: Zgon–Krutyń

Continuing northward on Lake Mokre, on the right you pass the Królewska Sosna nature reserve. The Dąb nad Mukrem—the oak on the Mokre—is an enormous, three-hundred-year-old tree, definitely worth a stop. After Lake Mokre, you carry your canoe for a brief stretch, then enter the picturesque Lake Krutyńskie, nestled in the woodlands. This is also the border of the Krutynia nature reserve, which includes the lake itself and part of the Krutynia River, its tributary. The first section of the river, from Lake Krutyńskie to the village of Krutyń, is a delight and a reward for the difficulties encountered on Lake Mokre. It is a place to paddle slowly, admiring the beauty of nature. The water is very shallow and crystal clear, which allows you to see the fish under the canoe. There is just one difficulty (or perhaps attraction): the tree trunks in the water and the tourist boats.

At Krutyń you can stop for a few days: horse lovers will find stables nearby at Gałkowo, while nature lovers can get up early to see the sun rise above the mist-covered lakes of the Zakręt nature reserve. The Krutynia River is a paradise for anglers, but the area also offers many treats for cyclists. In the evening, you can visit one of the many restaurants that serve fried whitefish (a typical Masurian dish) and bilberry-filled pancakes.

DAY 6: Krutyń–Ukta´

In the morning, you prepare to cross the Piska forest. After paddling for about an hour, you reach another stretch where you have to carry your canoe, near the old water mill at Zielony Lasek. Along the road, there are some cafés. Back to the river, after another hour, you arrive at Rosocha, where a landscape of meadows begins and the water is deeper. The trees gradually thin out, and rushes appear, leaving the canoeists without any protection from the sun. Before Wojnowo you can turn from the Krutynia River into the Dusianka tributary and thus reach Lake Duś to admire the Monastery of the Old Believers (the Old Believers are an Orthodox religious movement). Returning to the main route, you paddle to the village of Ukta, where you find the way station.

DAY 7: Ukta–Kamień–

From this point onwards the itinerary crosses the Krutynia Dolna M. Wańkowicz reserve. At first the course of the Krutynia river is surrounded by trees that form a sort of roof over the water; in this section we encounter numerous tree trunks, but we can go round them without leaving the canoe. Later, the woodland starts to change, it no longer offers protection from the sun and the area becomes marshy. The depth of the river can reach 23 feet (7 m) in this stretch, but despite this, the dense fluvial vegetation sometimes blocks our way. We paddle through the marsh for at least two hours, until we finally see the bridge of Nowy Most, where it is a good idea to stop for a rest and to eat something, because we will only encounter civilization again at Iznota. We set out again and enter the Pierwos reserve, which we will leave only when we leave Lake Malinówko. Here the river becomes much less winding, passing through vast beds of rushes to Lake Gardyńskie, where the Krutynia river ends. Keeping to the right and swerving around the sandbanks, we reach a small canal that leads to Lake Malinówko. Later we enter Lake Jerzewko, which leads to the town of Iznota. Here we continue to the bridge by the same name, we pass it and, a few hundred feet further on, we reach the Iznocka bay on Lake Bełdany. Keeping to the right bank, we reach the way station of Kamień, where we stop for the night.

DAY 8: Ruciane-Nidy

The next morning, you continue on Lake Bełdany. You keep to the right and pay attention to the other craft. You pass the island of Mysia and Wygryńska Bay. After about 1.2 miles (2 km), you reach the Guzianka lock, and you go along the Guzianka Mała River and enter Lake Guzianka Wielka. You reach the port of Ruciane-Nida, where your wonderful canoe trip concludes.

> **ECO-TIPS**

DO NOT LEAVE TRASH ALONG THE ROUTE, AND DO NOT THROW PLASTIC INTO THE WATER (USE A CANTEEN FOR DRINKING). DO NOT DISTURB THE WILDLIFE OR GATHER PLANTS OR FLOWERS. RESPECT THE ENVIRONMENT, AND LEAVE EVERYTHING AS YOU FIND IT.

Useful Websites
polonia.travel/en
mazury.travel/en/Find_information
-Tourism_services

Descent of the Ardèche

Start: Vallon-Pont-d'Arc
Finish: Saint-Martin-d'Ardèche
Distance: 19 mi (30 km)
Time: 2 days
Difficulty: easy
Accommodation: tents

France is a fascinating and attractive country, from the beaches packed with tourists to the more hidden and wild ones; from the magnificent Ville Lumière to small towns rich in perfumes, markets, and colors; from the imposing mountains capped with glaciers to quiet, dense oak woods and vast plains that stretch to the horizon. The numerous travelers who choose this country every year bear witness to the diversity of its territory. In addition to enjoying the cities with their historical sights, they also appreciate outdoor activities, perhaps opting for exciting pursuits like climbing, extreme trekking, spelunking, or descending rapids and rivers in a kayak.

The perfect place for kayaking is the Rhône-Alpes region, in the south, where you find the Réserve Naturelle Gorges de l'Ardèche. Founded in 1980 to protect this extraordinary environment, the reserve follows the course of the Ardèche River, offering both amateurs and pros the opportunity to follow it in some sections, from 4 to 20 miles (6–32 km), according to the season and the level of the water. In fact, the Ardèche is calm for long stretches, but it also has strong currents in the rapids. Many agencies hire out canoes or kayaks and organize the transfer from the arrival point to the point of embarkation.

164 *The Ray-Pic waterfall falls from a petrified basalt lava flow.*
165 *The Pont d'Arc, which crosses the Ardèche River, is a natural arch with a length of 197 feet (60 m) and a height of 177 feet (54 m). Vallon-Pont-d'Arc, the town in which it is located, is well-equipped for tourism.*

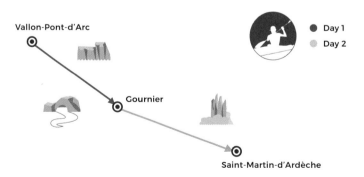

Vallon-Pont-d'Arc

Gournier

Saint-Martin-d'Ardèche

● Day 1
● Day 2

Eco because: The Réserve Naturelle Gorges de l'Ardèche was founded to protect this unique landscape from mass tourism and urbanization. The site is managed by a syndicate that sets out the rules for circulation and behavior within the reserve. For example, it limits the number of campers that each company can host during summer weekends.

IT IS FORBIDDEN TO CAMP OUTSIDE
THE MARKED AREAS AND TO
ABANDON WASTE OR TRASH: CARRY IT
WITH YOU TO THE FINAL DESTINATION.
IN ORDER TO ENJOY THIS EXPERIENCE
IN NATURE TO THE FULLEST, IT IS
BETTER TO CHOOSE WEEKDAYS.

Useful Websites
france.fr/en
gorgesdelardeche.fr
ardeche.com

TRAVEL TIPS

When to go: The best time, when the temperature is mild and the river is swollen with water, is between May and June. In the summer, the area becomes heavily crowded and there is less water in the river.

How to get there: The nearest airport is Marseilles, about 125 miles (200 km) by car from Vallon-Pont-d'Arc, while Lyon airport is about 137 miles (220 km) away by car.

What to pack: Backpack, sleeping bag, and tent. Bathing suit. Headlamp, kayaking glasses, life jacket, and helmet. Canteen. Biodegradable soap, sunscreen, mineral supplements. Insect repellent. Sandals, long pants, long-sleeved T-shirts. The waters of the Ardèche are not drinkable, so it is necessary to carry a canteen of drinking water. You will find water, barbecues, and charcoal at the campsites, so we recommend you bring food to cook on the barbecue. All luggage is placed in a large waterproof bin fixed to the kayak.

DAY 1: Vallon-Pont-d'Arc–Gournier

You start to kayak from Vallon-Pont-d'Arc. Thousands of plant species (many protected) grow in this karst park along the river, a tributary of the Rhône, which winds through woody slopes dominated by oaks and steep limestone cliffs, more than 820 feet (250 m) high.

In the first section, you encounter small beaches where you can take a relaxing swim. You paddle gently for an hour and a half and pass the first rapid, Charlemagne. It's an easy one but not to be taken for granted. After Pont d'Arc, the magnificent natural arch about 197 feet (60 m) above the Ardèche, you come to Chames, another rapid, the most challenging on the trip. Once you have passed this rapid, you find the first campsite, Gaud. Or you can also paddle on and spend the night at the next campsite, Gournier, if you have booked in advance.

DAY 2: Gournier–Saint-Martin-d'Ardèche

The next morning, you put your kayak back in the water and paddle to Cathédrale, an impressive and characteristic rock formation. Its slim columns rise toward the sky, their shape similar to a cathedral. You then encounter the Pastière rapid, easy and great fun. You paddle along quiet waters to Saint-Martin-d'Ardèche, your destination, where a bus picks up kayakers to take them back to Vallon-Pont-d'Arc.

166 View of the Cirque de la Madeleine in the Gorges de l'Ardèche. This series of river gorges forms a canyon from Vallon-Pont-d'Arc to Saint-Martin-d'Ardèche (19 miles [31 km]).

167 top The plant species in the gorges are typical of permeable terrains that do not hold water but rather allow it to flow into numerous underground tunnels and rivers.

167 bottom left From the Belvédère de la Cathédral, you can enjoy an incredible panoramic view of the river. The gorges are cut into a massif covered in Mediterranean scrub.

167 bottom right Saint-Martin-d'Ardèche is the end of your canoe trip. The canyon is a tourist attraction and attracts over a million visitors a year.

ITALY

Start: Marina di Campo
Finish: Marina di Campo
Distance: 91 mi (147 km)
Time: 7 days
Difficulty: easy
Accommodation: tents

168–169 Portoferraio is the most important town on Elba. In addition to being the municipality with the highest population, it also has enchanting coves that begin from Le Ghiaie Beach and reach the Capo d'Enfola.

Eco because: Elba is situated within the Pelagos Sanctuary, and as you paddle silently around the island, you will frequently sight shoals of fish, loggerhead sea turtles, dolphins, and whales. The sanctuary is a protected marine area located in the territorial waters of France, Italy and the Principality of Monaco. The habitat is characterized by its remarkable biodiversity, which is vulnerable to the impact of environmental change and human activities.

Kayaking Around Elba

The natural beauty of Italy makes it a must-visit destination. From the Alpine ranges to the coasts, from the rolling hills to the volcanic peaks, from the woods to the plateaus, it is an incredible landscape, diverse and attractive. It is enhanced by an unequaled cultural and artistic heritage, which makes this country a true delight. It is not by chance, therefore, that Italy holds the record for cultural and natural sites protected by UNESCO.

Elba, with the other islands in the Parco Nazionale dell'Arcipelago Toscano, is one of the UNESCO biosphere reserves. This island, one of the greenest in the Mediterranean, offers numerous activities for eco-friendly tourism: whale watching, hiking along the trails inland, sailing, cycling, and the opportunity to study the more than fifty species of butterflies that live here. One of the most exciting and picturesque ways to slowly explore the 91 miles (147 km) of coastline with its cliffs, beaches, and bays, is to circumnavigate the island in a kayak.

● Day 1   ○ Day 5
● Day 2   ○ Day 6
● Day 3   ● Day 7
○ Day 4

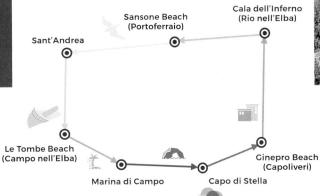

Sant'Andrea

Sansone Beach
(Portoferraio)

Cala dell'Inferno
(Rio nell'Elba)

Le Tombe Beach
(Campo nell'Elba)

Marina di Campo

Capo di Stella

Ginepro Beach
(Capoliveri)

169 The lives of farmers, fishermen, and sailors depend on the forces of nature: there are churches scattered all over the island dedicated to prayer for the protection of the land and the sea.

When to go: From June to September, but in July and August the island is packed with tourists, so it is better to avoid these months.

How to get there: On the island, a little more than one mile (2 km) away from Marina di Campo, there is an airport that links Elba with Pisa and Florence, which both have international airports. Otherwise, it is possible to take the Piombino train from Florence (about three hours), and a number of ferries reach Portoferraio in an hour. From here, Marina di Campo is about 9 miles (14 km) away by bus.

What to pack: Tent, lightweight summer sleeping bag, mattress. Headlamp, sandals, high protection sunscreen, hat or bandana, sunglasses, gloves to avoid blistered hands, snorkeling mask, bathing suit, large towel, a couple of T-shirts, a fleece sweater, and long pants for the evening. Biodegradable soap for personal hygiene. A canteen for water, energy bars, insect repellent, personal plate and cutlery (fork, multi-use knife, spoon, and cup) to avoid generating excessive waste.

170 *Sansone Beach, to the north of the island, has incredibly clear water.*
171 *Capo Bianco, near Portoferraio, is a beach with small white pebbles, like the seabed: they create wonderful reflections in the clear water.*

DAY 1: Marina di Campo–Lacona–Capo di Stella

From the beach of Marina di Campo, the starting point for this kayak trip, you paddle past Camping La Foce, and after Punta di Mele, you arrive at Buca dell'Acqua, a small cave with a freshwater spring. In Lacona Gulf, you make a first stop for a swim, lunch, and a rest. You take the kayak again to circumnavigate Capo di Stella, observing the coast covered in Mediterranean scrub. After leaving the gulf, you stop and prepare the campsite for the night.

DAY 2: Capo di Stella–Ginepro Beach (Capoliveri)

In the morning, you set out again, and shortly afterward, you swim in the clear and inviting sea at Acquarilli Beach. When you reach Lido di Capoliveri, you pass a number of beaches until you reach Innamorata Beach, where you stop to eat and rest. You put your kayak back into the sea. On the cliffs stand the ruins of buildings from the mining industry, abandoned in 1981 and now nestled between the sea and the scrub. Finally, you reach Ginepro Beach, where you stop for the night.

DAY 3: Ginepro Beach (Capoliveri)–Cala dell'Inferno (Rio nell'Elba)

Early in the morning, you put your kayak into the sea, pass Capo Calvo and the islet of Liscoli, to reach Forte Focardo and cross the gulf of Porto Azzurro, under the bastions of Forte di Longone. The next stage is Terranera Beach, where the emerald waters of the small lake by the same name glitter. After passing the islet of Ortano, you paddle toward Rio Marina. You then reach Cavo, and leaving Isola dei Topi to the east, you pass Capo Vita. After you pass the wonderful inlets of Mandriola and Mandolina, you stop for the night at Cala dell'Inferno on a pebble beach immersed in nature, which lies before the cove of Nisporto, a small tourist resort.

DAY 4: Cala dell'Inferno (Rio nell'Elba)–Sansone Beach (Portoferraio)

You continue your journey toward Portoferraio: in this stage you are to the north of the island. Having passed Punta di Nisporto and Punta Falconaia, you paddle along the coast until you glimpse the walls that surrounded Napoleon's Villa dei Mulini and reach Le Ghiaie Beach. You continue between the sandy beaches and steep cliffs that mark this extraordinary landscape. The destination of this stage is Sansone Beach, where, once you have drawn up your kayak, you can swim in the inviting waters. You spend the night here.

DAY 5: Sansone Beach (Portoferraio)–Sant'Andrea

Today you pass Capo d'Enfola, a nature reserve home to a rare nesting site of the Audouin's gull. There is also an ancient tuna factory, now the headquarters of the Parco Nazionale dell'Arcipelago Toscano. Paddling along the coast, you pass the Gulf of Viticcio and Punta Penisola, and discover the splendid bays of Forno, Scaglieri, and Biodola. You arrive at Procchio, and once you have passed Punta Crocetta, you reach

Marciana Marina and its seafront fishing village. On the hill you can see the towns of Marciana and Poggio, nestled in the chestnut woods. You continue westward and reach Sant'Andrea, where you spend the night.

DAY 6: Sant'Andrea–Le Tombe Beach (Campo nell'Elba)

This stage runs along the western coast of Elba, and after passing the clear waters of Cala della Cotaccia, you come to Punta della Zanca and Punta Polveraia. Along the way, you see the village of Pomonte, at the foot of the valley by the same name. Then you reach the cliff of Ogliera to discover, a few feet below the water, a diving site with the relic of the *Elviscott*, a ship that sank in 1972. You stay here for the night on Le Tombe Beach.

DAY 7: Le Tombe Beach (Campo nell'Elba)–Marina di Campo

This is the last day in your kayak. You pass Punta di Fetovaia, a promontory that protects a bay with white sands and crystal-clear water. You paddle past the granite cliffs sculpted by the sea and by time to Le Piscine, rock pools where you can swim in warm sea water. You come to the beach of Seccheto, a small ancient village, and from there continue toward the coast of Cavoli, a popular meeting point for young people. You head toward the Grotta Azzurra, passing the gulf of Galenzana, which has wonderful fields of Posidonia, a marine plant that grows only in clean water. Finally, you reach the end of your kayak trip on the beach of Marina di Campo, from where you started the circumnavigation of Elba.

FLORIDA (USA)

Start: Gulf Coast Visitor Center (Everglades City)
Finish: Gulf Coast Visitor Center (Everglades City)
Distance: 48 mi (77 km) (6 hours per day in a kayak)
Time: 5 days
Difficulty: medium
Accommodation: tents and chickee huts (stilt houses)

172–173 Often described as a "river of grass," the Everglades are home to coastal mangroves, swamps covered with sawgrass, and pinewoods that are the habitat of hundreds of animal species.

Eco because: Visiting the Everglades means exploring an infinite variety of flora and fauna, within diverse ecosystems. This delicate and fragile landscape is a paradise for bird watching.

Kayaking Through the Everglades

Florida is a tropical Eden, with dreamlike beaches, crystal-clear sea, and entertainment for everyone. However, travelers are also attracted by the less hyped aspects of its natural environment: the springs, the tropical forests, the swamps, and the exotically beautiful wildlife. This is another reason why the Sunshine State is involved in responsible tourism and in the preservation of this paradise for future generations. This commitment is also implemented through cutting-edge projects in the field of renewable energy, like the recent Babcock Ranch project, a highly technological, smart, green city relying entirely on solar power.

In the south of the country, the Everglades National Park includes a vast area of 1.5 million acres (600,000 ha) of wetland and the Everglades and Dry Tortugas Biosphere Reserve. This area is also a UNESCO World Heritage Site and home to more than 350 species of birds, 500 species of fish, and dozens of species of mammals and reptiles. To see turtles, herons, alligators, and manatees while sliding silently through the mangroves in a kayak, we recommend you enter the park from the Gulf Coast Visitor Center at Everglades City.

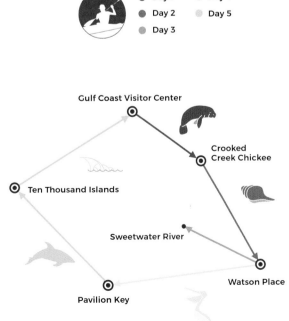

- Day 1
- Day 2
- Day 3
- Day 4
- Day 5

Gulf Coast Visitor Center

Crooked Creek Chickee

Ten Thousand Islands

Sweetwater River

Watson Place

Pavilion Key

173 You can either bring your own kayak or hire one in the park. Alternatively, you can go with an authorized guide, who will supply you with equipment and guide you in your adventure.

174 The Everglades are recognized as a World Heritage Site. They are a Wetland Area of Global Importance and a UNESCO biosphere reserve. The Everglades are one of only three places on the planet with all three designations.

175 top The western swamphen is one of the many avian species in the area.

175 bottom The park is an excellent place to see the Mississippi alligator and the American crocodile living side by side, go on cycling or kayak excursions, pitch a tent, or relax surrounded by nature.

176–177 The Everglades National Park, which extends from Lake Okeechobee in the north to the Gulf of Florida in the south, celebrated its 85th anniversary in 2019.

► ECO-TIPS

IN ORDER TO RESPECT THE ENVIRONMENT, CHOOSE A CANTEEN OVER PLASTIC BOTTLES. IT IS FORBIDDEN TO WALK ON THE DUNES OR TO PICK PLANTS. IT IS ALSO NOT ADVISABLE TO GO ONTO THE BEACH AT NIGHT, TO USE A FLASHLIGHT, OR TAKE PHOTOGRAPHS USING A FLASH (THE LIGHT DISTURBS THE NESTING TURTLES). ANOTHER GOOD HABIT IS TO DISPOSE OF WASTE AND TRASH CORRECTLY, IN ORDER TO KEEP PREDATORS AWAY.

Useful Websites
visitflorida.com/en-us.html
nps.gov/ever/index.htm
floutdooradventures.com/guides/

DAY 1: Gulf Coast Visitor Center–Crooked Creek Chickee

You start the day at the visitor center for a briefing and a description of the itinerary. Today you will explore the mangroves of the saltwater estuary, where manatees can be spotted. After a day spent paddling through the quiet landscape, you visit the Crooked Creek Chickee for a truly unique camping experience. *Chickee* is a Native American word for "home," or an open-sided stilt house. Camping in a chickee allows visitors to sleep between the stars and the water, surrounded by the sounds of nature. Daily life and stress are nothing but a distant memory.

DAY 2: Crooked Creek Chickee–Watson Place

You are woken up at dawn by the light reflecting on the water. Today you paddle through a section of the Wilderness Waterway. This navigable channel is the only marked path through the national park, and it runs from Everglades City to Flamingo, between protected inlets and shallow bays. Your destination is the infamous Watson Place. Legend says that Edgar Watson, the owner of a sugar plantation, used to kill his workers rather than paying them. The campsite here stands on an island of shells, originally built by the Calusa people, who lived in the Everglades before the arrival of the European colonists.

DAY 3: Watson Place–Sweetwater River–Watson Place

A second night at Watson Place allows you to explore this fascinating area to the fullest. In your kayak, you venture into the heart of the Sweetwater River, the preferred habitat of the American alligator, which is harmless unless you disturb it. In the afternoon, you explore Watson Place on foot. The area has been completely swallowed by the jungle, and it is impossible to recognize Watson's sugar plantation of the early 20th century. Nevertheless, many ruins are still waiting to be discovered.

DAY 4: Watson Place–Pavilion Key

Today you paddle along the Chatham River to the Gulf of Mexico, where dolphins, turtles, and white pelicans flaunt themselves. You set camp on the beach of Pavilion Key, one of the largest and most open islands. The soft, shiny, white sand is made of calcium carbonate from the shells of marine creatures, very different from the light brown sand of the Atlantic beaches of Florida.

DAY 5: Pavilion Key–Ten Thousand Islands–Gulf Coast Visitor Center

On the last day you paddle through the Ten Thousand Islands, an area of the park (not far from Pavilion Key) famous for its "hammocks," islets of mangroves growing in the shallow estuary. At high tide, the islands are inaccessible because they are completely submerged, while at low tide they are surrounded by boats beached on the muddy flats. Here you can admire the migratory and resident birds, including flocks of ibis, ospreys, and roseate spoonbills. The return journey ends at Everglades City, at the Gulf Coast Visitor Center.

When to go: The ideal time is between November and April, during the dry season, when it is easy to move around this untamed area and the mosquitoes are less troublesome.

How to get there: Miami international airport is the closest to the area. From here you take a bus to Naples, changing there for Everglades City (about two and a half hours).

What to pack: For this guided tour, the equipment for kayaking and camping is supplied. Take kayaking clothing and sunglasses, sunscreen, bathing suit, insect repellent, toiletries with biodegradable soap, first-aid kit.

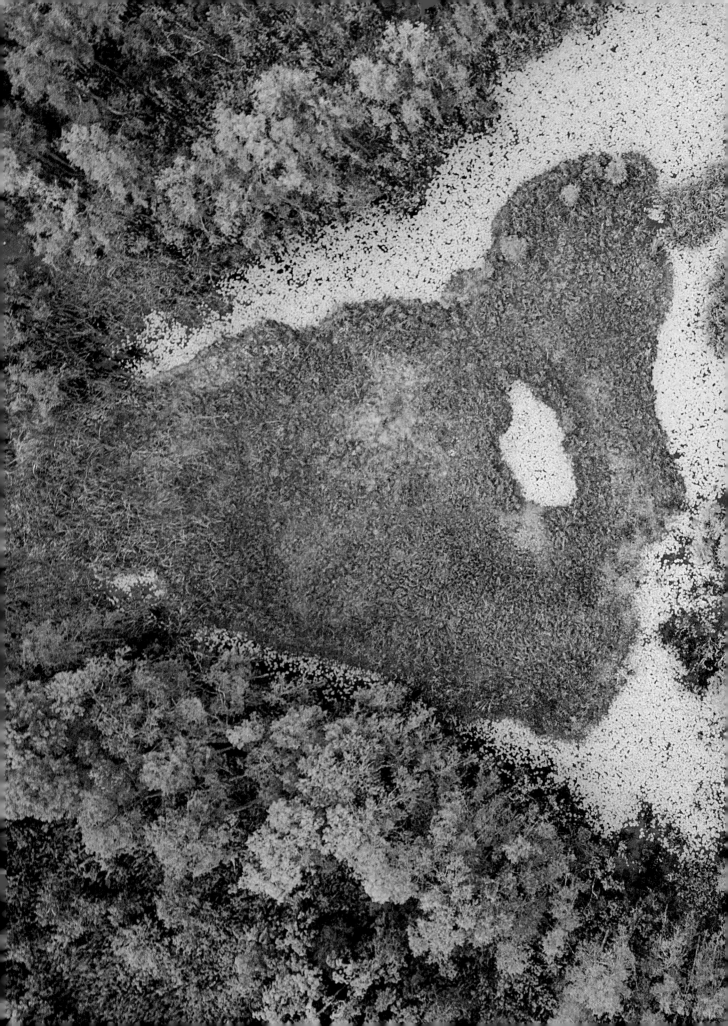

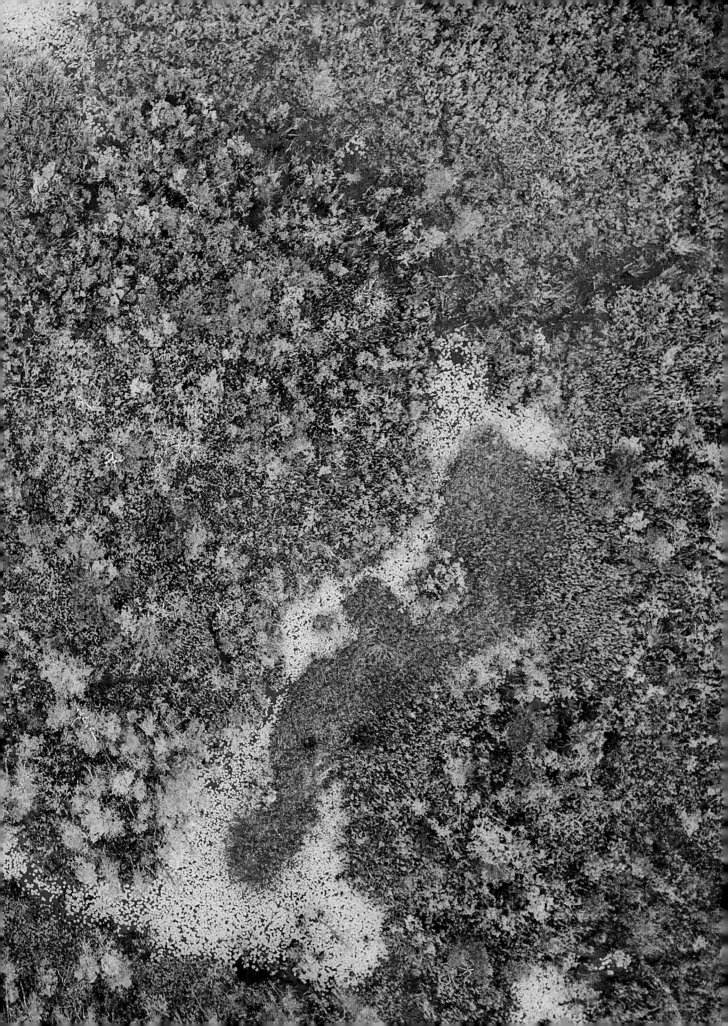

Abel Tasman National Park

Geysers, waterfalls, beaches, volcanoes, mountains, lush and abundant flora and fauna, rare species—the natural landscapes of New Zealand inevitably attract a constant flow of tourists. The country is a vast and peaceful nature reserve, in addition to being a virtuous example of environmental management and conservation. Its vast forests and numerous animal species are well protected in the many national parks, the protected areas, and the maritime parks, which make up about 30% of the country.

The recommended itinerary follows the northwestern coast of the South Island in the Abel Tasman National Park, the smallest national park in New Zealand. The park offers 34 miles (55 km) of sandy beach, turquoise waters, warm and shallow where you can swim, and splendid animal reserves with herds of seals and dolphin pods.

178 top It is by no means unusual to find seals in Tonga Bay. Tonga is the island off Onetahuti in the Abel Tasman National Park.

178 bottom The park takes its name from Abel Tasman, who was the first European explorer to see New Zealand, in 1642. He anchored near Golden Bay.

Awaroa

Onetahuti

Anchorage

Marahau

● Day 1
● Day 2
● Day 3

Start: Awaroa
Finish: Marahau
Distance: approximately 21 mi (34 km)
Time: 3 days
Difficulty: easy
Accommodation: tents

178–179 *Natural pools of turquoise water and splendid beaches in the smallest national park in New Zealand: its area is only 92 square miles (238 sq km).*

Eco because: The park allows limited access in order to preserve the environment. The tour by kayak is the best low-impact solution, allowing you to explore golden beaches, quiet inlets, lagoons, and offshore islands, and to admire the wildlife and the native forest along the granite coastline.

When to go: Between December and March, it is possible to swim in a pleasant sea.

How to get there: The nearest airport is in Nelson. From here you take the bus to Marahau (about 37 miles [60 km]) and then the water taxi to Tōtaranui (20 miles [32 km]).

What to pack: Canteen, sleeping bag, sunhat, sunscreen, insect repellent, towel, bathing suit, windbreaker, a change of clothing. Camera and first-aid kit. For the evening, long pants, T-shirt, warm sweater (wool or fleece), sneakers and socks, waterproof jacket, flashlight.

DAY 1: Awaroa–Onetahuti

Starting from Awaroa, you paddle along the coast, exploring the imposing granite rocks and secret lagoons, hoping to encounter herds of seals. When you reach Onetahuti, near the main beach, you find the Onetahuti Bay Campsite, where you stay for the night. The small island of Tonga lies out to sea. The native wildlife is an essential and precious part of the landscape.

DAY 2: Onetahuti–Anchorage

In the morning, you set out to sea and paddle in the direction of the Bark Bay Beach, which can only be reached by kayak. The northernmost tip of Bark Bay is also the start of the marine reserve of the island of Tonga, extending north to Awaroa Head. Proceeding along the coast, you reach Anchorage, where you camp for the night.

DAY 3: Anchorage–Marahau

In the morning, you put your kayak back in the water and paddle from Anchorage toward Marahau. At midday you can stop for lunch in the harbor of Astrolabe. Then you reach Marahau and its two long, white beaches. This is the end of the tour: you hand in the kayak at the base camp of Abel Tasman Kayaks, who organized the tour.

180 top and bottom *Mosquito Bay (bottom) and Bark Bay (top) are two marvelous coves that you can reach by canoe. In the first there is no drinking water, while in the second there is.*
180–181 *A trekker walking along the Abel Tasman Coastal Track through a windswept forest: the track is 37 miles (60 km) long within the national park, from Marahau to Wainui.*

> ## ECO-TIPS

DRINKING WATER IS AVAILABLE IN TŌTARANUI, BARK BAY, AND ANCHORAGE. ANY OTHER WATER MUST BE TREATED. THE PARK IS COMMITTED TO REDUCING CO_2 EMISSIONS, COMPENSATING THEM WITH CERTIFIED EKOS CARBON CREDITS.

Useful Websites
newzealand.com
newzealand.com/int/feature/national-parks
-abel-tasman
abeltasman.com
www.abeltasmankayaks.co.nz
For the campsites
www.doc.govt.nz

Itineraries on Horseback

Exploring the world on horseback is a wonderful feeling and offers experiences and memories that will linger in your heart forever. The relationship between man and animal is unique—every horse is different, just as every person is. During a trek, your horse becomes your peerless traveling companion, and this relationship must be built on reciprocal respect and trust. While riding and galloping through a magnificent landscape, you understand how magical this combination is: at times it seems as if the rider and the horse become one. There is an exchange of energy and you live in the moment, all concerns swept away while you enjoy a sense of freedom and great joy.

Equestrian tourism is one of the most genuinely low-impact ways of exploring every corner of our planet, far from mass tourism. In the saddle, you have the feeling of not disturbing nature, even of becoming part of it. It is a slow and active tourism, and you can visit remote areas inaccessible by other means. It is a great way to make contact with the local people and their culture. The more natural and unspoiled the environment, the more stimulating it is for the rider: it remains intact, fertilized and marked only by the hoof prints.

Every trek among those suggested here has different requirements and difficulty levels according to the trip chosen. In any case, in order to enjoy it to the fullest, we recommend riding experience and good physical fitness.

During the trek, it is best to avoid riding in the hottest hours. It is important to make short stops, to allow the horse to rest and drink. Meals should be given at the right time, not too close to physical activity. Horses must be groomed before saddling and at the end of the day. In the morning and the evening, they should be checked to see if they are well and whether they have any sores from the repeated rubbing of the harnesses. Check the hooves and remove any stones. Finally, never forget to carry a first-aid kit for both the horse and the rider.

183 Two horse trekkers explore the Göreme National Park. Discovering new places by horse trekking is an exceptional experience, also because of the relationship created between human being and animal.

 SPAIN

Sierra Nevada on Horseback

Start: Bubión
Finish: Bubión
Distance: 99 mi (160 km)
Time: 6 days
Difficulty: medium
Accommodation: guesthouses

Andalusia, in southern Spain, is bordered by the Mediterranean Sea and the Atlantic Ocean, separated from Africa by the Gibraltar Strait. Its territory offers a wide variety of landscapes, from the coastal plains to the mountains of the Sierra Nevada, the highest on the Iberian Peninsula. It has a strong, magnetic personality, also thanks to its past, marked by the passage and integration of various civilizations, whose heritage still attracts tourists. Among its peculiarities, Andalusia has a deeply rooted equestrian tradition, as witnessed by the Royal Andalusian School of Equestrian Art at Jerez de la Frontera (Cádiz). There are numerous stables, farms, and riding schools in the area, and many trips to make on horseback.

Among these, Alpujarra is a great area to explore on horseback, between the provinces of Granada and Almería, at the foot of the Sierra Nevada. Rich in waterways, vineyards, and almond groves, it has seen a considerable development of rural tourism, hiking, and trekking, thanks to its untamed natural landscape. Thanks to the Parque Nacional de Sierra Nevada, Alpujarra has one of the largest legally protected extensions in Europe.

The starting point for this ride is a small village, Bubión. The path follows historical herders' routes, passing through valleys rich in waterways and forests, until you reach the summer grazing in the mountains.

During the ride, you can stop to enjoy local hams and cheeses with freshly made bread. At dinner you taste local dishes and excellent Spanish wines, staying in characteristic inns and guesthouses.

184 top *The white village of Capileira is situated in the Poqueira gorge, between the Mediterranean coast and the Sierra Nevada.*
184 bottom *A street in Bubión. The architectural layout is typical of Berber villages: steep streets and houses with flat roofs, adapted to the mountainous terrain.*
185 *Horses grazing in a field in the Poqueira gorge, near the village of Capileira. The Poqueira River is formed from the confluence of watercourses with sources near the peak of Mulhacén.*

- ● Day 1
- ● Day 2
- ● Day 3
- ● Day 4
- ● Day 5
- ● Day 6

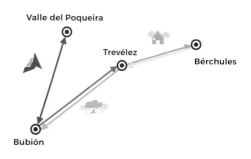

Eco because: You cross the Parque Nacional de Sierra Nevada, which, due to its isolated position in southern Europe, protects areas of great botanical value.

186 *Spanish horses are strong, know the paths well, and are sure-footed and agile on the trails: they are the jewels of the equine species.*

187 *The Sierra Nevada's mild climate, also in summer, is an excellent incentive for hiking and mountain biking, as well as horse riding.*

DAY 1: Bubión–Valle del Poqueira–Bubión

Bubión is a small village at 4,265 feet (1,300 m) above sea level, home to the stables from which the ride departs. The Spanish horses know the trails well, and they are surefooted and agile. You ride out to explore the most remote part of Valle del Poqueira, one of the most picturesque of the Alpujarra region, climbing toward the highest peak in continental Spain, Mulhacén (11,414 feet [3,480 m]). To reach the valley, you follow trails through meadows, across plateaus, and over streams. After a picnic, you descend the mountain by the trails through the pine forests and return to Bubión for dinner and to stay the night.

DAY 2: Bubión–Trevélez

After breakfast you set out again, following the mule tracks that traverse the countryside to the villages of Pitres and Pórtugos, where you stop for lunch. In the afternoon, you canter along the trails through the oak woods to reach Trevélez, the highest village in Spain, at 4,842 feet (1,476 m) above sea level. Here you stop for dinner and stay the night.

DAY 3: Trevélez–Bérchules

Today you ride toward the village of Bérchules. The first part of the stage involves a 15-minute walk to leave the village and reach the mountain trail. You start riding along a steep and rocky lane that passes between mountainside cabins and through meadows carpeted with aromatic wild herbs. You reach a peak of about 8,200 feet (2,500 m), from which, on a clear day, you can see the mountains of Morocco to the south and the highest peaks in Spain to the north. After lunch, you continue through the southern part of the Parque Nacional de Sierra Nevada, in the heart of Alpujarra. In the park, there are more than 2,100 species of plants, more than 60 of which are endemic and unique to this area. You can see alpine ibex, golden eagles and Bonelli's eagles, European wildcats, kestrels, barn owls, and little owls. The final stretch involves 30 minutes on foot as you cross the village of Bérchules and reach the stables. You stay the night in a hotel.

DAY 4: Bérchules

The following morning you prepare to reach an area that looms over Bérchules at a height of 7,218 feet (2,200 m), traversed by the Chico and Grande Rivers, tributaries of the Guadalfeo

River. You leave the village behind and climb steep trails through terraced kitchen gardens and orchards, until you reach a forest where you can gallop. Beyond the forest are meadows with a view over the Mediterranean Sea. You picnic and then descend by the old mule tracks to Bérchules for the night.

DAY 5: Bérchules–Trevélez

Today you return to Trevélez, through a continually changing landscape. In fact, you leave behind the forests and enter groves of olive, almond, and fig trees. In the late morning, you cross a spectacular ravine to reach the small village of Juviles for a lunch break. In the afternoon, you continue toward Trevélez, the end for today's ride.

DAY 6: Trevélez–Bubión

The last day in the saddle involves a brief excursion through the pine and oak forests to the stables near the Poqueira mountain shelter. This trail offers splendid views of the mountains of the Sierra de la Contraviesa and the Mediterranean Sea. Here, in some stretches, you can gallop. At Capileira you can stop for lunch, then you return to the trail and head for Bubión, where your ride through the Sierra Nevada ends.

FRANCE

Chemin de Stevenson

In France, tourism is one of the most active and thriving sectors. Apart from UNESCO sites, the country offers diverse tourist destinations: cities of culture, beaches, ski resorts, and rural destinations. Visitors seem to particularly appreciate the latter, and in fact every year there are thousands of walkers who, inspired by sustainable tourism, follow long-distance paths (GR or Grande Randonnée) to discover a surprising, lesser-known France.

Among these we should mention the Chemin de Stevenson (GR70), traced in 1878 by the Scottish writer Robert Louis Stevenson, who in 12 days walked 137 miles (220 km) through the land of the Camisards (rebellious Calvinists in the early 17th century). In his diary, *Travels with a Donkey in the Cévennes*, he recounted his progress through four regions—Velay, Gévaudan, Mont Lozère, and Cévennes—that today are classified as a UNESCO biosphere reserve. You, too, can make this journey on horseback (just check if the accommodation chosen has facilities for horses). Another useful tip is to take donkeys along: they will cheer you up as well as carry your baggage. You will feel a little like Stevenson!

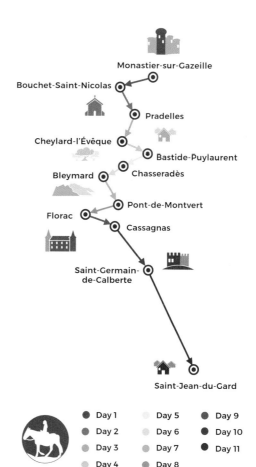

Monastier-sur-Gazeille
Bouchet-Saint-Nicolas
Pradelles
Cheylard-l'Évêque
Bastide-Puylaurent
Chasseradès
Bleymard
Pont-de-Montvert
Florac
Cassagnas
Saint-Germain-de-Calberte
Saint-Jean-du-Gard

- Day 1
- Day 2
- Day 3
- Day 4
- Day 5
- Day 6
- Day 7
- Day 8
- Day 9
- Day 10
- Day 11

188 top *Le Monastier sur Gazeille, the Romanesque Benedictine abbey. The apse of the church and the monastery buildings date from the 11/12th century.*
188 bottom *Pasture near Le Bouchet-Saint-Nicolas, a village in the Haute-Loire where a wooden statue commemorates Robert Louis Stevenson and his donkey Modestine.*

Start: Monastier-sur-Gazeille
Finish: Saint-Jean-du-Gard
Distance: 132 mi (212 km)
Time: 11 days
Difficulty: easy/medium
Accommodation: *gîtes d'étapes*
(hotel-type accommodation along the paths)

188–189 An ancient stone bridge
on the trail creates a fairy-tale
atmosphere.

Eco because: The Chemin de Stevenson was recognized as a Cultural Route by the Council of Europe in 2015. It is a great way to escape from chaos and traffic for a couple of weeks. It consists almost entirely of mule tracks and country roads, and crosses a wide variety of quiet, peaceful landscapes amid natural country life.

DAY 1: Monastier-sur-Gazeille–Bouchet-Saint-Nicolas

Monastier, built around a 7th-century Benedictine abbey, is the starting point of the trail. After crossing the farmed plateau and the village of Saint-Martin-de-Fugères, the Stevenson trail descends to the Loire gorges and then enters the village of Goudet, dominated by Beaufort Castle, a bulwark protecting the citizens during the religious wars. The descent from Prémajoux to Goudet is particularly steep and narrow: be very careful. You then continue to Bouchet-Saint-Nicolas, a typical Velay village with black stone houses grouped around a church. A mile north of Bouchet lies the lake of the same name.

DAY 2: Bouchet-Saint-Nicolas–Pradelles

After Bouchet-Saint-Nicolas, you continue the trip southward through Landos, a village of 900 people with an 11th-century Romanesque church. You ride through the fields and the last meadows of Velay until you reach Pradelles, the destination of the second stage.

DAY 3: Pradelles–Cheylard-l'Évêque

Pradelles is ranked among the most beautiful villages in France. It has various monuments, such as the historic fortified gates that recall a tumultuous past of religious wars. From here, you proceed toward Langogne: this stretch is difficult for the horses, as the bridge at the entrance has no sidewalks. Be very careful. After passing Gévaudan, you reach the pretty village of Cheylard-l'Évêque.

DAY 4: Cheylard-l'Évêque–Bastide-Puylaurent

Between Cheylard and Luc, you ride through flowery pastures (in spring) and beech and birch woods. As you descend toward Luc and the Allier gorges, you notice the remains of a castle from the 12th century. You then follow the valley as far as Bastide-Puylaurent.

This town developed in the 19th century with the advent of the Marseille-Paris railroad, which crossed Lozère and the Massif Centrale mountains. The Chemin de Stevenson here leaves the valley for a moment to climb up through the woods to the monastery of Notre-Dame des Neiges in Ardèche. Founded in 1850, the Cistercian-Trappist monastery can accommodate trekkers.

DAY 5: Bastide-Puylaurent–Chasseradès

After Bastide-Puylaurent, the path separates from the Regordane trail and heads for the village of Chasseradès in the southwest, with the historical church of Saint Blaise from the 12th century. As you move toward Mont Goulet, the trail follows the railroad line to Mende over the Mirandol railway viaduct across the Chassezac valley.

TRAVEL TIPS

When to go: In May and June, the flowers are at their best and the days are longer. October, on the other hand, is recommended if you love the colors of fall and like fewer people along the way.

How to get there: The nearest airport is at Lyon, then you can reach Puis-en-Velay by train, and then by bus as far as Monastier-sur-Gazeille (a total of about 106 miles [170 km]).

What to pack: Sleeping bag, light, quick-drying clothes, riding boots, and riding pants. Hiking boots, hat, sunscreen, first-aid kit with arnica cream, a map of GR70. Sufficient water. Raincoat, bathing suit, sandals, and headlamp. It is useful to take a first-aid kit for the horse, a hoof boot in case the horse should lose its shoe, and nail pullers. An invaluable traveling companion is obviously *Travels with a Donkey in the Cévennes* by Robert Louis Stevenson!

ECO-TIPS

FREE CAMPING IS FORBIDDEN. DO NOT TRAMPLE CROPS AND FRAGILE PLANTS, AND NEVER DISTURB THE WILDLIFE. PICK UP AND RECYCLE YOUR TRASH, RESPECT THE PRIVATE PROPERTY YOU CROSS, CLOSE GATES YOU HAVE OPENED, AND SLOW DOWN TO LET PEDESTRIANS PASS. DURING THE HUNTING SEASON, BE CAREFUL AND AVOID HUNTING AREAS.

Useful Websites
us.france.fr/en
chemin-stevenson.org
fctl.fr

DAY 6: Chasseradès–Bleymard

The Lot River flows down the southern slope of Mont Goulet. It is one of the longest rivers in France and a tributary of the Garonne. In the village of Bleymard, the chapel of Saint Jean de Bleymard (12th century) is worth a visit: it, too, is a historical monument.

DAY 7: Bleymard–Pont-de-Montvert

Between Bleymard and Pont-de-Montvert, the trail crosses the Mont Lozère area with its highest peak, the Pic de Finiels (5,574 feet [1,700 m]), in the middle of the Parc National des Cévennes, the largest in France. You then continue toward the village of Pont-de-Montvert.

DAY 8: Pont-de-Montvert–Florac

At Pont-de-Montvert you can visit the Mont Lozère ecomuseum, which shows the natural and cultural heritage of this mountain, and stroll in the village spanning the Tarn River with its rocky bed. You follow the route that climbs up granite and the schistous Mont Bougès, which is partly covered in woods, mainly beech and conifer, and partly in moorland, juniper, and pastures on the south slope. From the summit, you can take in the Cévennes range as far as the eye can see. The road comes down Mont Bougès to the west and leads to Florac, a little village of 1,900 inhabitants at the meeting of Causses, Mont Lozère, and Barre-des-Cévennes, from which the Tarnon River flows through the city. At Florac, the 12th-century castle houses the administrative center of the park; you should also see the ancient Templar house with a noteworthy facade and the Protestant temple. From Florac to Alès, mulberry growing and silkworm raising dominated the economy until the mid-19th century, when an epidemic devastated the farms. When the silkworm declined, most of the labor force migrated to Alès, where industrial coal mining began; this contributed significantly to the desertification of the Cévennes.

DAY 9: Florac–Cassagnas

When you leave Florac, the road leads to the east along the granite valley of Mimente, toward Cassagnas. You walk through pine and chestnut woods. For centuries, chestnuts, along with livestock, have been the main food resource of the Cévennes: if dried, they could be preserved for months and were the staple food during the winter.

DAY 10: Cassagnas–Saint-Germain-de-Calberte

After Cassagnas, the route winds south and then southeast toward Saint-Germain-de-Calberte. Here, the castle (11th century) and the church bell tower (14th century) loom over the heart of the historic Cévennes region. The village preserves the iconic symbols of its past: Protestant culture, Pélardon cheese, and houses with slate roofs.

DAY 11: Saint-Germain-de-Calberte–Saint-Jean-du-Gard

The route continues and after 5.5 miles (9 km) you reach Saint-Etienne-Vallée-Française, where you see various fortified sites, such as Cambié Castle. It dates from the 14th century and was built by the family of Raymond de Calberte, but today it is a *gîte* for tourists. As you continue southward, the Chemin de Stevenson crosses the forest of Gardon, with chestnut trees, conifers, and robinia trees, goes through the Saint Pierre pass, and then descends to the little town of Saint-Jean-du-Gard, the end of the stage. The descent from Col de Saint-Pierre, before Saint-Jean-du-Gard, is very steep and narrow, which makes it almost impracticable for horses. You can avoid it by leaving the GR70 at Pont de Burgen (before Saint-Etienne-Vallée-Française) and following the GR67A and then the 44D, and then rejoining the GR70 at Col d'Uglas, between Saint-Jean-du-Gard and Alès. At Saint-Jean-du-Gard you can take a walk in the old town to visit the market place—here, on Tuesdays you can try the *pissaladière* or *fougasse* with an aperitif—and the clock tower, what remains of the 12th-century Romanesque church destroyed during the religious wars. To the north of Saint-Jean-du-Gard, in the village of Mialet, you can visit a museum documenting the history of Protestantism in the Cévennes and the Camisard war.

192 top *Sainte-Marie-des-Chazes near the Allier gorges. The Allier River, which is longer than the Loire, into which it flows, has created a deep valley with views of villages, woods, basalt gorges, and escarpments.*

192 bottom *Florac Castle houses the administration of the Parque National des Cévennes, created in 1970, and the museum with all the information concerning it.*

193 *Horse trekkers near Saint-Germain. The trail mainly runs along mule tracks and country roads, but it has a lot of accommodation for every need.*

Monte Catria on Horseback

Marche has it all: seaside, hills, countryside, caves, mountains, cities, art, all in the same region. It is a combination of everything Italy has to offer, surprising visitors with the beauty and gentleness of its landscapes. Montefeltro is one of its districts, shared between the province of Pesaro-Urbino and the region of Emilia Romagna (province of Rimini), the Republic of San Marino, and the province of Arezzo in Tuscany. It is a little-known area, ready to be explored, where the strong, generous horses of Monte Catria—a breed named after the mountain—graze. It is an absorbing experience in the heart of the Apennines: a slow ride through villages and monasteries, with pauses to swim in the rivers. During the ride, you can admire the wonderful local fauna, the rock partridges, the mouflons, and the golden eagles.

194 top *Monte Catria in the early dawn.*
194 bottom *A day in the saddle bestows well-being and happiness: well-trained horses are the ideal companions for riding.*

Start: Fermignano
Finish: Fermignano
Distance: approximately 155 mi (250 km)
Time: 5 days
Difficulty: medium (6/7 hours on horseback each day)
Accommodation: tents and farmhouses

194–195 *Fermignano, the land of the famous architect Donato Bramante, is situated on the left bank of the Metauro River. The Torre delle Milizie (Tower of the Militia) defends the three-arched Roman bridge spanning the river.*

Eco because: Riders will enjoy exploring the territory and meeting the people. This trek is ideal for anyone who wants to lose themself in the silence and the harmony of nature. It is also a chance to spend the night at a farm refurbished to become a green building and that grows and cooks biodynamic food.

196 The plant species that grow in rocky settings and stony meadows of the Gruppo del Catria have been divided into as many as 8 protected areas instituted by the Regione Marche.

197 top The Catria horse has ancient origins, and it is characterized by the strength and frugality necessary for survival on the natural mountain pastures.

197 bottom left Monte Catria is characterized by extensive wooded areas and centuries-old tall beech woods, along with orchids, primroses, violets, gentians, crocuses, narcissus, and yet other flowers.

197 bottom right The Fonte Avellana Monastery dates from the end of the 10th century, when some hermits chose the slopes of Monte Catria to build their first cells.

DAY 1: Fermignano–Frontone

From the Ca' Maddalena farm, you ride toward the hills of Montefeltro until evening, when you reach the small town of Frontone, at the foot of Monte Catria. Here you set up your tent for the night in a campsite.

DAY 2: Frontone–Monte Catria

Today you reach the hermitage of Fonte Avellana, at the foot of Monte Catria (2,297 feet [700 m]). It dates from the end of the 10th century, when a group of hermits chose to build the first cells. Their spirituality was influenced by Saint Romuald of Ravenna, the founder of the Camaldolese order. From here you climb Monte Catria to the peak (5,580 feet [1,700 m]), stopping here for the night in tents or a shelter (Cupa delle Cotaline, at 4,593 feet [1,400 m]).

DAY 3: Monte Catria–Monte Petrano

You descend from Monte Catria and, on horseback, climb Monte Petrano, a vast plateau from which you can admire the Catria massif, with the silhouette of Monte Acuto in the foreground and Monte Nerone behind it. From up here you overlook the Adriatic coast and the landscape of central Italy. Along the way, you pass through landscapes scattered

TRAVEL TIPS

When to go: From spring to autumn. Best in summer.

How to get there: The nearest airport is Ancona, then you can take either a train or a bus to Fermignano, about 62 miles (100 km) away; you need to take a car to reach Ca' Maddalena (7.5 miles from Urbino) where the ride starts.

What to pack: A bag or haversack with anything necessary for the evening; sleeping bag, long trousers, change of clothes, towels, toiletries. Swimsuit, hiking boots, gaiters, waterproof garments, headlamp.

with beech trees, maples, and holm oaks, where horses, mules, cattle, sheep, and goats graze. In summer, there are wonderful blankets of narcissus, violets, and orchids beside the trail. You can spend the night in your tent at the foot of Monte Petrano.

DAY 4: Monte Petrano–Bacciardi

In this stage you pass through the perfectly intact Tecchie wood and cross the Nerone massif to the characteristic village of Bacciardi, with its typical stone houses. Here you have dinner and sleep at the Slowcanda, a late 19th-century stone house refurbished to be a green building and almost completely energy self-sufficient. Here the vegetables are grown using the principles of biodynamics.

DAY 5: Bacciardi–Fermignano

Today you make a series of small fords within the Fosso dell'Eremo valley and climb Monte Montiego to arrive once again in the splendid hills of Montefeltro, which lead you back to Ca' Maddalena at Fermignano.

ECO-TIPS

TRAVEL LIGHT AND RESPECT THE NEEDS OF YOUR HORSE: A GOOD RELATIONSHIP WITH YOUR MOST IMPORTANT TRAVELING COMPANION WILL MAKE THIS RIDE THROUGH NATURE PERFECT! DO NOT THROW FOOD OR TRASH ON THE TRAIL, AND ABOVE ALL DO NOT LEAVE CIGARETTE BUTTS IN THE ENVIRONMENT. KEEP AWAY FROM THE HERDS OF WILD HORSES: THE STALLIONS COULD ATTACK YOUR HORSE TO PROTECT THEIR MARES. SOME PATHS REQUIRE RIDERS TO DISMOUNT AND LEAD THEIR HORSES.

Useful Websites
en.turismo.marche.it
www.montecatria.com
horseback.it
camaddalena.com
www.asmontecatria.com

TURKEY

Cappadocia on Horseback

Start: Avanos
Finish: Avanos
Distance: approximately
100 mi (160 km)
Time: 7 days
Difficulty: difficult
Accommodation: tents and hotel

Lapped by four seas and suspended between Europe and Asia, with the Bosphorus Sea marking the southern border between the two continents, from the Marmara Sea to the Dardanel Straits, Turkey is a land of inestimable artistic and cultural treasures. In addition to monuments and archaeological sites, there is a unique and picturesque landscape that ranges from golden beaches to rocky formations in the valleys and rolling hills in the hinterland.

Among all the environments that beautify this extraordinary country, the most exciting is Cappadocia, a UNESCO World Heritage Site in the heart of the Anatolian peninsula. Its land, carved by nature and by mankind, is a fairy-tale landscape of canyons, gorges, hoodoos or peribacasi (fairy chimneys) and cave homes. A landscape of amazing beauty that preserves traces of the civilizations that were born and developed here: Assyrians, Hittites, Persians, Christians, Byzantines, Mongols, Greeks, Ottomans . . .

To explore the valleys of the "Land of Beautiful Horses"—the meaning of the name Cappadocia—nothing can be better than riding the lively, agile horses, native to Anatolia. The level of difficulty of this route is advanced. Being a mountainous area, with particularly rocky terrain, you often ride at a walk: sometimes, when the trail is very steep, it is necessary to lead the horse on foot.

198 top A beautiful image of the Red Valley, perfect for horse trekking.
198 bottom One of the many underground cities in Cappadocia: the layers are of volcanic granite.
199 It is exciting to ride through this land formed by lava, the wind, and water over millions of years. Here nature reigns unchallenged.

	Day 1	Day 5
	Day 2	Day 6
	Day 3	Day 7
	Day 4	

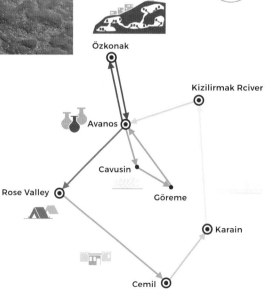

Eco because: In this unique landscape, sculpted by nature, the tour is minimally invasive and respects the local culture. You spend most nights in tents and enjoy the specialties of Turkish cuisine, prepared by the locals. The well-being of the horses is a major concern for the operator, who organizes the trek and promotes responsible and sustainable tourism.

RIDERS ARE RESPONSIBLE FOR
THE WELL-BEING OF THEIR HORSE.
TAKE ALL TRASH WITH YOU,
NEVER LEAVE IT ALONG THE TRAIL.
RESPECT THE ENVIRONMENTAL
FRAGILITY OF THIS AREA.

Useful Websites
turkey.com
goturkey.com
ktb.gov.tr
inthesaddle.com

200 *The Göreme National Park has multicolored rocks, the result of high concentrations of iron oxides and other minerals.*

201 top *The ancient cave village of Cavusin, with cliff houses, on the edge of Göreme. The Church of St. John the Baptist is probably one of the oldest cliff churches in the region.*

201 bottom *The main tourist attraction in the city of Derinkuyu is the underground city of the same name, opened in 1996.*

202–203 *Dawn in the Red and Rose valley in April makes this enchanted place even more magical.*

DAY 1: Avanos–Özkonak–Avanos

You start at the stables in Avanos, a town renowned for its ceramics. You ride from Avanos to Özkonak, one of the three most extensive and fascinating underground cities in Cappadocia. Dug into the tufa rock, the town has ten levels and is linked to a complex ventilation system and water supply. Nowadays, only four levels are open to the public. After the visit to the subterranean settlement, in the afternoon you return to the stables, crossing the Ziyaretdagi mountain, which dominates Avanos.

DAY 2: Avanos–Rose Valley

In the morning you ride through the Dereyamanli valley, where a Christian church dating from the 6th century is carved into the rock. Along the way you can see a number of small vineyards. You then reach the White valley, near the hoodoos. After lunch you cross the Göreme valley, from

where you can admire the Rose valley and the Red valley and even see Ortahisar with its honeycomb natural fortress, comprising caves and tunnels well hidden by the vegetation. With its red, pink, and ochre rock citadels, this is the most spectacular valley in the Cappadocia. You camp for the night in the Rose valley.

DAY 3: Rose Valley–Cemil

From the Rose valley you ride toward Ortahisar and Mustafapasa, a village of Greek origin, once known by the name of Sinasos. The next destination is the rock-cut Byzantine monastery of Keslik, built between the 7th and the 13th centuries. The monastic complex has two chapels, a refectory, dormitories, and living quarters carved out from the rock. The Church of St. Stephen is situated about 164 feet (50 m) from the monastery and contains rare and beautiful frescoes. You camp for the night outside the village of Cemil.

DAY 4: Cemil–Karain

In the morning you cross the Cemil valley, between the plateaus, the magnificent basins, and the hoodoos—tall tufa pyramids with a rock balanced on the top, placed there by a divinity, according to the legends. On horseback, you climb the beautiful canyon to reach the village of Taskinpasa. Before you reach the camp at Karain, you can visit the 14th-century Karamanid mosque.

DAY 5: Karain–Kizilirmak River

In the first part of this stage, you reach the Akkoy plateau, where you can admire unending panoramas. Once you reach Sofular, on a clear day you can admire the silhouette of the Ericyes volcano in the distance (12,854 feet [3,900 m]). You continue along an ancient caravan and trade route from the 13th century—the Uzun Yol, which means "the long road." You camp for the night near the Kizilirmak River ("the Red River") the longest in Turkey.

DAY 6: Kizilirmak River–Avanos

This day is dedicated to a ride along the bed of the Kizilirmak River, where you can take long gallops. After four nights in a tent, you return to the hotel in Avanos.

DAY 7: Avanos–Cavusin–Göreme–Avanos

On the last day of your ride, you explore the area around Avanos, in the direction of Göreme. You ride through the spectacular Rose valley and the Red valley to Cavusin, an ancient rock village. From Cavusin you can gallop across the steppe. In the afternoon, you visit the open-air museum of Göreme, with its many chapels, monasteries, and small churches only accessible by staircases and tunnels carved into the rock, which lead to the discovery of splendid frescoes. It is a good way to end an exciting tour.

When to go: From the beginning of April to October.

How to get there: You arrive at Nevşehir Kapadokya airport and then travel by car to Avanos (about 22 miles [35 km]).

What to pack: Sleeping bag, riding clothes, helmet, gaiters or chaps. Comfortable boots for riding and walking, with a rubber sole. Comfortable clothes for when you are not riding, fleece sweater, gloves, scarf or bandana. Headlamp, canteen, towel, and toiletries. Battery charger for mobile phone and camera. Sunscreen, sunglasses, bathing suit, sandals. Personal medicines, diarrhea tablets, insect repellent.

KYRGYZSTAN

Start: Tamchy
Finish: Dobo
Distance: 23 mi (37 km)
Time: 3 days
Difficulty: easy
Accommodation: tents and guesthouses

204–205 Some yurts (circular tents that are the home of nomadic peoples in Asia) near the salt lake of Issyk-Kul, a UNESCO biosphere reserve. It is the second-largest mountain lake in the world.

Eco because: This trek on horseback allows you to travel through the Chong Kemin National Park, in landscapes still little-known. Contrasts are strong, from deserts to coniferous forests and green hills: a plunge into intact nature. This trek also allows you to experience the Kyrgyz culture, living in close contact with the local people. In fact, the itineraries are often based on a network of visits to local families, including the yurt makers and the falconers who still hunt using birds of prey. An authentic and fascinating world to be discovered without prejudices.

Lake Kol-Kogur on Horseback

Kyrgyzstan—"the land of the Mountains of Heaven" on the ancient Silk Road that linked China to the Mediterranean—is a mountainous country dominated by the Tien Shan chain (the Mountains of Heaven, precisely) and the high plateau of Pamir. If offers numerous treks on horseback or on foot, and thanks to its many national parks and forest reserves, it preserves its natural beauty intact in its diverse forms: a dream for any ecotourist who loves adventure. Kyrgyzstan has also maintained its traditions of nomadic life: in fact, even today, in the warm season, the shepherds and their families take their animals to the grazing grounds, which are dotted with yurts, the packable homes built on a wooden frame and covered in sheep wool rugs.

The trek we propose visits the region of Chong Kemin, in the national park of the same name, rich in rocky gorges, desert plateaus, forests, meadows, and lakes, including Lake Kol-Kogur at 6,562 feet (2,000 m) above sea level, accessible only on foot or on horseback. The park protects more than 780 species of plants and rare animals, like the snow leopard (whose numbers have fallen dramatically in recent years), the brown bear, the Eurasian lynx, the golden eagle, the Himalayan vulture (*Gyps himalayensis*), the bearded vulture, the saker falcon, and the sable.

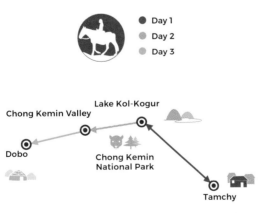

205 *Lake Issyk-Kul, 2,300 feet (700 m) deep, a UNESCO biosphere reserve.*

206 top left *In Kyrgyzstan, horse wrestling is one of the national sports. Kirghiz people are semi-nomadic herders: they live in the mountains and tend sheep, horses, and yaks (Tibetan oxen).*

206 top right *A stubborn mule ridden by a child is pulled by a man in order to cross a wooden bridge over a watercourse.*

206 bottom *Central Asia is the cradle of the ancient tradition of hunting with eagles: it is passed on from generation to generation. It was fundamental for obtaining furs and food.*

207 *There are various horse riding trails in the province of Issyk-Kul: often there is no way of reaching certain places apart from on horseback or on foot.*

DAY 1: Village of Tamchy

The tour starts with a stay in the village of Tamchy, at 5,249 feet (1,600 m) above sea level, on the northern bank of Lake Issyk-Kul, a UNESCO biosphere reserve, 2,297 feet (700 m) deep. Fun fact: this lake never freezes despite the altitude; in fact, it is known as "the hot sea." Local people, in addition to preserving the ecosystem and its biodiversity, jealously safeguard their nomadic traditions, the national songs and dances, and the ancient skills of Kyrgyz carpet making. You spend the night in a guesthouse.

DAY 2: Tamchy–Lake Kol-Kogur

On horseback, you begin the first major crossing: the Koltor pass, 10,892 feet (3,320 m) above sea level. From here you have a panoramic view on Lake Issyk-Kul. You then continue toward Lake Kol-Kogur, in the Chong Kemin National Park, where the river by the same name flows. Once you arrive on the banks of

Lake Kol-Kogur, surrounded by the Küngöy Ala-Too mountains and the coniferous forests, at 6,562 feet (2,000 m) above sea level, you can finally relax and stroll by the lake. You camp in tents for the night.

DAY 3: Lake Kol-Kogur–Village of Dobo

The next morning, you continue toward the Chong Kemin valley. Along the trail you can stop on the banks of the river. You ride through the mountain passes you encounter along the trail, until you reach the village of Dobo, the final stage of your ride, 4,593 feet (1,400 m) above sea level. Here you can attend a concert of local music and find accommodation in one of the local guesthouses.

When to go: From mid-May to mid-September is the ideal time, while in autumn and winter the yurts are dismantled and tourist accommodations are closed.

How to get there: From the airport of the capital, Bishkek, you can take a bus or a train, or rent a car to reach Tamchy, the starting point of the trip, which is about 143 miles (230 km) away. The ride is organized by ecotourism companies specializing in trips through Kyrgyzstan and central Asia. You can also rent horses at the CBT (Community Based Tourism) offices. During the ride, the baggage and camping equipment are carried on packhorses.

What to pack: Anyone who decides not to contact the specialized companies must buy maps before arriving in the country because they are very difficult to find on the spot. Since the trail reaches average altitudes of 9,285 feet (2,830 m) above sea level, be prepared for difficult weather conditions. It is advisable to bring warm clothing for sleeping in the tents, waterproof jacket, comfortable shoes and hiking boots for the high plateaus, a hat, high protection sunscreen, and soft bags, rather than rigid suitcases.

▶ ECO-TIPS

THE PHILOSOPHY OF THE JOURNEY LIES IN RESPECT FOR THE FRAGILE BIODIVERSITY OF CENTRAL ASIA—TRYING TO REDUCE THE CONSUMPTION OF NON-RENEWABLE RESOURCES—AND FOR THE LOCALS, WHO ARE VERY SOCIABLE AND HOSPITABLE. IF YOU STAY WITH THEM, EVEN JUST FOR LUNCH, PLEASE RESPECT THEIR TRADITIONS.

Useful Websites
caravanistan.com
www.discoverkyrgyzstan.org
cbtkyrgyzstan.kg

On Horseback in the Wilds of Yukon

Yukon, in the furthermost northwestern corner of Canada, is one of the three Canadian territories included in the cold regions overlooking the Arctic, on the border with Alaska. It was named after the river that runs through it, which in the language of the Gwich'in people means "great river."

Far from the obvious tourist itineraries, Yukon offers splendid wild panoramas with glacier valleys, highlands, rivers and lakes, forests, taiga, and tundra. Its territory appears mainly wild and unspoiled, with a very low population density: a genuine natural paradise. Its residential centers have adopted a policy of sustainable development: for example, Whitehorse, the capital of Yukon, has drawn up the Whitehorse Sustainability Plan, a program to be implemented between 2015 and 2050, with twelve goals concerning the environmental impact of urban activities, the protection of green areas, the decrease of energy waste, and the encouragement of collective participation and social inclusion.

To enjoy a truly eco-friendly adventure, you ride strong, reliable horses. These animals generally live in the wild, even during harsh winters, and they are accustomed to mountainous terrain and fording rivers. The itinerary we propose is suitable for riders with experience of camping and trekking of several days, with a spirit of adventure and a desire for a unique experience.

208 Horses ready for trekking. These strong animals live all year round in the wild, and they are used to carrying weights, fording rivers, and tackling mountainous terrain.

- Day 1
- Day 2
- Day 3
- Day 4–5
- Day 6
- Day 7
- Day 8
- Day 9
- Day 10

Start: Shinevalley (Fish Lake Valley)
Finish: Shinevalley (Fish Lake Valley)
Distance: approximately 224 mi (360 km)
Time: 10 days
Difficulty: difficult
Accommodation: cottages and tents

208-209 A magnificent aerial view
of the fall colors and the lakes in the
Bonneville area.

Eco because: The spirit of this trek lies in seeing the experience itself as an
immersion in an environment and a culture other than one's own, respecting
the landscapes and the traditions. Not just an adventure for its own sake, but an
"environmental awareness" tour. The guides teach visitors how to appreciate the
beauty of the territory and encourage a kind of behavior that helps to protect the
uncontaminated landscapes of Yukon.

When to go: The best time for this horseback trek is summer, when the weather is mild.

How to get there: By plane to Whitehorse airport in the capital of Yukon, then by car to Shinevalley (about one hour)

What to pack: Mattress, sleeping bag, canteen, riding hat (compulsory), boots, gloves and jodhpurs, chaps to protect the legs when riding through dense woodland. The temperature varies between 40°F (5°C) at night and 85°F (30°C) in the day, so it is a good idea to take a hat, warm gloves, comfortable shoes, and warm, casual clothing for the evenings, in addition to a windbreaker. Sunglasses, thermos, bathing suit, small towel, personal medicines, camera, and spare batteries.

210 top A family of common loons, considered a species in danger of extinction.
210 bottom left One of the lakes of Yukon: the different colors of foliage distinguish the different plants in the area.
210 bottom right Beavers are part of the local fauna. Yukon's vegetation is classified as subarctic and alpine. The boreal forests cover 57% of the land, and there are over 200 species of wildflowers.
211 Mount Vanier and Kusawa Lake, one of the main lakes in the region, are near your horseback trek.

DAY 1: Shinevalley–Bonneville

The trek starts at the Shinevalley ranch, in the Fish Lake valley, where you spend the night and enjoy the midnight sun. In the early morning, you prepare to leave, after weighing the saddlebags and distributing them among the packhorses. Finally, you leave on horseback, traveling through the Bonneville region, with the first massifs and the wide-open spaces of Yukon. In the evening, you set up camp.

DAY 2: Bonneville–Ibex Lake

After breakfast, you take down the camp and ride toward Marmot Pass, a narrow mountain pass at 5,900 feet (1,800 m) above sea level, which leads to a plateau often visited by caribou, moose, and grizzly bears. You reach Ibex Lake, high in the mountains, where you camp for the night.

DAY 3: Ibex Lake–Rose Creek

In the morning, you ride across open ground to Mud Lake, a lake formed by glaciers. You ford some streams before stopping for lunch, then you rest while the horses graze. Back in the saddle, you look out for wolf dens as you head for Rose Creek and your campsite for the night. You spend the night beside the campfire, with a wonderful panoramic view of the valley.

DAY 4: Rose Creek–Rose Lake

After breakfast, you ride through the forest, following an old trail that overlooks the valley carved out in the ice age. You reach Rose Lake with its rich and varied wildlife: eagles, ducks, geese, and many other migratory birds. You can also see dams built by beavers. Fresh food supplies are delivered here by float plane to the camp set up for the night.

ECO-TIPS

YOU WILL BE RESPONSIBLE FOR YOUR OWN HORSE, ITS FEEDING AND GROOMING. TAKE BIODEGRADABLE DETERGENT AND SOAP FOR PERSONAL HYGIENE. DO NOT LEAVE ANY TRASH ALONG THE TRAIL.

Useful Websites

www.canada.travel
pc.gc.ca/en/index
cheval-daventure.com
www.yukonshinevalley.com

212 top *A black bear (Ursus americanus) eating raspberries along the border between British Columbia and Yukon. You can meet bears along the trail.*

212 bottom *A caravan of horses carrying provisions and baggage between the ranches on the itinerary.*

212–213 *An aerial view of a lake in the Watson Lake area. Yukon is a sparsely populated region, but it is rich in natural beauty, small lakes, and mountains, the highest in Canada.*

DAY 5: Rose Lake

This is a rest day for horses and riders. You can relax by fishing, swimming (if the water is not too cold), paddling in a canoe, or walking through the woods, immersed in a variety of flora and fauna. In the evening, you eat around the campfire and prepare for the night in your tent.

DAY 6: Rose Lake–Big Ben

You set out for Big Ben, an old trapper cabin. The trail leads through open meadows to a ridge of alpine forest overlooking the Watson River. You spend the night in your tent.

DAY 7: Big Ben–Watson River

You head off on the Watson Trail, following the river through the forest. After fording the river, you stop for lunch on the river bank.

In the afternoon, you ride to a small clearing in the forest with a view of the mountains and the meadows where the moose graze. You enjoy an evening beside the fire and spend the night in your tent or under the stars.

DAY 8: Watson River–Alligator Lake

Here you travel through the forest that leads to the highlands, an ideal place to observe wildlife: in summer, caribou and moose migrate here to find abundant grazing. At the end of the day, you descend to Alligator Lake valley, where the glacial activity has left islands of fine sand. Dinner and a night in the tents.

DAY 9: Alligator Lake–Upper Fish Lake

The next morning, after breakfast, you are back in the saddle, traveling across a high plateau, in the area between Alligator Lake and the southern banks of Fish Lake, the ideal place to find caribou. You reach a high point overlooking the lake, where you camp. It's the perfect place to enjoy the sun setting behind the mountains and your last night in the wilderness.

DAY 10: Fish Lake–Shinevalley

After taking down the tents and saddling up, you start the last day of the trek. You pass through mountainous terrain and tundra before descending at the northern tip of Fish Lake to reach the Shinevalley ranch, where you rest, have dinner, and sleep.

Yellowstone–Bechler River Trail

On March 1, 1872, the Congress of the United States and President Ulysses S. Grant inaugurated the Yellowstone National Park, the first in the nation and in the world. It is mostly situated in the state of Wyoming and part in Montana and Idaho. It is now a UNESCO World Heritage Site and the core of the Greater Yellowstone Ecosystem, one of the largest intact ecosystems in the temperate belt of the Northern Hemisphere. About 5% of the park is covered in water, 15% is prairie, and 80% is occupied by forests that include unique plants. Hundreds of species of mammals, birds, fish. and reptiles live here, including some that are at risk of extinction or threatened: this is the kingdom of grizzly bears, wolves, bison, and moose.

The ride we propose runs through Wyoming and Idaho, in the Bechler region (also known as Cascade Corner), and heads toward Silver Scarf and Dunanda Falls. You ride through meadows, passing rivers, waterfalls, and hot springs where you can swim, enjoying the vast scenic panoramas.

214 Horses tethered in Yellowstone National Park, awaiting riders for the trek through the park.

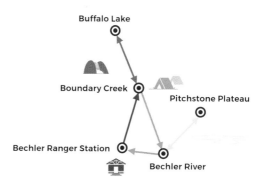

Buffalo Lake

Boundary Creek

Pitchstone Plateau

Bechler Ranger Station

Bechler River

- Day 1
- Day 2
- Day 3
- Day 4
- Day 5

Start: Bechler Ranger Station
Finish: Bechler Ranger Station
Distance: 30.3 miles (48.9 km)
Time: 10 days
Difficulty: medium
Accommodation: tents

214–215 The Bechler River in the fall: this wide, remote river flows entirely within Yellowstone National Park, as far as its confluence with the Fall River in the southwest.

Eco because: Yellowstone Park is home to a variety of wildlife that is easy to see and spectacular natural panoramas; the unspoiled landscape makes it one of the most visited parks in the world.

When to go: July, August, and September are the best months (the first two are the hottest).

How to get there: The nearest airport is West Yellowstone. From here you travel by car (approximately 34 miles (55 km)) to the West Yellowstone Park entrance, open from April to November.

What to pack: Tent, sleeping bag, canteen. Waterproof travel bag, waterproof cape and pants, riding clothes. Boots (either hiking boots with a small heel or cowboy boots), hat, sunscreen, sunglasses. Insect repellent and mosquito net. Bathing suit, toiletries. Headlamp, camera, video camera, binoculars, fishing rod.

ECO-TIPS

THIS RIDE FOLLOWS THE LEAVE NO TRACE PHILOSOPHY: THE ONLY ACCEPTABLE SIGNS OF YOUR PASSAGE ARE HOOFPRINTS. VISITORS SHOULD ADOPT SUSTAINABLE BEHAVIOR: KEEP YOUR DISTANCE FROM THE WILDLIFE, CLEAN AND DRY FISHING GEAR BEFORE ENTERING THE PARK AND BEFORE MOVING FROM ONE WATERCOURSE TO ANOTHER, RECYCLE AS MUCH AS POSSIBLE, AND PUT ANY OTHER TRASH IN THE BEAR-PROOF BINS. IF ONE BIN IS FULL, FIND ANOTHER ONE: NEVER LEAVE TRASH IN THE PARK. IT IS FORBIDDEN TO TAKE AWAY HORNS OR ANTLERS, ROCKS, PLANTS, OR ANYTHING ELSE FROM THE PARK.

Useful Websites
nps.gov

DAY 1: Bechler Ranger Station–Boundary Creek

The trail begins at the Bechler Ranger Station in the southeastern corner of Yellowstone National Park. As you ride, you can have some fun fording Boundary Creek. You camp for the night beside the creek, where you can fish and swim, or relax on its banks, watching the horses graze peacefully in the meadows.

DAY 2: Boundary Creek–Dunanda Falls–Buffalo Lake–Boundary Creek

Today's ride takes you to Dunanda Falls, a few miles from Boundary Creek. The waterfall is 148 feet (45 m) high and was discovered by Europeans only a century ago. At the base of the falls there is a warm pool where you can swim, enjoying a perfect view of the falls. Nearby is the Silver Scarf Falls: the water of the stream that feeds the waterfall is warmed by several hot springs to the north. When you leave the waterfalls, you climb the canyon to Buffalo Lake, in Idaho, with its iconic thermal springs. You then return to Boundary Creek, where you camp for night.

DAY 3: Boundary Creek–Bechler River

This stage involves the transfer to the second camp, which is about 7.5 miles (12 km) away on the Bechler River, near the confluence of the Phillips Fork, Gregg Fork, and Ferns Fork Rivers (Three Rivers Junction). The meadows are perfect for the horses. You camp here.

DAY 4: Bechler River–Pitchstone Plateau–Bechler River

On the fourth day, you make a brief excursion to the hot springs upstream of a fork that leads to Ferris Fork Pool, or "Mr. Bubbly" as the locals call it, where you can enjoy swimming. You can also ride up to the Pitchstone Plateau, created by rhyolite lava flows seventy thousand years ago. You then return to your camp on the Bechler River.

DAY 5: Bechler River–Bechler Ranger Station

In the final stage, you return toward the ranger station you started out from, along the last stretch of the Bechler River Trail, crossing the Rocky Ford. You can stop for a picnic along the Fall River. Then you set out again, riding through some of the most beautiful meadows of Yellowstone National Park, until you arrive at the Bechler Ranger Station, where the trail ends.

216 Terraced waterfall in the southwest of Yellowstone National Park.
216–217 A cowboy leads a packhorse caravan across a stream in Yellowstone National Park.

Avenue of Volcanoes Trail

Straddling the equator, from which it takes its name, Ecuador is also known as the "country of four worlds" for its natural environments: the Amazon rain forest, the Andes, the Galápagos Islands, and the Pacific coast. It is one of the so-called "megadiverse" countries, with an enormous wealth of fauna and natural landscapes, and a very high density of biodiversity per square mile. Ecuador's attention to its natural heritage is demonstrated by its legislative decisions, and in fact the "rights of nature" are safeguarded in this country by the constitution.

For travelers who love adventure, riding through the magnificent landscape of the Avenue of Volcanoes Trail, perhaps wearing a traditional poncho, is an unforgettable experience. This trek is for expert riders. Running between the central plateaus of Parque Nacional Cotopaxi, it was the first trail to be marked on the mainland and has rare species of flora, exotic fauna, and amazing rock formations. Cotopaxi (19,118 feet [5,800 m]) is one of the highest active volcanoes in the world and dominates the entire landscape of this protected area, which also includes the smaller volcanoes Morurco (16,010 feet [4,880 m]) and Rumiñahui (15,489 feet [4,720 m]). The trek unfolds at more than 9,842 feet (3,000 m) above sea level, with spectacular craters and snow-capped peaks in the background. The predominant ecosystem in the park is the *páramo* (an alpine tundra ecosystem) with its montane vegetation, dominated by pajonal and small shrubs.

218 *La Basílica del Voto Nacional in the old town of the capital Quito. It is the largest neo-Gothic church in the Americas; it was built in 1884 but technically it is "unfinished."*

San Clemente

Valle Zuleta

Quito

- Day 1
- Day 2
- Day 3
- Day 4
- Day 5
- Day 6-7

Refugio de Vida Silvestre Pasochoa

Parque Nacional Cotopaxi

Cerro Quilindaña

Start: Quito
Finish: Quito
Distance: approximately 124 mi (200 km)
Time: 7 days
Difficulty: medium
Accommodation: inns and farms

218–219 Trekking on horseback begins from Quito, a UNESCO World Heritage Site, where you are advised to spend a little time to acclimatize.

Eco because: The local guide for the trek is a *chagra*, an Ecuadorian "cowboy" who looks after the land, the cattle, and the horses, and who was born and raised in the Andes, with expert knowledge of the territory. These *campesinos*, or countrymen, promote responsible and sustainable tourism and are committed to protecting the environment and contributing to the communities they work with.

DAY 1: Quito–Valle Zuleta

Before starting the trek, we recommend you spend at least a couple of nights in Quito (UNESCO World Heritage Site) in order to acclimatize and visit the largest and best-preserved old town in Latin America. From Quito you move to the riding school in Valle Cayambe to meet the guide and the horses that will be your companions on the trek. You can also take a trial ride, to ensure you have chosen the right mount. From here you explore Valle Zuleta with its hills draped in Andean wildflowers: iris, puya hamata, gentians, and lupin beans. You reach Hacienda La Merced, located in the valley, where you stay for the night.

DAY 2: Valle Zuleta–San Clemente

After breakfast you ride toward an area sculpted by the retreating glaciers during the ice age. Breathtaking panoramas mark the climb up the valley, through pine forests that cover the slopes of the inactive Imbabura volcano (15,121 feet [4,610 m]). According to the season, if you are lucky, you will see

TRAVEL TIPS

When to go: It is advisable to go between June and February; the driest season is between May and October.

How to get there: The nearest airport is Quito. From there you take the Pan American Highway, if traveling by car, or the train to reach the entrance to Parco El Caspi: from here the local guides take you to the riding school in Valle Cayambe, where the itinerary starts.

What to pack: Wear layers of clothes: at high altitudes there can be a considerable day-to-night drop in temperature (86°F [30°C] to near 32°F [0°C]). Hat, sunscreen, sunglasses, canteen.

220 Snow-covered Cotopaxi. At 19,118 feet (5,872 m), it is one of the highest active volcanoes. In the Quechua language, its name means "neck of the moon."
*221 **left** A hummingbird on a Chuquiragua plant.*
*221 **right** Andean landscape in the Zuleta valley, with fields growing lupins and wildflowers such as irises, puya hamata, and gentians.*

the brightly colored tanagers and the vermilion flycatchers. A pause for lunch in the midst of nature and then you ride toward San Clemente, where you spend the night at an inn.

DAY 3: San Clemente–Refugio de Vida Silvestre Pasochoa

In the morning, you set out for another ride, flanking small farms and fields, meeting the people who live and work here. You reach the ridge of Valle San Pablo, from which you can admire the lake by the same name. Along the trail, you encounter flocks of sheep and pass beside fields of quinoa and lupin beans. In the afternoon, you continue toward the Avenue of Volcanoes Trail and reach on foot the Pasochoa volcano (13,780 feet [4,200 m]). You spend the night at Hosteria Cucayo, within the protected area Refugio de Vida Silvestre Pasochoa.

► ECO-TIPS

BESIDES TAKING CARE OF THE ENVIRONMENT, WHERE YOU SHOULD LEAVE ONLY MINIMAL SIGNS OF YOUR PASSAGE, REMEMBER TO RESPECT THE HORSES. TO ENJOY THE TREK, IT IS ESSENTIAL TO BE IN TUNE WITH THE ANIMALS, PERHAPS LEARNING FROM THE *CHAGRAS*.

Useful Websites
ecuador.travel/en
ambiente.gob.ec/parque-nacional-cotopaxi
ilmondoacavallo.com
inthesaddle.com
losmortinos.com
tierradelvolcan.com/es/hacienda-el-tambo

222–223 *Alpacas, raised for wool in flocks that graze at an altitude between 11,400 and 16,400 feet (3,500–5,000 m), and llamas, which are stronger, at the foot of the volcano Pasochoa.*

223 **top** *One of the rivers flowing within the Parque Nacional Cotopaxi.*

223 **bottom** *A farmer leads his livestock near Quito.*

DAY 4: Refugio de Vida Silvestre Pasochoa–Parque Nacional Cotopaxi

Today you follow the trail through the meadows where the Spanish bulls for bullfighting are grazing. They were introduced by the Jesuit priests centuries ago with the aim of preventing cattle rustling. You are in Parque Nacional Cotopaxi, which includes the volcano by the same name, the third-highest active volcano in the world. The park offers spectacular views of the *páramo*, the splendid neotropical high mountain biome. This area is home to sword-billed hummingbird and to birds of prey, such as the Andean condor. It is also the habitat of the puma, the Andean fox, and bears. Often, during a walk, you can see deer or herds of wild horses grazing in the park, and you can gallop across the vast plains. Following an ancient Inca path, you reach Hacienda Los Mortiños, where you stay the night, 1 mile (1.6 km) from the northern entrance to the park. This is a strategic area from which you can admire the four magnificent Andean peaks: the Rumiñahui, the Pasochoa, the Sincholagua, and the Cotopaxi volcanoes.

DAY 5: Parque Nacional Cotopaxi–Slopes of the Cerro Quilindaña

The itinerary for the day features a ride of about 28 miles (45 km). You cross Parque Nacional

Cotopaxi to the north, avoiding the most popular paths and venturing in the wild. Your destination is the slopes of the Cerro Quilindaña (16,000 feet [4,880 m]), a remote place where the night sky is scattered with thousands of stars and it is often possible to see the Southern Cross. Also, in this area there is a good chance to see condors, hawks, and eagles. Occasionally, you will meet a shepherd and his dog. You spend the night at Hacienda El Tambo, nestled in an unspoiled and remote corner of the Condor Bioreserve, on the eastern slopes of Cotopaxi, at 11,811 feet (3,600 m) above sea level.

DAY 6: Parque Nacional Cotopaxi–Cerro Quilindaña

Today you visit the area of Cerro Quilindaña with the *páramo* vegetation that precedes the snow-covered area with grasses, giant rosette plants, and low shrubs. You follow a circular path in the company of the *chagras*, the local horsemen. These guides illustrate their daily work,

inviting visitors to take part in their activities. Riding with the *chagras* is a great honor and a unique opportunity to fully understand their culture. You sleep at the same hacienda as the previous evening.

DAY 7: Cerro Quilindaña–Quito

This is the last day of your trek. You wake up to a spectacular view of the peaks of Cotopaxi and Quilindaña, and if you are lucky, you can see the Antisana volcano (18,875 feet [5,753 m]). On horseback you reach the foot of Cotopaxi: the view is magnificent with rocky peaks and snow-covered glaciers. In some areas you ride over layers of volcanic rock. You continue along the riverbed. The pine trees and the forests give way to wide sandy tracks and green paths, the ideal terrain for enjoying one of the last gallops of this spectacular trek. In the afternoon you reach the entrance to the park, where you leave the horses and the guides. From here you return to Quito.

Bike Itineraries

Bike traveling is a way of life. Those who have tried it hardly stop. You can go wherever you like, stop wherever you like, park wherever you like. Bikes do not pollute, and they are silent, a great workout, a cheap means of transport, suitable for everyone, and easy to use and maintain. We owe them to the creativity of Karl Drais of Karlsruhe, who conceived and presented a prototype on July 12, 1817, in Mannheim, Baden-Württemberg, in Germany. The draisine, named after its inventor, had no pedals and had to be pushed with the feet, but it laid the foundation for the birth of the modern bicycle. Today there are different types and models on the market: road, tourism, racing, mountain, snow, trekking…

The number of bike travelers is growing. Networks of cycle tracks are being created within and outside cities, and bike-friendly hotel facilities, which cater to cyclists' needs, are more and more common, as are dedicated apps to find, monitor, trace, and share information. There are also many resources online, specialist sites and web tutorials on the organization of a bike trip, the equipment, the accessories recommended, bikepacking, and so on.

So, what is all this hype about? Whether it's island hopping—moving from one island to another to see nature—cycling around a lake, crossing a land wrested from the sea, a trip to the countryside or a nature reserve, or the exploration of an ocean coast or an old railroad transformed into a trail, cycling at an average speed of 9 miles (15 km) per hour is thrilling and liberating.

Here we present several itineraries. Note that before starting your trip, you need to have a precise idea of the actual distance, the altitude, the type of road surface, and the location of accommodation. You must assess well your physical fitness, be used to sitting on a saddle, and be able to cycle on slopes and dirt roads, bearing in mind that you are carrying the extra weight of baggage. And be well equipped: it is better to take a paper map, check your position with GPS, and follow route signs and directions.

All this is to have a unique and satisfying experience. It is no accident that someone described the bicycle as humanity's noblest invention. Are you ready to leave?

225 *Autumn colors along one of the ascents of the Otago Trail. The bicycle is becoming one of the most common ways to travel, as it is economical and suitable for everyone.*

Lofoten Islands

226–227 A panoramic view of the town of Svolvaer, with the splendid mountains and the surrounding coast, from the summit of the Tjeldbergtind peak.

To be truly in touch with nature, there is no better way than visiting Norway: fjords, mountains, glaciers, and islands are scattered around one of the best European destinations for adventure tourism. Norway is one of the most advanced countries with regard to environmental protection, headed by Oslo, voted European Green Capital 2019 with ambitious aims to reduce CO_2 and other greenhouse gas emissions. Although Norway is one of the top gas and oil exporters in the world, the green economy is evident here. For example, 98% of the electricity comes from renewable sources and the rate of electric car sharing is the highest in the world.

Among its iconic destinations, the Lofoten archipelago is wonderful. The picturesque fishing villages have wooden houses painted in bright colors with drying racks for cod, a symbol and economic resource for these islands. They are surrounded by rich marine life, including the largest deep water coral reef in the world. To explore Lofoten, we recommend pedaling along the roads that wind through this archipelago, where, although you are near the Arctic Circle, the climate is mild.

Start: Svolvaer
Finish: Å
Distance: 85 mi (137 km)
Time: 5 days
Difficulty: easy/medium
Accommodation: hotel or *rorbu* (traditional fishermen's cottages, refurbished as tourist accommodation)

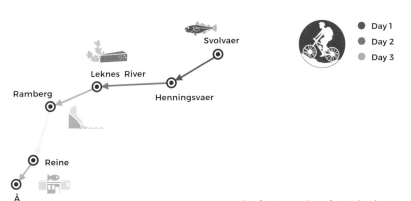

Svolvaer
Leknes River
Ramberg
Henningsvaer
Reine
Å

● Day 1
● Day 2
● Day 3
○ Day 4
● Day 5

Eco because: The Lofoten Islands are among the so-called "sustainable destinations." This is a Norwegian certification that covers the quality and sustainability of tourist destinations. Thanks to the sustainable development of companies and towns, it safeguards the environmental and cultural heritage and the well-being and economic growth of local communities.

When to go: We recommend taking the E10, the backbone of the archipelago, between May and July: the midnight sun is a unique and unforgettable experience.

How to get there: You arrive at the airport or the station of Bodø: the best way to reach Lofoten is the ferry between Bodø and Svolvaer, the starting point for any excursion on the archipelago (the crossing lasts about three and a half hours). Direct flights are available from Bodø to Svolvaer (about half an hour).

What to pack: Bicycles can be rented locally. You will need a helmet, sunglasses, mobile phone, headlamp, first-aid kit, canteen, bags for trash, plug adapters, gloves, padded cycling shorts, leg warmers, pump and puncture kit, a map, a waterproof backpack, and a compass.

DAY 1: Svolvaer–Henningsvaer

You start from Svolvaer following the E10 and reach Kabelvåg, where you find the Coastal Administration Museum and the aquarium. Here you can admire the Lofoten cod, also known as skrei: the core of the local fishing industry, it has been one of the most common fish in Europe for centuries. You pass through a tunnel and reach the junction of Rorvin, where you take road 816 for Henningsvaer. The village stands on two islands, with the traditional buildings overlooking the fjord. You stay here for the night.

DAY 2: Henningsvaer–Leknes

On the second day, you return to Rorvin and take the E10 to the bridge for the island of Vestvågøy, an oasis in the center of the archipelago, a large agricultural area where you find cheeses

ECO-TIPS

FOLLOW THE PATHS AND AVOID CREATING ANY NEW ONES. TRASH MUST ALWAYS BE DISPOSED OF IN THE DESIGNATED SITES. DURING THE RIDE, ALWAYS USE PUBLIC TOILETS AND RESPECT THE NATURAL ENVIRONMENT. FOR YOUR OWN SAFETY, BE CAREFUL WHEN CYCLING, ESPECIALLY IN THE TUNNELS AND ALONG THE NARROW ROADS. WE SUGGEST YOU ORGANIZE ALL ACTIVITIES THROUGH A LOCAL TOUR OPERATOR.

Useful Websites
visitnorway.com
lofoten.info/Visitlofoten

and herbs from the local producers. On the island you can take either the E10 to Borg (there, at Lofotr, you can visit the Viking Museum) or the less busy road 815.
Both run through beautiful landscapes. You sleep at Leknes, in the heart of Lofoten.

DAY 3: Leknes–Ramberg

The plan for today is a ride along road 818 to Ballstad, a fishing village. You return by the E10, passing through the underwater Nappstraum Tunnel to reach Napp on the island of Flakstadoya. You descend toward Vareid and follow the signs for Nusfjord, another fishing village and a very picturesque viewpoint. You return toward Flakstad, pedaling in the direction of Ramberg to reach Kvalvika Beach. In this isolated bay, you see the emerald green sea lapping the sand and the cliffs rising steeply to the sky. You spend the night at Ramberg.

DAY 4: Ramberg–Reine

From Ramberg you head south (with a small detour) to Sund and then, crossing the bridge, you reach Hamnøy, the oldest fishing village in Lofoten. It is small but incredibly beautiful. The local museums and galleries will introduce you to local culture and history. After a visit to the village, you pedal towards Reine, situated among the Norwegian fjords, another remote gem that is well-known to tourists. You stay here for the night.

DAY 5: Reine–Å

Å is the last letter of the Norwegian alphabet and the last town in Lofoten, again on the E10 (here called King Olaf V's Road). The cycle tour ends here, with a visit to the Lofoten Stockfish Museum and the Norwegian Fishing Village Museum.

228 left A cyclist pedaling toward Raftsundet.

228 right A road flanked by flower fields toward the town of Leknes, the largest center in the Lofoten Islands. Vesterålen is a good lookout point for the aurora borealis.

229 Reine is a true gem: popular with tourists, it is usually described as the most beautiful village in Norway, nestled at the foot of the mountains.

THE NETHERLANDS

Cycling Along the Northern Ring

"God created the earth, but the Dutch created the Netherlands." It is called the Netherlands, and in fact it is: almost half its land is below sea level. But humans have drained the waters and recovered farmland (the *polder*), now protected by 1,491 miles (2,400 km) of dams. This country, which is very flat, is the ideal destination for cycling: there are many traveling options within the intricate cycle network, which boasts more than 19,884 miles (32,000 km) of tracks.

The Northern Ring is an iconic itinerary in the Netherlands: windmills, *polder*, tulips and other flowers, bridges over rivers, little fairy-tale villages, and nature reserves. The trail starts and ends in Amsterdam. You cycle northward in brief stages, suitable for budding cyclists, but for those who want to add a couple more days to the itinerary, a half hour's ferry crossing links Den Helder to the island of Texel. Here you can cycle to discover the Dunes National Park and Ecomare. You can do the same from Hoorn to Marken.

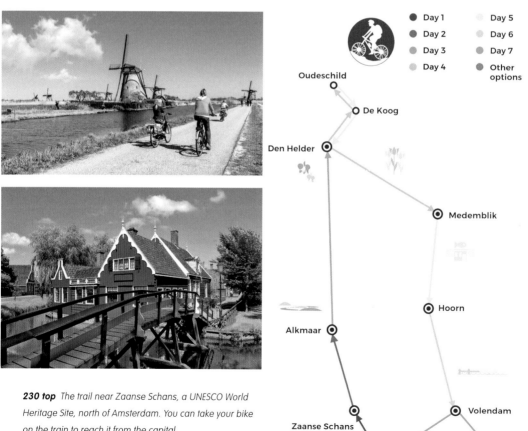

Day 1 Day 2 Day 3 Day 4 Day 5 Day 6 Day 7 Other options

Oudeschild
De Koog
Den Helder
Medemblik
Hoorn
Alkmaar
Zaanse Schans
Volendam
Marken
Amsterdam

230 top The trail near Zaanse Schans, a UNESCO World Heritage Site, north of Amsterdam. You can take your bike on the train to reach it from the capital.
230 bottom Zaanse Schans is also famous for its small wooden houses and its canals, as well as its cheese production.

Start: Amsterdam
Finish: Amsterdam
Distance: 139 mi (223 km)
Time: 7 days (with options of added stages)
Difficulty: easy
Accommodation: farms, B&Bs, hotels

230–231 Near the Zaanse Schans canal, there is the iconic countryside with tulips and mills. At one time, the locality had more than 700 mills, and ships were built and wooden clogs made in the village.

Eco because: The trail crosses flat areas where nature reigns, and it is not difficult to spot wild geese, mallards and horses, goats and grazing cows. Moreover, part of the trail is equipped with solar panels that supply clean, renewable energy!

When to go: We recommend spring, for the climate and incredible blooms.

How to get there: You land at Amsterdam international airport and you are already at the starting point of the itinerary.

What to pack: Bikes can be rented locally, also electric ones. The weather in the Netherlands is very changeable and it often rains, so it is advisable to take cycling clothing that dries quickly and waterproof shoe covers. You also need a helmet, sunglasses, mobile phone, headlamp, first-aid kit, canteen, bags for your trash, electrical adapter, gloves, padded cycling shorts, pump and puncture repair kit, map, waterproof backpack, compass, bike lock.

DAY 1: Amsterdam–Zaanse Schans

The trail begins in Amsterdam, which is worth a visit before undertaking the tour. Then you choose one among the many northbound trails to reach Zaanse Schans. For example, you can cycle through the Buikslotermeer quarter as far as junction 36, turn left, and stay on the LF7a even after junction 4. After Landsmeer and junction 20, you cycle toward Het Twiske, and after De Haal you follow the signs for Zaanse Schans. You arrive in this village on the Zaan River, which is famous for its windmills (once there were more than 700) and the typical Dutch wooden houses and buildings from the 17th century: a leap into a fairy-tale world. You spend a magical night here.

DAY 2: Zaanse Schans–Alkmaar

You cover the mile after Zaanse Schans on a cycle track paved with solar panels, Solar Road, which is able to produce clean electric power. This brief stretch linking Wormerveer and Krommenie has solar cells in crystalline silicon installed on the concrete and covered with a layer of tempered glass. You continue cycling to reach Alkmaar, well known for its cheese market, which is held in spring and summer.

ECO-TIPS

NATURE SHOULD ALWAYS BE RESPECTED: DON'T PICK, BURN, SPOIL, OR DAMAGE NATURE. WHEN YOU CYCLE, ALWAYS FOLLOW THE PATHS, WHICH ARE VERY WELL MARKED, AND AVOID CREATING NEW ONES. ALWAYS COLLECT YOUR TRASH DURING THE JOURNEY AND THEN DISPOSE OF IT IN THE ASSIGNED PLACES.

Useful Websites
holland.com/global
npduinenvantexel.nl
ecomare.nl

DAY 3: Alkmaar–Den Helder

In the morning, you leave Alkmaar to head for the North Sea. You pedal through Koedijk and continue as far as Petten on the coast, with its beautiful beaches and dunes. With the sea in the west, among shores, woods, and *polder*, you ride as far as Callanstsoog. Not far is the Het Zwanenwater nature reserve: here you can see spoonbills nesting, great white herons, and fields of orchids. Still following the beach and the dunes, you reach Den Helder, where you stop for the night.

DAY 4: Den Helder–Medemblik

You leave Den Helder along a trail across the *polder*. South of the city you find the largest area in the world dedicated to the growing of bulbs: in spring, there is an explosive blooming of tulips, hyacinths, and narcissus, which creates a waving multicolored picture. Near Van Ewijcksluis, you cycle along the banks toward Westerland, with the Amstelmeer basin on the right. You turn left toward Wieringerwerf-Zuid and then continue as far as Medemblik, where you have dinner and stay the night.

DAY 5: Medemblik–Hoorn

The next morning, you pedal toward the fishing village of Enkhuizen on the IJsselmeer. Besides the old town, you should see the open-air museum at Zuiderzee, which relates the history and culture of this unique region. The trail continues as far as Hoorn, once a very rich city: like Enkhuizen, it was part of the Dutch East India Company (the so-called VOC, Vereenigde Geoctroyeerde Oostindische Compagnie). You stop at Hoorn for the night.

DAY 6: Hoorn–Volendam

In the morning, you leave Hoorn and cycle southward along the coast, first touching Schardam, then Warden, and finally Edam, famous for its cheese. Volendam, the destination for the day, is almost 2 miles (3 km) away. It is a fishing village with the traditional wooden clogs hanging from the doors of the houses and narrow alleys between canals and drawbridges.

DAY 7: Volendam–Amsterdam

You leave Volendam along the road, in the midst of nature, to return to Amsterdam, where the tour concludes.

OPTION 1

DAY 4: Den Helder–Oudeschild (Island of Texel)–De Koog

The day begins with a half-hour ferry crossing, from Marsdiep to the port of Oudeschild, in the southwest of the island of Texel. You then get on your bike to explore the island, with De Koog as your destination, a seaside resort on the western coast with a long sandy beach on the North Sea. From here, you reach the Dunes National Park of Texel and Ecomare, with an aquarium and a museum. This detour is 11 miles (18 km) long.

DAY 5: De Koog–Oudeschild

Today you cycle among white beaches and dunes, and explore the scenic Thijsse-route in the south of the island, a track that after about

11 miles (18 km) at the end of the day leads back to Oudeschild. From here the next day you take the ferry again to return to Den Helder.

OPTION 2

DAY 7: Volendam–Marken

From Volendam you take the ferry and in half an hour you arrive in the fishing village of Marken with its traditional colorful houses: a dream. Here you stop for the night. This detour involves about 24 miles (38 km) more on a bike.

DAY 8: Marken–Amsterdam

The next morning, you leave from Marken, crossing the area of Waterland, among scattered small lakes and canals. It is 13 miles (21 km) more on a bike. Finally you reach Amsterdam, where the journey ends.

232 left The Kasteel Radboud in Medemblik dates from the 12th century. Today, it belongs to the state and it can be visited, with various reconstructions of daily life in the Middle Ages.

232 right The old town of Hoorn, the "pearl of Lake IJsselmeer," an important center of the Dutch East India Company, which became extremely rich in the 17th century.

233 left Volendam, a village and fishing port on Lake Markermeer, has a maze of narrow streets in the old quarters of Dijk and Doolhof to explore.

233 right Near Marken, which has been a peninsula since 1957, you bike along the trail crossing the "Waterland" area among its numerous small lakes and canals.

Lake Constance Cycle Path

234–235 Stein Am Rhein is a delightful town in German Switzerland on Lake Constance. It is characterized by half-timbered houses with painted facades and old churches.

235 Saint Mary's and Saint Mark's Church on the Island of Reichenau, which is famous for vegetable production and vineyards. A nature reserve is located near the island.

The Bodensee-Radweg is a well-marked bike path, 168 miles (270 km) long, around Lake Constance, the third-largest lake in Europe. The path is generally traveled clockwise, is suitable for all, and can be personalized: a pleasant and unchallenging tour, recommended for budding cyclists and families seeking a holiday on two wheels in the midst of nature.

Far from roads and traffic, this mainly level path starts from and arrives at Constance and, along the banks of the lake, passes through three countries (Germany, Austria, and Switzerland), offering an amazing variety of landscapes and panoramas. The surrounding hills are draped in vineyards and also boast typically Mediterranean glimpses, with lemon groves and gardens blooming with bougainvillea in the summer. Cyclists can rent bicycles on site.

Start: Constance
Finish: Constance
Distance: 168 mi (270 km)
Time: 6 days
Difficulty: easy/medium
Accommodation: B&Bs, hotels, guest-houses

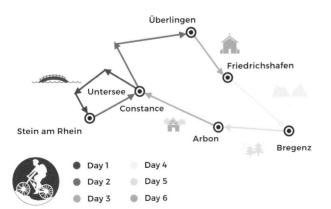

Day 1
Day 2
Day 3
Day 4
Day 5
Day 6

Überlingen
Friedrichshafen
Untersee
Constance
Stein am Rhein
Arbon
Bregenz

Eco because: The natural beauty of Lake Constance is remarkable: from the mainly intact landscapes surrounding it to the organic crops dotting the hills, to the goodness and quality of its water, drinkable for five million people.

236 There are different crops grown around Lake Constance.

237 top The pile dwellings on Lake Constance in Unteruhldingen. The open air museum is one of the oldest in Europe, and it relates the life of fishermen, farmers, and traders three thousand years ago.

237 bottom The island of Mainau has the largest butterfly house in Germany and thematic gardens, among which are a rhododendron slope, an Italian rose garden, a dahlia garden, and a hortensia path.

▶ ECO-TIPS

YOU CAN GLIDE SILENTLY OVER THE LAKE ON THE SUN-POWERED HELIO CATAMARAN: FOR MANY YEARS IT HAS WELCOMED VISITORS ABOARD, WITHOUT POLLUTING THE WATER, FOR A FIFTY-MINUTE TOUR. THE DEUTSCHE BAHN (THE GERMAN RAILWAY) IS WELL EQUIPPED AND ORGANIZED FOR THE TRANSPORT OF BIKES.

Useful Websites
germany.travel/en
bodensee.eu/en
https://www.cycling-lake-constance.com/lake-constance
https://www.bodensee.eu/en/what-to-experience/travelling-around-lake-constance/tour-suggestions/lake-constance-bike-route_touroute594

DAY 1: Constance–Stein am Rhein

The trip starts from Constance and follows a circular path around the lower lake (Untersee). In the first stage it passes through the Wollmatinger Ried nature reserve, to reach the island of Reichenau, a UNESCO World Heritage Site, linked to the mainland by a bridge. The island is famous for its monasteries and for its organic, integrated farms and vineyards, whose high quality is also due to the climate. You arrive, cycling by the Untersee, at the peninsula of Höri, where writer Hermann Hesse and painter Otto Dix lived for a time. The cycle path then runs along the Swiss bank to Stein am Rhein, a small medieval hamlet with half-timbered houses and painted facades, standing at the point where the lake flows into the Rhine.

DAY 2: Stein am Rhein–Überlingen

This stage follows the Überlinger See, the northwestern part of the Obersee (upper lake). In the morning, from Stein am Rhein, you return to Constance, pedaling toward the island of Mainau, which has splendid gardens to visit. In April, millions of flowers are in bloom: crocus, narcissus, tulips, camellias, and magnolia. The sea of colors and flowers lasts all year round. On the island, there is also the Butterfly House, with about 120 species, and the Palm House, where the most important exhibition of orchids in Europe is held. From Mainau you return to the mainland and continue toward Wallhausen, Bodman-Ludwigshafen, and Sipplingen, until you reach Überlingen, where you spend the night. The largest Gothic cathedral on Lake Constance stands here.

DAY 3: Überlingen–Friedrichshafen

From Überlingen, you cycle through picturesque vineyards to Friedrichshafen: along the way is the baroque church of Birnau, a pilgrimage destination. You reach Uhldingen, with its replica stilt houses in the lake, and Meersburg, an ancient village. You proceed through Hagnau, famous for its wine, and Immenstaad to reach the day's destination, Friedrichshafen. It was here, in the mid-20th century, that the Zeppelin airship was built, and its story is told at the Zeppelin Museum.

DAY 4: Friedrichshafen–Bregenz

Today you continue to Kressbronn, and in the morning, you reach the Bavarian town of Lindau, situated on the island of the same name and linked to the mainland by two bridges, on the border between Germany and Austria. It is an elegant, lively town with multicolored houses. Crossing the Austrian border, you arrive in Bregenz, another famous tourist destination between the mountains and the lake and an important cultural center. You stay here for the night.

DAY 5: Bregenz–Arbon

From Bregenz you cycle through an important nature reserve in the Rhine delta, between Austria and Switzerland. At Hard, you cross a bridge over the Rhine before it runs into Lake Constance. Passing the border at Gaißau you return to the Swiss bank, where at Altenrhein, artist, architect, and environmentalist Friedensreich Hundertwasser built an indoor market. Leaving the city, you visit Rorschach, Steinach, and Arbon, where the stage ends.

DAY 6: Arbon–Constance

On the last day, you reach the Romanshorn region, passing through many villages with traditional half-timbered houses. From the center of Romanshorn, which has the most important harbor on the Swiss side, you flank the lake until you reach Kreuzlingen, before crossing the Swiss-German border to Constance. Here the unforgettable bike tour ends.

When to go: The best time for this trip is in spring, when the flowers are blooming.

How to get there: The nearest airport is Zurich, then it's a one-hour train ride to Constance, which is about 43 miles (70 km) away.

What to pack: Bicycles are rented locally. We recommend using a well-equipped bicycle suited to use on the road. Cycle in the correct lane because fines are considerable. It would be useful to carry saddlebags or a backpack. It is also advisable to take a helmet, glasses, a mobile phone, a headlamp, a first-aid kit, a canteen, bags for trash, gloves, padded cycling shorts, a pump, a puncture kit, a map, and a compass.

Tauern Cycle Trail

Start: Krimml
Finish: Passau
Distance: 192 mi (310 km)
Time: 5 days (8 days if staying extra nights at any point in the journey)
Difficulty: generally easy, with some occasional difficulties
Accommodation: bike hotels

Set in the heart of Europe, Austria is rich in traditions, artistic and historical testimonies to imperial glory, baroque cities, and Alpine landscapes. To preserve its natural heritage, the country encourages sustainability through environmentally friendly tourist structures, campsites that use renewable energy, and biological hotels and spas that adopt energy-saving strategies. Citizens and tourists are made aware of and encouraged to use public transport, leaving their cars in parking lots, which are often underground, but, above all, to move around on a bicycle. In fact, Austria attracts cyclists from all over the world not merely thanks to its splendid landscapes and the more or less challenging cycle routes and the hospitality of its people, but also thanks to its infrastructures designed to respect nature.

The Tauern Cycle Trail (Tauernradweg) begins at the Krimml Waterfalls and ends in Passau (the city of three rivers) in Germany, where it meets with the Danube Cycle Path. It is one of the most spectacular cycle paths in Europe, encountering parks, gorges, waterfalls, villages, and the beautiful town of Salzburg along its way. It is an easy route with only a few gentle hills.

238 *Tourists cycling on the road to Krimml: a light backpack and a helmet are indispensable for this adventure on two wheels.*

239 *The Krimml Waterfalls in the intermediate phase in the Pinzgau mountains: they are the highest in central Europe, at 1,240 feet (380 m).*

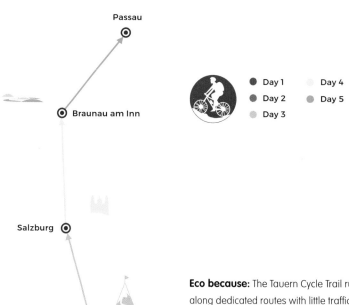

Passau

Braunau am Inn

Day 1   Day 4
Day 2   Day 5
Day 3

Salzburg

Bischofshofen

Zell am See

Krimml Waterfalls

Eco because: The Tauern Cycle Trail runs along dedicated routes with little traffic, often surrounded by woods and valleys, a true paradise for lovers of sustainable tourism. Cyclists pedal through an unspoiled environment, enjoying environmentally sustainable tourism with zero impact on the land.

DAY 1: Krimml–Kaprun (Zell am See)

The starting point is the Krimml Waterfalls in the Hohe Tauern National Park in the Salzburg region. These are the highest waterfalls in Austria, and their power is inspiring. Nearby, in the Kitzbühel Alps, is the source of the Salzach River, which will accompany cyclists all the way to Salzburg. From Krimml you cycle toward Vorderkrimml and then follow the railway to Rosental, a small village from which you can admire the glaciers on the peak of the Großvenediger. You go on until you reach the Untersulzbachfall waterfall, passing through the Obersulzbachtal valley with its scenic pastures. After Neukirchen am Großvenediger, you reach Bramberg am Wildkogel, home to a museum of local culture. The trail touches on a number

When to go: The best time is between May and October, when nature is waking up and reaches its utmost splendor. Also, the weather is generally good at this time of the year.

How to get there: Innsbruck and its airport are the destination for those wishing to reach Krimml, which is 62 miles (100 km) away. Alternatively, it is possible to take a train from Innsbruck to Aschau Im Zillertal and continue by car for about 28 miles (45 km) to Krimml.

What to pack: Cycle helmet (cyclists under the age of 12 must wear a helmet at all times) and panniers, sunglasses, headlamp, first-aid kit, canteen, gloves, padded cycling shorts, bathing suit, reflective vest (useful in tunnels and after dark), legwarmers, bicycle pump, puncture kit, waterproof backpack, map, compass. Comfortable and waterproof clothing.

of interesting localities, including Mühlbach, Dorf, Hollersbach im Pinzgau, Mittersill, and Uttendorf. When you reach the Zell am See lake, the town of Kaprun is the ideal place to stay overnight. Here it is possible to follow the bike path around the lake or to swim in its refreshing waters.

240–241 Lake Zell, around which there is a bike trail. In winter it ices over and winter sports take place, while in summer boat races are held.
241 top A hairpin bend descending toward Lake Zell: the water quality, which is continuously monitored, is as good as that of drinking water, as in other Austrian lakes.
241 bottom Another beautiful view of the lake, early in the morning. The little town of Zell am See, from which the lake takes its name, is a well-known health resort.

DAY 2: Kaprun (Zell am See)–Bischofshofen

The following day, you pedal from Zell am See to the village of Bruck, where a trail leads up to the Glockner Mountain, the highest peak in Austria. Passing through Niederhof, St. Georgen, and Pülzl, you come to Taxenbach. Following the Salzach River to Lend, you head toward Schwarzach im Pongau. From here you continue toward St. Johann im Pongau, where it is possible to visit the Liechtensteinklamm gorge. This leg of your journey ends in Bischofshofen, a town well known for summer and winter sports.

DAY 3: Bischofshofen–Salzburg

On the third day, the trail leaves Bischofshofen and takes you north to Werfen, a historical town with an imposing fortress built in the 11th century, where falconry events are often organized. Continuing along the trail, you pass through Tenneck, where

ECO-TIPS

KEEN CYCLISTS CAN RELY ON THE VAST NETWORK OF HOTELS AND ACCOMMODATION DISPLAYING THE "BETT & BIKE" SIGN (BIKE-FRIENDLY ACCOMMODATION). WHEN TRAVELING, IT IS NECESSARY TO CARRY BAGS FOR TRASH AND TO AVOID ABANDONING ANYTHING ALONG THE WAY. FOR RESPECT AND SAFETY, IN AUSTRIA IT IS FORBIDDEN TO CYCLE ON THE SIDEWALK.

Useful Websites
www.tauernradweg.at
www.austria.info/en
www.nationalpark.at/en
www.europareservat.de
www.bettundbike.de

the gorges of the Salzach River form. In the area, it is possible to visit the Eisriesenwelt, a great ice cave that runs for more than 26 miles (42 km), one of the most important underground networks in the world. To reach it, you must take the cable car. From Tenneck, you descend toward Golling: here it is possible to make an excursion to the Bluntautal valley or the Gollinger Wasserfall. The next stop is Hallein, of Celtic origin and famous for the extraction of rock salt. The salt mine is now a museum and visits are made more entertaining by using the slides from one floor to the other.

Then you leave for Salzburg. The city where Mozart was born is now a UNESCO World Heritage Site, and for those who wish to stay here a couple of days, it is well worth a visit.

DAY 4: Salzburg–Braunau am Inn

From Salzburg you travel north following the Salzach River,

which flows into the Inn River: the two rivers form the border with Germany. Following the trail, you reach Oberndorf and then continue to the Gothic city of Braunau am Inn, on the border with the Europareservat Unterer Inn (Lower Inn European Nature Reserve), one of the largest fluvial conservation areas in Europe, which can be explored by bike. Here you can see beavers, migratory birds, and various species of eagle, including the sea eagle.

DAY 5: Braunau am Inn–Passau

The following morning, you pass by the baroque town of Schärding, which, with Braunau and Hallein, is one of the "small historical towns" subject to particular conservation criteria that make a visit to them truly special. Then you cross the border with Germany at Passau, the city of three rivers: the Danube, the Inn, and the Ilz. This is where the Tauern Cycle Trail ends.

242 top and 242 bottom left The Gollinger Wasserfall (sometimes called Schwarzbachfall) are among the most beautiful in Austria. They are situated at Golling in the Salzburg region.

242 bottom right A cyclist travels along the river bike trail at Passau, the final destination of your cycling tour.

243 A small, abandoned wooden water mill above the Gollinger falls.

FRANCE

From Nantes to La Rochelle

From Brittany to the Basque coast, along the Atlantic coast, the Vélodyssée is an invigorating cycle trek through beautiful, unspoiled landscapes. The route follows the national scheme for bike trails and greenways: it is part of the European cycle network, EuroVelo, one of the 15 cycle circuits linking the European countries into a single network. It is the longest bike trail in France and has brought together local authorities and tourist boards in an ambitious project of collaboration to promote sustainable transport.

From Roscoff (on the English Channel) to Handaye-Olage (on the Spanish border), cycle tourists are spoiled for choice: they can cover the whole route in about 38 stages, a total of 745 miles (1,200 km), or only do part.

Among the various sections of the route, the one linking Nantes and La Rochelle is particularly interesting for its landscape and nature. As you cycle southward, you will experience sandy coves, jagged coasts, little seaside resorts, marshy areas, woods, salt flats, fishing villages, and oyster farms.

244 top The sun sets over the port, the beach, and the brightly colored houses of Paimbœuf in France.
244 bottom The "Route bleue" crosses the bridge over the Loire, linking Saint-Nazaire on the north bank to Saint-Brevin-les-Pins on the south bank.

- Day 1
- Day 2
- Day 3
- Day 4
- Day 5
- Day 6
- Day 7
- Day 8
- Day 9
- Day 10

Start: Nantes
Finish: La Rochelle
Distance: 222 mi (358 km)
Time: 10 days
Difficulty: easy/medium
Accommodation: hotels, campsites, cottages, B&Bs, youth hostels for cyclists

244–245 *Panoramic aerial view of Nantes, on the banks of the Loire, a city at the same time elegant and lively, also described as the "Venice of the West" because of its canals and islands.*

Eco because: The proposed tour is ideal for those who prefer a sustainable, zero-impact trip. The itinerary is part of the Vélodyssée, France's longest cycling path; an unspoiled, vibrant route that runs along the Atlantic. Seventy percent of the itinerary is on traffic-free routes and on greenways, attesting to the eco-sustainability of the project.

When to go: The temperatures are mild all year round; it rains more often in winter.

How to get there: You arrive at Nantes airport or railroad station, from where the cycle route begins.

What to pack: Helmet, cycling glasses, mobile phone, headlamp, first-aid kit, canteen, bags for trash, cycling gloves, padded cycling shorts, raincoat, pump and puncture kit, map, waterproof backpack, compass. Comfortable clothing for free time, light or heavy according to the season.

DAY 1: Nantes–Le Pellerin

Before you get on your bike, we recommend a visit to Nantes, the starting point of the tour. Be very careful when cycling in the city: the traffic is heavy and the signage for the bike trail is not easy to see. You follow the EuroVelo1 signs until you enter the trail: this stretch is shared with the Loire à Vélo cycle path and flanked by works of contemporary art. You arrive in Le Pellerin, on the bank of the Loire, and you stay the night.

DAY 2: Le Pellerin–Saint-Brevin-les-Pins

This section crosses a coastal area comprising the last stretch of the Loire, marshes, farmed fields, and the Martinière canal. You pedal a little further to arrive in Paimboeuf, a port town once

popular with artists. This is the last section of the Loire à Vélo and a new beginning along the ocean for the Vélodyssée, with tides ever present. You arrive at the Loire estuary, immersed in a new maritime atmosphere. You stop for the night at Saint-Brevin-les-Pins, the starting point for EuroVelo 6 toward the Black Sea.

DAY 3: Saint-Brevin-les-Pins–Pornic

In this stage, you cycle only a few miles from the vast sandy beaches, flanked by the pines of Saint-Brevin, as far as the fascinating coves of Pornic, dotted with fish farms. Pornic is a seaside resort with a 14th-century castle and a maze of streets and alleys in the old town. Be careful: in summer traffic can be heavy.

Day 4: Pornic–Bouin

The last stage in the Atlantic Loire region begins at Pornic. At La Bernerie-en-Retz, you can try fishing from the water's edge,

a strong local custom. As you approach Les Moutiers-en-Retz, you can see beaches divided up by wooden poles. A sea of fish farms marks the landscape. The bike trail moves further into the Bay of Bourgneuf. This is the land of the oyster, as you can see from the many oyster farms. You stop for the night at Bouin, a little further on.

Day 5: Bouin–La Barre-de-Monts/Fromentine

This last stage in the Bay of Bourgneuf leads to Port-du-Bec, also called "Chinese port" because of its numerous piers and pontoons with wooden poles evoking an Asiatic country. You spend the night on a campsite with bungalows near La Barre-de-Monts/Fromentine.

Day 6: La Barre-de-Monts/Fromentine–Saint-Gilles-Croix-de-Vie

You pedal further on the bike trail, which goes through the forest of Pays de Monts for 11 miles (18 km), then leads to the dunes and finally to the vast beach of Saint-Jean-de-Monts, on the Atlantic Ocean. The trail arrives at Saint-Gilles-Croix-de-Vie before reaching the Bay of Vendée and its famous rocks at Sion-sur-l'Océan. Here you stop for the night.

DAY 7: Saint-Gilles-Croix-de-Vie–Les Sables-d'Olonne

Saint-Gilles-Croix-de-Vie, famous for its bluefish, sardines, and mackerel, is also a renowned seaside resort with the Grande Plage beach, where you can pause and take a walk. The trail then continues toward Brétignolles-sur-Mer and Brem-sur-Mer. It winds along the Avocette road through the Olonne forest and the ancient salt flats stretching between Brem, the island of Olonne, Olonne-sur-Mer, and Les Sables-d'Olonne, a world-famous sailing resort and your destination for this stage.

246 left *Fishermen's stilt houses in Pornic. The seaside resort is popular for its beaches and biking and trekking trails; the view alternates between ocean and woodland scenery.*
246 right *The coast between Brétignolles-sur-Mer and Saint-Gilles-Croix-de-Vie. Behind the beaches of Brétignolles-sur-Mer, which offer sports like surfing, sailing, and kitesurfing, there is quiet green countryside.*
247 *Walks and bike tracks among the saltwater marshes in Olonne-sur-Mer.*

DAY 8: Les Sables-d'Olonne–La Tranche-sur-Mer

From Les Sables-d'Olonne you move southward. We recommend a stop at the Payré estuary; after walking on the salt flats, you can enjoy oysters in the ports of Illaude and La Guittière. After Saint-Vincent, the Vélodyssée goes through the great national forest of Longeville-sur-Mer, touching the sea in two places, where you can easily access splendid beaches, like Les Conches (a plunge here is unmissable). You stop at La Tranche-sur-Mer for the night.

DAY 9: La Tranche-sur-Mer–Marans

This stage of the Vélodyssée crosses the lagoon at La Belle-Henriette, which is separated from the sea by a narrow band of sand, and then La Faute-sur-Mer, which extends toward the

point of Arçay. The route then heads for Saint-Michel-en-l'Herm through the Parc Naturel Régional du marais Poitevin, a great stretch of marshes and crops studded with farms and stables. These 247,105 acres (100,000 ha) of exceptional biodiversity have a maze of canals, in which centuries-old trees and European otters share an ecosystem with no less than 250 species of birds, 38 species of fish, 60 species of dragonflies, 80 species of butterflies, and 126 species of plants unique to this area. Crossing the Sèvre Niortaise River at Pont du Brault, you proceed along the Marans canal. Marans, capital of the dry marshes, was once a very important lookout point. You can visit it before dinner.

TO BE CLOSER TO NATURE, YOU CAN SLEEP IN A *PÊCHERIE PERCHÉE* (ONE OF THE OLD STILT HOUSES FROM WHICH PEOPLE FISHED WITH ROD AND LINE, WHICH ARE NOW SMALL WOODEN TREE HOUSES) OR IN A *CABADIENNE*, A "WOODEN PUP TENT" IN THE FOREST.

Useful Websites
us.france.fr/en
cycling-lavelodyssee.com

DAY 10: Marans–La Rochelle

After Marans, you follow a greenway for pedestrians and cyclists along the canal linking Marans to La Rochelle (an exception is a small crossroad section at Dompierre-sur-Mer). The bike trail enable you to reach easily the old ocean port of La Rochelle, where your route ends. Be sure to visit the Old Port in La Rochelle; it's the pride of the city. The streets of the old city are lined with renaissance dwellings and antique half-timbered houses, making it the perfect way to end the tour.

248–249 The port of Pornic and the castle. Built in the 13th century, today it is a center of art and culture, organizing theatrical performances and exhibitions throughout the year.
249 top The Marais Poitevin, between Charente-Maritime and the Vendée, alternates between sandy beaches, dunes, woods, cliffs, and Venise Verte (Green Venice). You can discover it on foot, on a bike, in a boat, or in a canoe.
249 bottom La Rochelle belongs to the Charente-Maritime, which enjoys an exceptional microclimate. Its seaside resorts are very popular, thanks to its beaches of fine sand and its coves.

SPAIN

Start: Pedralba
Finish: Siete Aguas
Distance: 25 mi (40 km)
Time: 2 days
Difficulty: medium
Accommodation: hotels

250–251 The mountain village of Chulilla from the Mirador de la Cruz. It is a very popular destination internationally, as well as among rock climbers.

Eco because: This itinerary enables you to discover the biodiversity and beauty of the natural heritage, the villages, the places, the traditions, and the people who are part of them.

Camino Natural Turia–Siete Aguas

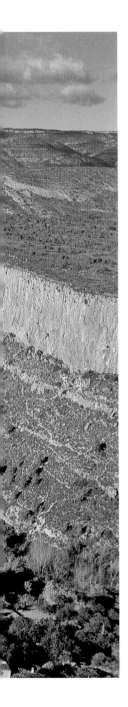

Spain is a multifaceted country. Prehistoric settlements, the Roman and Islamic presences, the golden age of the empire and the colonies are an impressive heritage that attracts many travelers. In the country with the largest number of UNESCO biosphere reserves, the Ministry of Agriculture, Fishing and Food has launched the "Camino Natural" project, the objective of which is to promote and improve the existing trekking paths. Such an improvement, in fact, contributes to the sustainable development of rural areas by reusing old abandoned transport infrastructure, cattle paths, railways, trails, and traditional routes, or opening new roads.

The Camino Natural Turia–Siete Aguas, in the province of Valencia, is the first section of the Turia-Cabriel trail. It crosses four protected natural areas—one of them is a UNESCO World Heritage site, part of the category Rock Art of the Mediterranean Basin on the Iberian Peninsula. The path has a few difficult sections, where you must get off your bike and walk. The region has an irrigation system created in ancient times that is still working and enhances the flourishing citrus production and a verdant landscape.

The trail is scented and sunny, with spectacular views in every direction. It starts from the orange groves of Turia, crosses the mountains, and ends among olive groves and vineyards.

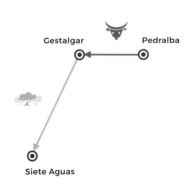

Gestalgar   Pedralba

Siete Aguas

● Day 1
● Day 2

251 *A street in Chulilla. In the background are the crags famous for rock climbing.*

When to go: The trail can be covered all year round, but it is better to avoid July and August, when the heat is oppressive and the route is crowded.

How to get there: The nearest airport is Valencia. To reach Pedralba, about 25 miles (40 km) away, take a car or a taxi.

What to pack: You can rent bikes locally. You need a helmet, cycling glasses, a mobile phone, headlamp, first-aid kit, a canteen, food, bags for your trash, gloves, padded cycling shorts, leg-warmers, a pump and puncture kit, map, waterproof backpack, compass, bike lock.

DAY 1: Pedralba–Gestalgar

This biking itinerary begins on the edge of the city of Pedralba, within the Parque Natural del Turia. The path winds along a paved road among orange and tangerine groves, in an area once dedicated to agriculture that has now become residential. You cross the Barranco de Chiva and the Cordel de Castilla, a trail used for the transhumance of cattle, passing grazing areas. Then pavement turns into dirt, and you arrive in the Special Protection Area for the birds of the Alto Turia and Sierra del Negrete. You continue as far as La Muela rest area: from here on, ups and downs will put your muscles and breath to the test. As you continue, you see a well-preserved cistern, once a watering place for cattle and horses. Shortly afterward, you find the Corral de la

ECO-TIPS

DON'T FORGET TO LEAVE THE TERRITORY EXACTLY AS YOU FOUND IT. THIS IS THE APPEAL THAT THE SPANISH MINISTRY OF AGRICULTURE, FISHERIES AND FOOD (MAPA) MAKES TO ALL EXCURSIONISTS WHO VISIT. PRESERVING THESE ROUTES AND THE LANDSCAPES THEY TRAVEL THROUGH DEPENDS IN PART ON THE RESPONSIBLE BEHAVIOR OF TOURISTS.

Useful Websites
spain.info/en
parcdelturia.es/actividades/camino-natural-turia-cabriel

Balsa, a former shelter for cattle, and you reach the crossing with the Colada de Cheste in Chulilla: it is a transhumance way for short journeys between the pastures of Serranía de Cuenca and Sierra de Javalambre and the mountain chains of the Valencia coast, a wintering area. At this point, you make a detour of 361 feet (110 m), which takes you to another shelter, the Corral de los Calzones, which is used for the night when work in the fields does not allow enough time to return home. The view on clear days takes in Valencia and the Mediterranean Sea. After an upward path, you come across a building of the hunting society, while shortly afterward you cross the Colada de Bugarra, the cattle way linking Cheste and Chulilla. About 6 miles (10 km) later, you take a path crossing a small area teeming with young Aleppo pines.

Then you reach a few houses surrounded by fields and later the intersection of the Camino Natural and the CV-379 road. This stretch is hard for cyclists. You ride carefully until you meet a group of country houses with vineyards and olive groves. A little further you find the Corral del Carnicero, an old building that maintains its role of cattle raising thanks to many restorations. You continue to a rest area at Alto de Cazoleta. The technical difficulty of this stretch is greater than in the previous stretch, and we recommend you proceed on foot. The steep ups and downs end in a rest area with stupendous views. The route crosses the Vereda Real de Gestalgar in Godelleta, a sheep way connecting the Cordel del Mas del Pinar with the coastal mountains. You then arrive at the Microrreserva Umbría de las Carrasquillas, from which the Camino Natural descends as far as Gestalgar, where you stay for the night.

DAY 2: Gestalgar–Siete Aguas

Halfway between the towns of Gestalgar and Chulilla, the route crosses a sheep way, the Vereda de Chiva in Chulilla. Here the vegetation is dominated by oak forests and rosemary undergrowth. The infrastructure for cattle farming is constant along all the Camino Natural, such as the Corral de Medineta, which is now used as accommodation. Here you see vineyards and olive and almond groves. You then enter the Parque Natural Municipal de la Sierra de Chiva, where the trail runs for several miles. Near the boundary between the towns of Chiva and Siete Aguas, there is another rest area, with tall pines creating pleasant shade,

which is very rare on this route. Afterward, the path crosses Tejera Azagador, another cattle way. You pedal on for less than a mile, with detours on the right and left. The first, after covering just over 1,148 feet (350 m), leads to a hydraulic construction called a cenia, a wheel on a river that is moved by the current to draw water for irrigation. The second detour leads after 656 feet (200 m) to the recreational area of La Vallesa, where a poplar wood and a fountain that gives its name to the place precede a space with stone and wooden tables, bike stands, and barbecues: the place is designed to enable cyclists and hikers to regain their strength in pleasant shade.

On the way back to the Camino Natural, you reach a third path, 2 miles (3 km) long, which delves into an oak wood. This is not a bike trail: cyclists have to use a paved track from the recreational area of La Vallesa to near Siete Aguas, enabling them to rejoin the trail. At mile 23 (km 37) you find a splendid Aleppo pine, from which the descent begins: after Peña Rubia the Camino Natural is a wide dirt road toward Siete Aguas, preceded by the springs of Gota, Roca, and Garbanzo. The traveler enters the town center along the Fuente de la Gota avenue: here the first section of the Turia-Cabriel path ends, near the spring of Siete Chorros.

252 left The suspension bridge over the Turia River. The river has dug a deep gorge with vertical walls through the limestone, creating a spectacular canyon.
252 right Orange and almond groves are a constant feature of the landscape on this bike tour.
253 A cyclist among fields of poppies. The trail has some difficult stretches where it is necessary to push your bike.

 **CROATIA**

Parenzana Bike Route

Start: Muggia
Finish: Poreč
Distance: 76 mi (123 km)
Time: 3 days
Difficulty: medium
Accommodation: hotel and Bike & Bed

254 top *The Salt Works of the Sečovlje Nature Park, the northernmost ones in the Mediterranean. The park's purpose is to preserve the local biodiversity.*
254 bottom *Sign of the Parenzana trekking and biking path. The trail starts in Italy and its longest stretch, through varied and very attractive scenery, crosses Slovenia and Croatia.*
255 *Mountain biker riding along the Parenzana. The trail begins by following the narrow gauge railroad.*

Nestled on the eastern coast of the Adriatic Sea with numerous islands and islets, inland Croatia abounds in vineyards, woodlands, national parks, and picturesque small towns. Often known and appreciated for its seaside resorts, which are undoubtedly blessed with enchanting coastlines and crystal-clear waters, the country also offers hidden artistic treasures and delicious food and wine.

In terms of eco-sustainable tourism, it offers the tempting option of the Parenzana, a bike route that crosses three countries (Italy for 8 miles [13 km], Slovenia for 20 miles [32 km], and Croatia for 48 miles [45 km]), passing along the coasts and through the hills and the woodlands. The landscapes were once admired from the windows of the train that ran along the narrow gauge railway commissioned by Emperor Franz Joseph I of Austria in 1902. The railway line was a major engineering feat that linked the city of Trieste with Poreč in Croatia, a feather in the cap of the Austro-Hungarian Empire. It had fifteen stations and was decommissioned in 1935. After various vicissitudes in the early 21st century, it was transformed into a bike trail.

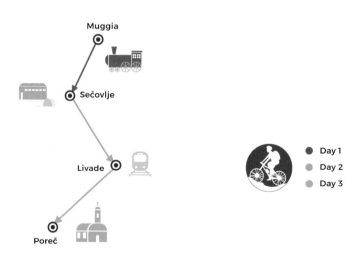

Muggia

Sečovlje

Livade

Poreč

- Day 1
- Day 2
- Day 3

Eco because: The social reuse of a decommissioned but not abandoned railway that links three countries is an excellent way to promote slow tourism, respecting the resources and territories it passes through. Safeguarding the heritage, both natural and man-made, starting with the refurbishment of abandoned or disused structures, is a mark of sustainable and responsible tourism.

SINCE THE TRAIL RUNS THROUGH THE
COUNTRYSIDE, IT IS ESSENTIAL TO AVOID
FRIGHTENING THE ANIMALS AND THE
WILDLIFE, AND DISTURBING GRAZING
ANIMALS WITH SUDDEN MOVEMENTS OR
LOUD NOISES. CYCLISTS SHOULD ENSURE
MINIMAL ENVIRONMENTAL IMPACT,
LEAVING NO TRACE OF THEIR PASSAGE
AND NEVER CREATING NEW PATHS OR
SHORTCUTS, OR CUTTING CORNERS.

Useful Websites

www.istria-bike.com/en/information/parenzana_route

https://muggia.green/en/parenzana-biking-on-the-old-railway-trail/

https://www.cicerone.co.uk/pedalling-the-parenzana-a-long-distance-cycle-route-in-croatia-slovenia-and-italy

DAY 1: Muggia–Sečovlje

The bike path starts in Muggia, near Trieste, and runs along the Rio Ospo to enter Rabuiese. After a short climb, the trail takes the route of the old railway track. Once you cross the border with Slovenia, you continue up a gentle slope to Škofije. Following the D8 and passing through woodland, you reach Dekani, with its well-preserved station. All around are countryside and vineyards. After the Rižana River, you come to the more urban section, which crosses the Škocjan Zatok Nature Reserve (an estuarine-marshy biotope and a national nature reserve) and arrive at the port city of Koper. From here you pedal to Izola on the promenade and then turn inland. After passing through the first tunnel in Saleto, you pass between the small gardens and olive groves of Strunjan until you reach the longest tunnel on the route, under Mount Luzzan. At the mouth of the tunnel, there is a splendid glimpse of the sea: you overlook the spa town of Portorož on the Gulf of Piran. The trail runs along the coastline to the salt marshes of Sečovlje, where you stop for the night.

DAY 2: Sečovlje–Livade

The trail runs through the salt farms flanked by the little houses of the workers, who still mine salt in the traditional manner. Between May and June, many species of birds nest here. You continue through the countryside to the Slovenia-Croatia border, after which you follow the yellow signs with the logo of the Parenzana trail. Riding alongside the road to Salvudrija and Umag, you reach the junction with the highway and take a short section on the road before rejoining the railway, which leads to the hamlet of Kaldanija. Here you again dive into woodland and fields until you reach Buje. Leaving the town on the right and passing the old station, you again follow the dirt road to Grožnjan, known as the "town of artists," which is worth a visit. You now descend toward the valley of the Mirna River, pass Biloslavo, and take the Kalcini Tunnel to the junction with the white road that climbs toward Završje. You continue to descend along viaducts and through tunnels to reach a clearing in the woods, where the station of Oprtalj once stood. The cycle path continues to descend in wide curves between woodland and clearings. Finally, you arrive in Livade, the city of truffles, with its perfectly preserved station. At the end of the dirt road, you emerge among houses. Here stands the Parenzana museum.

DAY 3: Livade–Poreč

In the morning you take the road across the bridge over the Mirna River to the foot of the hill on which the village of Motovun stands; it is well worth a visit and will repay the tiring climb to reach it. Leaving Motovun behind you, you enter a long stretch in the woods. There are splendid views of the Mirna River valley and the highland of Buje on the other side of the river. After a few miles, you reach Vižinada, teeming with olive groves and farmed fields, then you proceed across the red soil of the plateau that slopes gently toward the sea.

After the hamlet of Baldaši you return to the robinia woods and the countryside until you reach one of the last historical stations, that of Višnjan. Further on is Nova Vas with the Baredine caves, which are open to visitors, where an endemic amphibian, the *Proteus anguinus*, lives. The trail again crosses the road and a stretch of woodland and joins the paved road. After a few miles, you reach Poreč, where a visit to the early Byzantine Euphrasian basilica, a UNESCO World Heritage Site, is a must. Near the historical center of the town and a few feet from the coast, is the last station of the Parenzana trail.

TRAVEL TIPS

When to go: May and June, September and October are the best months: it is not too hot and there are not many tourists around.

How to get there: The airport and the station of Trieste are respectively about 34 miles (55 km) and 9 miles (15 km) from Muggia.

What to pack: Make sure your bike is outfitted with lights, since the trail runs throughout unlit tunnels. You will need a helmet, sunglasses, a headlamp, first-aid kit, canteen, bags for trash, gloves, padded cycling shorts, leg warmers, a pump and puncture kit, a waterproof backpack, and a compass.

256 *Every year, in Grožnjan, there are workshops for artistic education, dance, acting, and pacifist activism directed by renowned international experts.*

257 top *The Kotli falls with an old water mill on the Mirna River. It is augmented by the snow thawing on Učka and in Ćićarija or after the autumn rains.*

257 bottom *The Adriatic coast of Slovenia is your traveling companion. You breathe deeply in an incredibly beautiful landscape.*

Great Marsh

Start: Newburyport
Finish: Newburyport
Distance: 84 mi (136 km)
Time: 3 days
Difficulty: easy
Accommodation: hotels

Massachusetts has a lengthy tradition of government measures aimed at preserving the environment. Along the roads you encounter solar panels and wind turbines, tangible proof of the use of renewable energy sources. Hotels and restaurants are making considerable effort to reduce the consumption of energy and water, limit the production of waste, and provide a healthy environment for guests and employees. In the restaurant sector, local farmers and growers are involved in the production of delicious "zero miles" food. The Natural Resources Defense Council (NRDC) has recently nominated Boston the greenest city on the East Coast. The availability of public and private transport for car-free travelers within Boston and in many other areas of the state is also good, and there are plenty of easy bike paths.

The itinerary we suggest here is in the Great Marsh area, a saltwater marsh in New England that extends from Cape Ann in the northeast of Massachusetts to the southwestern coast of New Hampshire. It is an internationally important reserve and contributes to the preservation of many nesting and migrating birds. This unique complex of natural ecosystems adds ecological, economic, recreational, and cultural value to the daily life on the coast and inland.

258 The architecture of the old town of Newburyport, which was once an important trading port and center for silver working, has not changed much in 200 years.
259 The Plum Island Lighthouse, the only one remaining on the island, marks the narrow entrance of the mouth of the Merrimack River.

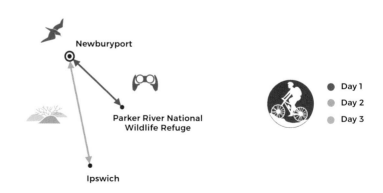

Newburyport

Parker River National
Wildlife Refuge

Ipswich

● Day 1
● Day 2
● Day 3

Eco because: It is an easy bike tour through diverse habitats: beaches, dunes, mudflats, salt flats, and coastal forests. You can do some bird watching in the Parker River National Wildlife Refuge, which has more than 300 species of birds, and there are also mammals, reptiles, amphibians, insects, and rare plants.

When to go: We recommend springtime, when you can see the return of the songbirds and the flowering of native azaleas and rhododendrons. Autumn is also an excellent time, with a fall foliage among the most spectacular in the world.

How to get there: The nearest international airport is Boston, then you reach Newburyport in about two hours by train.

What to pack: Bicycles can be rented locally. Bring a helmet, canteen, sunglasses, mobile phone and an adapter for recharging, headlamp. A first-aid kit, bags for trash. Padded cycling shorts, gloves, legwarmers, pump and puncture kit, maps, waterproof backpack, and a compass.

ECO-TIPS

ACCESS TO MOST OF THE BEACHES IS NOT ALLOWED DURING THE SUMMER NESTING SEASON, SO WE RECOMMEND CHECKING BEFORE PLANNING A VISIT. FOR YOUR STAY, CHOOSE HOTELS AND RESTAURANTS THAT ORGANIZE PROGRAMS IN FAVOR OF THE ENVIRONMENT.

Useful Websites
massvacation.com
/greatmarsh.org/
www.fws.gov/refuge/parker_river

DAY 1: Newburyport–Parker River National Wildlife Refuge–Newburyport

In the morning you set out from Newburyport and pedal toward the reserve of Joppa Flats: the first stop is Plum Island, named after the wild plum trees that grow on the beach. This barrier island is on a migratory route for many birds and is a busy nesting site. It has an excellent reputation among birdwatchers and environmentalists, with many observation points equipped with binoculars and video cameras. You then cross the marsh and the salt flats, and in the southern part of the island you enter the Parker River National Wildlife Refuge. Home to many hundreds of species of birds, plants, and animals, a visit to the refuge is definitely recommended to cyclists, nature lovers, and anyone looking for peace and quiet. You can hear the song of the American redstart, the summer tanager, and the green tanager, and at times you can see seal pups lying on the beach. It is a good idea to cross this island on the walkways through the marshes, the sand dunes, the black pines, and the woolly beachheather. You return to Newburyport to explore the town before dinner and your stay for the night.

DAY 2: Newburyport–Ipswich–Newburyport

After breakfast, you pedal inland, passing a number of historical farms along the road. Your destination is Castle Neck, a vast ecosystem of 1,200 acres (486 ha) of dunes and beach, with splendid views of the bays of Ipswich and Essex. The trail crosses the dunes covered in woolly beachheather and runs through the coastal forests, allowing glimpses of deer and foxes. You arrive at Crane Beach, one of the most beautiful beaches on the East Coast, and continue until you reach Castle Hill, declared a national historical monument in 1998. This former summer residence of Mr. and Mrs. Richard T. Crane comprises a historical building, twenty-one outbuildings, and landscaped grounds with views over Ipswich Bay. You continue along the road for Ipswich. Along the way you can stop at a winery, a farm, or an orchard to buy local products. The town of Ipswich has a considerable number of historical houses. In the evening you return to Newburyport.

DAY 3: Newburyport

You continue exploring the area around Newburyport, cycling through meadows that are home to the largest population of bobolinks and starlings in New England. You pedal carefree along the bucolic roads beside ponds and small farms, where horses, cattle, and llamas are grazing, enjoying this last day on your bike in this corner of paradise.

260 top Cycling through high dunes and the beaches on the edge of the Atlantic Ocean, in the midst of unspoiled and protected nature, is in itself an advantage for relaxation and well-being.

260 bottom The area has more than 6.2 miles (10 km) of sandy beaches, about 3.7 acres (1.5 ha) of water meadows, dunes, and a concentration of avian species for the joy of birdwatchers.

261 Bikes are hired locally, but it is important to check before planning the trip whether access to the beaches is permitted to visitors or if it is the summer nesting season.

NEW ZEALAND

Otago Central Rail Trail

Start: Clyde
Finish: Middlemarch
Distance: 94 mi (152 km)
Time: 3 days
Difficulty: medium/difficult
Accommodation: gangers sheds (used for shelter)

New Zealand is a welcoming, green land, where unspoiled nature still survives. The land is carefully watched over by government institutions. There are as many as 13 national parks, which cover an area of 9,653 square miles (25,000 sq km), which are distributed over the wilder South Island. The Department of Conservation, the national body that manages the country's environmental heritage, also administers more than 3,000 nature reserves and 21 marine reserves. Overall, protected areas make up over 20% of the land, a sign of a very well-developed environmental culture.

Visiting these wonders of nature is an absorbing, unforgettable experience, which can be achieved in various ways. For example, cycling in the Otago Central (the central area of one of New Zealand's 16 regions, in the southeast of South Island) is easy and enables you to travel through enchanting landscapes and old mining towns, to try excellent wines and beers, and to enjoy delicious fruit. From Clyde to Middlemarch, the bike trail follows the old railway line once used to transport minerals from the central regions to the coast. Today, the Otago Central Rail Trail is the most popular cycle route in the country, and certainly the most interesting.

262 top The Clyde Bridge on the Clutha River in Clyde is the departure point for the cycling itinerary. Today, the village is famous for its production of excellent wines.
262 bottom The Otago Central Rail Trail sign at Middlemarch, the end point of the trail.
263 In 1860, the Manuherikia River was one of the centers of the region's gold rush. Two important bridges cross it: Manuherikia No.1 Bridge and the bridge at Ophir on stone piers.

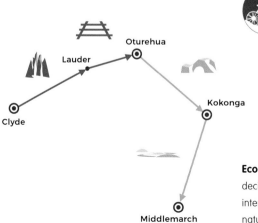

Day 1
Day 2
Day 3

Clyde
Lauder
Oturehua
Kokonga
Middlemarch

Eco because: In the Otago region, economic decisions are made keeping in mind both the interests of the community and respect for the natural environment.

DAY 1: Clyde–Lauder–Oturehua

Clyde is a little village on the banks of the Clutha River. It was founded during the gold rush of the 19th century (it preserves a surprising number of original buildings from the mining age) and is now a center for the production of some of the most prestigious wines in New Zealand. The itinerary begins from this village, following the signs for the bike trail at the intersection of State Highway 8 and Springvale Road. One of the sights of this stage is Muttontown, a viaduct 358 feet (109 m) long and 30 feet (9 m) high. After crossing this, you arrive in Alexandra. You cross the Manuherikia bridge No. 3 and arrive in Galloway: there are red lupin beans in bloom all along the road. As you continue, you pass the imposing Manuherikia bridge No. 2, 394 feet (120 m) long and 46 feet (14 m) high. From the bridge you can spot trout, or on hot summer days, you can swim in the river. Leaving the Manuherikia River, you follow Chatto Creek. Willows line the creek on the left and you smell the scent of thyme wafting among the schist formations on the right. You can pause for lunch at the Chatto Creek Tavern. After crossing State Highway 85, an information booth with a basic restroom indicates the next section of the Rail Trail. The path ascends slowly toward Tiger Hill, from which you have spectacular views of the mountains. You then arrive at Omakau, in the direction of Lauder, which is reached by crossing the Matakanui valley. Adjacent to the Rail Trail, you see deer, sheep, and cattle grazing. From here you can make out the snowy Dunstan Mountains and the Hawkdun Range, while the Raggedy Range remains to the left of the path. Finally, you reach Lauder, the intermediate stop of the stage, which boasts one of the cleanest and most pollution-free atmospheres in the world. The Lauder area is also known for the National Institute of Water and Atmospheric Research Center (NIWA), which is situated a few thousand feet outside the city: here, scientists measure climate variations and study atmospheric phenomena, such as climate change and the depletion of the ozone layer. At Lauder, the Rail Trail meets Highway 85, making this village a convenient meeting point for cyclists and support vehicles. The path then crosses the imposing Manuherikia bridge No. 1, 361 feet (110 m) long, with the Manuherikia Stream 46 feet (14 m) below. About 33 feet (10 m) before the entrance to the Poolburn tunnel No. 2, you find a path on the left with a safety line: if you follow this short detour, you reach the remains of Linemen's Base, the base for the construction of the railroad through the Poolburn Gorge. You continue through Poolburn tunnel No. 2, the longest on the path with its 751 feet (229 m); we strongly recommend the use of a headlamp as it is extremely dark in the central section. Shortly afterward you find the Poolburn viaduct, probably the most imposing structure on the Rail Trail. While you descend from the Raggedy Range, you have a splendid view of the spectacular Hawkdun Range. Here, after leaving the Poolburn Gorge, you reach the original site of the former Auripo station: the Ida valley, known for its extremely cold climate during the winter months and subject to fog in the valley bottom, opens up before you. Coming to the outskirts of Oturehua, you cross the Ida Valley Road and notice what is known locally as the Idaburn dam, a place that comes to life in winter when it is covered with ice and bonspiel, or curling competitions, are held. Also, the historic mud brick buildings are very interesting and evocative. Hayes Engineering, a company famous for its inventions, is clearly marked on the path and the Ida Valley Road. You spend the night at Oturehua.

DAY 2: Oturehua–Kokonga

On the outskirts of Oturehua, on Wedderburn Road, you find the sign for the 45th parallel south on a concrete monument. Nearby, you can visit the historic gold mine by leaving the path and following the clear signage for Reef Road. After a gradual ascent on Rough Ridge,

266 top Agricultural land and, in the background, the snowy Dunstan Mountains, in the Manuherikia valley. New Zealand grows cereals and fruit, and exports apples and kiwi fruit.
266 bottom Cycling the trail isn't always easy: here, the cyclist deals with a stretch in the water along the Otago Central Trail near Clyde.
267 Cyclists on the Poolburn viaduct over the gorge of the same name, 4.3 miles (7 km) into the Omakau and Ophir backcountry: a rocky land with an impressive engineering masterpiece of the old railroad line.

you cross the 45th parallel south once more. After pausing in the Seagull Hill gangers shed, you conquer the highest point on the Rail Trail, 2,028 feet (618 m) above sea level, before descending easily to the community of Wedderburn. As you approach, it is possible to see the golf course and, after the SH 85, the iconic warehouse immortalized on canvas by the local artist Grahame Sydney. From Wedderburn, there is a light, gradual descent down to Ranfurly: the stretch is quite easy and very pleasant, due to its gentle slope and favorable winds. This section of the trail gives you your first views of the vast Maniototo Plain, surrounded by several natural formations: Mount Ida, Rough Ridge, Hawkdun, Rock and Pillar Range, as well as the Kakanui mountains. Many of these high peaks are often covered in snow in winter and spring. Two sheds along this section of the Rail Trail are available for shelter in case

of bad weather. Ranfurly is known as the rural center of art deco in New Zealand, with its popular Art Deco Festival that every year attracts people from all the world. The section of the path leading from Ranfurly to Waipiata is in the heart of the Maniototo Plain: the vastness of this landscape and the "great sky" certainly convey a feeling of serenity. "Mani-o-toto" in the Maori language means "plains of blood"—a name recalling bloody episodes in the distant past. Around it, the mountain chains include the Rock and Pillar Range in the south, Rough Ridge in the west, Mount Saint Bathans in the northwest, Mount Kakanui in the east, and Mount Ida in the north. The contrast between the vastness of the plain, the mountains covered in snow in winter, and the great sky of Maniototo can prove particularly spectacular: the mountains enhance the most dramatic of dawns and sunsets. Along the way, you can stop in the Ranfurly Straight gangers shed to find a little shade or consult information boards on

the local area. As you approach Waipiata, you go through an underground passage near the Taieri River, the third-longest river in New Zealand (197 miles [317 km]), ideal for swimming, kayaking, and trout fishing.

The Taieri River Rail bridge, 318 feet (97 m) long and 20 feet (6 m) high, is the only Taieri River crossing point along the Rail Trail. Near to its banks you find one of the few free camping areas on the trail, but there is no running water and it is forbidden to light fires. Nearby you can also see the volcanic rocks created by Flat Cap, an extinct volcano that rises beside the trail. From Waipiata you head for Kokonga, a small township along State Highway 87, from which you can access some gangers sheds. At Kokonga the railway station and the warehouse have been removed, but the concrete platform survives. Kokonga, the final destination of the stage, offers splendid scenery and a quiet atmosphere.

DAY 3: Kokonga–Middlemarch

On the last stretch of the Rail Trail, the path runs next to State Highway 87, with the imposing Kakanui mountains to the east. About 2.5 miles (4 km) from Kokonga, you find the Daisy Bank Car Park, which is clearly signed and ideal for support vehicle parking. This section is quite easy for today's cyclists, but the bumpy road used to be a great obstacle for workers during the construction of the railroad line. You can camp at Daisy Bank, an excellent place to enjoy the wild nature (avoid lighting fires and creating dangers); the area has basic restrooms without running water. In any case, those who do not intend to stop for the night can relax under one of the many willows and admire the great rock walls of the nearby mountains, or else have a refreshing swim in the Taieri River, paying great attention to the level of the water. A mile further, you reach Tiroiti, where you can stay in a gangers shed. An information kiosk shows the route of State Highway 87 and the parking available. Not very far from the kiosk you find the Capburn historic railway bridge, 151 feet (40 m) long and 23 feet (7 m) high: it still preserves the original sleepers and railway lines. You must get off your bike to cross this bridge over the Capburn stream. Shortly afterward, the stream flows into the Taieri River. You continue

266 left The Blue Lake, at the foot of Mount Saint Bathans in the center of Otago, is one of the many important historic gold mines in the area.

266 right The entrance to the Poolburn Gorge tunnel, the longest on the trail. It is extremely dark in the center, and cycle headlights are necessary to light the way.

267 A cyclist on the dirt road along the Otago Central Trail: the difficulty of the trail varies, and therefore it is necessary to be well trained in biking on different terrains.

along the path as far as the spectacular iron-and-concrete Prices Creek Viaduct, which is 299 feet (91 m) long and 105 feet (32 m) high, one of the last structures built on the Rail Trail. Strong gusts of wind may make it difficult to cross, so you need to watch the weather closely. Continuing in the direction of Hyde, a walkway leads to the Taieri River to see the Hyde Tunnel, built to extract gold. From the walkway you can enjoy breathtaking landscapes, interesting stories, and great photographic opportunities (it is a highly recommended site). After Hyde Tunnel, the only completely bricked tunnel along the Rail Trail, there is a slight slope to the village of Hyde, where you stop in a public parking lot with an information kiosk. On the other side of Highway 87 you find the Otago Central Hotel, where you can enjoy a substantial meal. Another gold-mining town, Hyde was originally called "Eight Miles" for its distance from the Hamilton gold mine.

The mine employed most of the local residents. Although Hyde is a remote place, Main Street runs along State Highway 87 and this makes it perfect for rest and supplies (the nearest places offering food and drinks are quite far away: Waipiata is 18 miles (29 km) to the north and Middlemarch is 17 miles (27 km) to the south). There are also two churches on the main road, while on the other side of the highway Cooks Transport is a flourishing transport business. In the past, because there was too little flat land in Hyde, the station was built more than a mile away from the center, where there was a large enough area to load and unload wagons: Hyde station, now owned by the Otago Central Rail Trail Trust, still preserves some of the original wagons. Beside the station there are signs for cyclists to rejoin the trail. After Hyde Station you pass Straw Cutting, where a fatal railway disaster happened on June 4, 1943. The derailment of

the locomotive due to excessive speed caused the deaths of 21 people and injuries to 47 others. The Hyde disaster remains the second worst railway accident in the history of New Zealand. The Rail Trail goes very near to the commemorative site, which is clearly indicated from State Highway 87. The last section of the Rail Trail, between Hyde and Middlemarch, can be subject to strong winds, especially during the spring and summer. There are four gangers sheds along this section: Scrub Burn, Rock and Pillar Access (an excellent meeting point for support vehicles, since the Rail Trail crosses State Highway 87), Strath Taieri, and Rock and Pillar Station. There is a gentle slope toward Middlemarch, crossing the bridge over Five Mile Creek with the majestic Rock and Pillar mountains in the northwest and the Taieri Ridge in the southeast. It is very satisfying to make out the town of Middlemarch, the final destination of the Rail Trail, in the distance: here good food, drink, and hospitality conclude this exciting travel experience.

268 top *A bizarre rock formation along the trail. This area is the background for some scenes in the famous trilogy* The Lord of the Rings, *which was filmed at the beginning of the century.*

268 bottom *The old green goods shed, on the most popular bike trail in the country, serves as a reference point and shelter for cyclists.*

268–269 *Te Mata Peak in the Hawke's Bay region, which has many bike trails.*

Photo Credits

All the maps are by Giulia Lombardo

Shutterstock.com pages:

3, 11, 12-13, 16 center, 16 bottom, 17, 18,19, 20, 21 top, 21 center left, 21 center right, 22 center, 22 bottom, 22-23, 25, 26-27, 27 center, 27 bottom, 28, 29 top, 30-31, 32, 33 bottom, 34-35, 35 bottom, 36, 37 center left, 37 center right, 38-39, 39, 41 center, 41 bottom, 42-43, 43 center, 43 bottom, 44, 44-45, 46 center, 46 bottom, 48 center, 48 bottom, 50 bottom, 51, 52, 52-53, 54, 55 center left, 56-57, 57 center, 58-59, 59, 60 top, 60 center left, 62-63, 63, 64 center left, 64 center right, 65, 66-67, 68-69, 74 center left, 74 center right, 75, 78, 79 center left, 79 center right, 84 top, 84 center, 86 center left, 86 center right, 87, 89, 90 center, 90 bottom, 93, 94 center left, 94 center right, 95, 96-97, 98-99, 99 bottom, 100 bottom, 100-101, 102-103, 104 top, 108, 108-109, 110 center, 110 bottom, 111, 112 center, 112 bottom, 112-113, 114 bottom, 115, 116, 116-117, 120 center, 122, 122-123, 124 top, 126-127, 129 center right, 131 center, 131 bottom, 133 center, 133 bottom, 134 top, 134 center left, 134 center right, 137 top, 137 center, 138 top, 138 bottom, 139, 140, 141, 142, 144-145, 145, 147 center left, 148 top left, 148 top right, 148 center left, 148 center right, 149, 152,152-153, 154 center, 158, 158-159, 160, 161 top, 161 center left, 161 center right, 163, 164,165, 166, 170, 171, 172-173, 173, 174, 175 center, 175 bottom, 176-177, 178 center, 178-179, 183, 184 center, 184 bottom, 187, 192 center, 194 center, 194 bottom, 194-195, 196, 197 top, 197 center left, 197 center right, 198 center, 198 bottom, 200, 201 center, 201 bottom, 202-203, 204-205, 205, 206 center left, 206 center right, 206 bottom, 210 top, 210 center left, 210 center right, 212 top, 214, 214-215, 216, 218, 218-219, 221 center left, 221 center right, 222-223, 223 top, 226-227, 228 center right, 229, 230 bottom, 230-231, 232 center left, 232 center right, 233 center left, 234-235, 235, 236, 237 center, 237 bottom, 238, 239, 241 bottom, 242 top, 242 center left, 243, 244-245, 246 center left, 249 center, 249 bottom, 251, 252 center left, 252 center right, 253, 256, 257 center, 257 bottom, 258, 259, 264 bottom, 267, 268 bottom, 268-269

Page 5: Pavliha/Getty Images
Pages 8-9: Nathaniel Noir/Alamy Stock Photo
Pages 14-15: MARIA LUISA LOPEZ ESTIVILL/123RF
Page 15: Oleg Senkov/Alamy Stock Photo

Pages 24-25: ALAN OLIVER/Alamy Stock Photo
Page 29 center: Keith Fergus/Alamy Stock Photo
Page 33 center: David Ronald Head/123RF
Page 40: imageBROKER/Alamy Stock Photo
Pages 46-47: Evgeni Dinev/123RF
Page 49: Antonina Dattola/123RF
Page 50 center: FLAVIO VIERI/123RF
Page 55 center right: age footstock/Alamy Stock Photo
Page 57 bottom: Joana Kruse/Alamy Stock Photo
Page 60 center right: Aliaksandr Mazurkevich/123RF
Page 61: Rupert Oberhauser/Alamy Stock Foto
Page 70 top: © Frits Meyst/MeystPhoto.com
Page 70 center left: © Frits Meyst/MeystPhoto.com
Page 70 center right: © Frits Meyst/MeystPhoto.com
Page 71: © Frits Meyst/MeystPhoto.com
Pages 72-73: Victor Gector/Alamy Stock Photo
Pages 76-77: Yellow Single/Getty Images
Pages 80-81: Mauritius images GmbH/Alamy Stock Photo
Page 81: Hemis/Alamy Stock Photo
Page 82: Hemis/Alamy Stock Photo
Page 83 top: imageBROKER/Alamy Stock Photo
Page 83 center left: imageBROKER/Alamy Stock Photo
Page 83 center right: Hemis/Alamy Stock Photo
Page 85: Ed Callaert/Alamy Stock Photo
Pages 88-89: age fotostock/Alamy Stock Photo
Pages 90-91: imageBROKER/Alamy Stock Photo
Pages 92-93: sorincolac/iStockPhoto
Page 99 center: Lucas Vallecillos/Alamy Stock Photo
Page 100 center: H. Mark Weidman Photography/Alamy Stock Photo
Page 102: Veeravong Komalamena/Alamy Stock Photo
Page 104 center: Prisma by Dukas Presseagentur GmbH/Alamy Stock Photo
Page 105: Tina Kretschmer/Alamy Stock Photo
Page 106-107: Gabor Kovacs/Alamy Stock Photo
Page 114 center: Dmitrii Melnikov/Alamy Stock Photo
Page 118: Alex Ramsay/Alamy Stock Photo
Page 119 center left: Charles Mann/Alamy Stock Photo
Page 119 center right: INTERFOTO/Alamy Stock Photo
Page 120 bottom: SOURCENEXT/Alamy Stock Photo
Page 121: David Kleyn/Alamy Stock Photo
Page 124 center: Lukasz Kurbiel/123RF

Author

MADDALENA STENDARDI, a professional journalist from Milan, has worked on editorial staffs of travel magazines as a photo editor and an editor for more than 20 years. Moreover, she has created two online magazines: one dedicated to travel and the other to small producers of food excellence. As an avid nature lover, she enjoys walking and travelling. Due to her experiences, she became aware of the need to stop the vast acceleration of pollution and waste and to preserve the environment rather than destroy it. She therefore decided to share a choice that was more attentive to sustainability during the journey as well. With that in mind, she founded the site *Ecoturismonline* in 2010, which she still manages and is dedicated to travels, itineraries and places that have characteristics of eco-sustainability. Currently, she is the vice president of NEOS, an association of journalists and photographers specializing in travel reportage.

Project editor VALERIA MANFERTO DE FABIANIS

Editorial assistant GIORGIA RAINERI

Graphic design PAOLA PIACCO

WS White Star Publishers® is a registered trademark property of White Star s.r.l.

© 2020 White Star s.r.l.
Piazzale Luigi Cadorna, 6
20123 Milan, Italy
www.whitestar.it

ISBN 978-88-544-1665-9
2 3 4 5 6   25 24 23 22 21

Printed in Serbia